America, Germany, and the
Future of Europe

America, Germany, and the Future of Europe

GREGORY F. TREVERTON

A Council on Foreign Relations Book

PRINCETON UNIVERSITY PRESS

PRINCETON, NEW JERSEY

Library of Congress Cataloging-in-Publication Data

Treverton, Gregory F.
America, Germany, and the future of Europe / Gregory F. Treverton.
p.   cm.
"A Council on foreign relations book."
Includes bibliographical references and index.
ISBN 0-691-07859-9
1. Germany—Foreign relations—1990–   2. Germany—Politics and
government—1990–   3. Europe—Foreign relations—1945–   4. Europe—
Foreign relations—United States.   5. United States—Foreign
relations—Europe.   I. Title.
DD290.3T74   1992
327.7304—dc20   91-39420   CIP

This book has been composed in Linotron Berkeley

Princeton University Press books are
printed on acid-free paper and meet the guidelines
for permanence and durability of the Committee
on Production Guidelines for Book Longevity
of the Council on Library Resources

Printed in the United States of America

1   3   5   7   9   10   8   6   4   2

Contents

Preface   vii

Abbreviations   xi

INTRODUCTION   3

CHAPTER ONE
Dividing Germany   15

CHAPTER TWO
Creating Dependence   38

CHAPTER THREE
Integrating Germany, Engaging America   64

CHAPTER FOUR
Economics and Security   92

CHAPTER FIVE
Moscow's German Problem   119

CHAPTER SIX
Europe's Past, Europe's Future   153

CHAPTER SEVEN
A European Germany or a German Europe?   173

A FINAL WORD   206

Notes   215

Index   231

Preface

THIS BOOK was conceived before the fall of the Berlin Wall. Until then I had thought of my stock-in-trade as "alliance management." Influenced by studying and teaching political management at Harvard's Kennedy School and by my stints in government, I had borrowed the term from my Harvard teacher, later colleague, Francis Bator. Others borrowed it from me or came to it separately.

"Alliance management" presumed that the underlying structure of the trans-Atlantic alliance was tolerably stable and that the allies shared basic interests. In those circumstances, the task for policy was to manage the politics of alliance so that shared purposes were not lost in the babble of particular issues and pleadings.

By the 1980s—to put a precise date to it would falsify both history and autobiography—the managerial perspective no longer seemed tenable to me. Then, before Mikhail Gorbachev, it was not so much that new disruptions threatened underlying structures; rather, it seemed that the strains that had always been there might actually engender real change. Or at least the question was on the table in a way it had not been before, during the long years of perennial—but manageable—"crises" in the alliance.

The book thus began as an inquiry backward, to the beginning of the Cold War in order to imagine how it might end. A funny thing happened on the way to publication: for all intents and purposes, the Cold War ended. I was no better at predicting the fall of the Wall than anyone else. The closest I came to prophecy was a paper, presented to Germanists in early September 1989, a scant two months before the Wall came down, in which I argued that German reunification had become inevitable. I did not say soon. And still my colleagues, bemused, treated me as a provocateur. So I half-regarded myself.

Of my project, what survived the Wall's fall was its fundamental theme: that Germany is, and will remain, Europe's center, both literally and figuratively. What happens on the periphery can upset the status quo, but the decisive events are those at the center. It was so in 1989. Gorbachev's reform had set loose, however inadvertently, a political whirlwind in eastern Europe that became definitive when it came to Germany—the fall of the Wall. In the future, too, the central happenings will be those at the center, notwithstanding the dazzling rush of change in Europe's east.

This is a book about Europe, but its ultimate purpose is American policy. It seeks to understand what has happened in Europe, and what may happen, in order to illuminate American decisions, past and prospective. If, in working through the early history of the trans-Atlantic engagement I give pride of place to American deliberations, that does not necessarily imply a judgment about causation. If Stalin was the father of the trans-Atlantic alliance, Ernest Bevin, the British foreign secretary, was its godfather. My purpose, though, is assessing what Americans thought—about Europe, their own interests, and their domestic politics. My might-have-beens are, given my focus, primarily American.

Since I have worked, in and out of government, on what we came to call almost automatically the "Atlantic alliance" for my entire career, the book is also an exercise in personal history. It is perhaps more so since I and the alliance are the same age; I am two years younger than the postwar period, just as old as the division of Germany in 1947, and two years older than NATO.

Sorting out the parenthood of particular ideas is complicated because I have pondered the subject so long. But the nuclear argument in Chapter 6 was first presented to a West Point Senior Conference in 1987. Ideas in Chapter 7 were developed for the Working Group on Changing Roles and Shifting Burdens in the Atlantic Alliance, sponsored by the Johns Hopkins Foreign Policy Institute in 1990; another version of those arguments was published as "Elements of a New European Security Order," *Journal of International Affairs* 45, no. 1 (Summer 1991). A part of "A Final Word" was outlined, in an early version, in "America's European Engagement," Paper No. 6, *Beyond the Cold War: Current Issues in European Security*, Woodrow Wilson International Center for Scholars (November 1990).

I have been helped greatly by William Diebold, whose comments challenged me and convinced me more than ever that he should write his own personal account of Europe's construction during the early postwar years; and by Richard Ullman, Nicholas X. Rizopoulos, Robert E. Klitgaard, Richard E. Neustadt, and Charles Maier. These good people are more than entitled to the ritual disclaimer of responsibility for what follows, and more entitled still to my gratitude.

At various times I have been helped in ferreting out details by Raymond Baxter, Paola Cesarini, Robert Goldsmith, John Ray, Susan Monaco, and Steven Spiegel. To them I express my thanks.

Finally, my thinking about Germany and Europe has been advanced (I hope!) in myriad ways beyond my ken by my various projects at the Council on Foreign Relations. I have had the opportunity to inflict ideas on several Council study groups and to hazard some in print while editing two Council books, *Europe and America beyond 2000* (1989) and *The Shape of the New Europe* (1991). I am grateful to the sponsors of these activities: the Ford Foundation, the Rockefeller Foundation, and the German Marshall Fund.

New York, August 1991

Abbreviations

CAD   Civil Affairs Division (U.S. army)

CAP   Common Agricultural Policy (of the European Community)

CDU   Christian Democratic Union (Federal Republic)

CFE   Conventional Forces in Europe

CSCE   Conference on Security and Cooperation in Europe

CSU   Christian Social Union (Federal Republic)

EAC   European Advisory Commission

EC   European Community

ECA   Economic Cooperation Agency (United States)

ECSC   European Coal and Steel Community (also the Schuman plan)

EDC   European Defense Community

EMU   European (or Economic and Monetary) Monetary Union

EPU   European Payments Union (of the ECSC, later the European Political Union)

ERP   European Recovery Program (also the Marshall Plan)

FDP   Free Democratic Party (Federal Republic)

FRG   Federal Republic of Germany

GATT   General Agreement on Tariffs and Trade

GDR   German Democratic Republic (East Germany)

GNP   Gross National Product

GSFG   Group of Soviet Forces in Germany

JCS   Joint Chiefs of Staff (United States)

MSP   Mutual Security Program (later name for the Marshall Plan)

NATO   North Atlantic Treaty Organization

NSC   National Security Council (United States)

OEEC   Organization for European Economic Cooperation

OSS   Office of Strategic Services (United States)

SAC   Strategic Air Command (United States)

SED   Socialist Unity Party (East Germany)

SNF	Short-range Nuclear Forces
SPD	Social Democratic Party (Federal Republic)
UN	United Nations
WEU	Western European Union

America, Germany, and the
Future of Europe

Introduction

In MY OPINION, the center of readjustment, if readjustment is to be, lies in Germany, not in Russia or with us." So wrote Henry Adams in 1897.[1] For different reasons, Adams's judgment is applicable almost a century later. In today's turmoil in Europe, the center of readjustment is the center, Germany.

Looking back over the more than forty postwar years, they now seem a race in decline between the Soviet threat and the trans-Atlantic security order the threat justified. The threat shaped the postwar order in Europe and, especially, the American role in that order. It excused the bipolar structure of international politics and justified the Europeans' dependence on the United States, making that dependence tolerable, most of the time at any rate. With the fall of the Berlin Wall in 1989, the threat "won" the race in decline—a surprise to many people, less so perhaps to those who had asserted, even if they were not always confident they would be proven right, that trans-Atlantic firmness would eventually expose the weakness of communist societies.

Although the postwar order was justified in terms of the Soviet threat, it had as much to do with the balance within Europe. The extracontinental balancer, the United States, had to be engaged and seen as both necessary and acceptable to the western Europeans, who with the erecting of the Iron Curtain took for themselves the shorter title "European." Almost continuously before 1989 it seemed to many in Europe and America that the structure linking them might win the race in decline. Americans would lose interest in their European engagement, or Europeans would come to see their dependence as too costly, with each unravelling tendency abetting the other.

In the wake of all the change, all the surprises, this book is an inquiry into the future shape of Europe and its implications for the United States. Now that the old order in Europe is passing away, its central question is less "why?" than "what next?" The book concentrates on security, for it is there that the structure of European—and German—dependence on the United States was most acute, and therefore it is in that realm that the change is and will be most marked. Yet the economic and security strands of Europe's postwar reconstruction were intertwined.

They will remain so in Europe's future, and in America's engagement with it. My argument, to summarize, is that sustaining NATO and some American military presence in Europe will be sensible but more and more beside the point. Retaining some remnant of the existing security order will be insurance against an unpredictable future.

If, however, that future is a relatively happy one, the question of NATO and American troops will recede in importance. Already the weight of security considerations in trans-Atlantic relations has diminished. If the United States is to be as engaged in Europe as it has been for the last two generations, the basis of that engagement will have to change.

EXAMINING THE PAST

From one perspective, there are grounds for worry about Europe's future: relatively speaking, Germany is as strong as it has been for a hundred years, Russia as weak (apart from nuclear weapons), and eastern Europe as much a vacuum. Yet from another, this democratic Germany is very different from earlier ones, and it is enmeshed in institutional arrangements that are unusual historically. Of these, NATO is less important over the long run than the European Community (EC).

Europe's future plainly is unknowable. The subject does not admit of the same kinds of evidence and predictions as, say, economics (and look how badly *it* does). Looking backward does, however, help us understand the roots of existing structures in the circumstances of their creation. It then permits us to compare those circumstances with today, at this period of re-creation now that the old order in Europe has ended.

And so this book begins, in its first three chapters, by examining the critical instances that shaped the postwar order in Europe. Decisions about Germany were decisions about Europe, and vice versa. The dominant fear at the time was of course that of a Soviet invasion into western Europe. The Red Army did not march westward in those dark days of 1947–48, and it now appears reasonably clear—it will take *glasnost* coming to Soviet archives for us to know better—that Stalin, for all his menace, was not about to invade. But we can nonetheless empathize with those who felt the threat was imminent.

In those circumstances of fear and uncertainty, the achievements of postwar statesmen, European and American, are impressive, truly remarkable. Their response to the Soviet threat did have some side effects, both short-term and long, on Soviet mind-sets and East-West relations; the debate about the impacts of those side effects will rage on, and this book will not enter that debate directly, much less try to settle it. But the side effects of America's preeminence and western Europe's dependence *are* central to this inquiry.

Europe now faces the problems of success tantamount to victory, not of defeat and exhaustion. Such problems are naturally to be preferred to the alternative, but they do have the unfortunate attribute of fuzziness. They lack the brilliant clarity of the choices faced in 1947. Examining those choices may provide new insights into what might have been, and therefore helps us think about what might be today.

For instance, despite the clarity of the choices in retrospect, with Stalin in the Kremlin and western Europe impoverished by war, the postwar order took time to evolve. It emerged only step by step, and each step was not easily taken, especially not on the American side, where the engagement ran counter to the republic's history and inclinations. Against that history, it is imprudent to imagine now that grand new bargains, creations, or structures will emerge overnight in circumstances that make their creation much less urgent.

At the same time, it is striking that in the end the United States reached a clear decision, and a rough consensus, on the nature of the national task. Europe would be the centerpiece of American policy and the focal point of the nation's attentions. It is not as though there were no other contenders. But America's policymakers decided on, and its people assented to, that concentration.

The second step in creating Europe's dependence and America's engagement, the North Atlantic Treaty, the subject of Chapter 2, gets the most attention. But the first and third—dividing Germany, then integrating Europe and America in a military structure—were no less important. Viewed in hindsight, critical decisions by the end of 1946, decisions then regarded as provisional, set in motion much of what followed. In the first and third steps, discussed in Chapters 1 and 3, the theme, though not the principal actor, was Germany, a fact obscured in the third by preoccupation with the peril of Soviet military attack.

Building the postwar economic order in Europe, the subject of Chapter 4, began before the security order and continued after NATO was in place as a full-fledged alliance. The first key decision was American, the Marshall Plan of 1947, designed not as the start of a long-term American engagement in Europe but as a finite program to provide enough money to let Europe stand again on its own feet. Ever since, "Marshall Plan" has become the cry for those seeking rapid economic development. It is inescapable now as an analogy for rapidly bringing Europe's east to economic health.

Later, the crucial decisions were European, with economics and security entangled: if the Soviet threat required rearming (West) Germany, then that Germany was entitled to become a full partner; it could not be consigned to second-class status in the club of European nations. However, that in turn raised the old dilemma, especially for France: how to coexist with a dynamic Germany. France's answer, and bit by bit Europe's as well, was an epoch-making bet: "if you can't beat 'em, join 'em," the process of European integration beginning with the European Coal and Steel Community in 1950.

European integration created an irritant and raised a question. From the Coal and Steel Community in 1950 through the EC's 1992 program, if integration was not hostile to Europe's security partner, the United States, neither was it carried out for America's benefit. It was done by Europeans for Europe and thus discriminated in some degree against all others, but most visibly against the United States. From the beginning, the United States concluded that its broad interest in Europe, even a "United States of Europe," was worth the price of some trade discrimination, and so it encouraged Europe's integration. Trans-Atlantic arguments over particular trade issues, from chicken to beef hormones, were contained; they were mostly trivial in their economic weight if not always in their political heat.

The question concerns the connection between economic arrangements and the security order. Did security dependence imply economic leverage? Or did common security interests mute economic disagreements? Looking ahead, what effect will the lesser weight of security, and so the lessened dependence, have on economic quarrels?

Moscow's motives in the early postwar period will, like its actions, continue to be debated, none more so than those surrounding Stalin's note of March 1952. In it he offered, more specifically and with less polemic than he had before, to remove his troops from Germany and let it unify provided the western nations did the same, and provided that unified Germany was a member of no alliance. We cannot know for sure what Stalin intended or how far he calculated until Soviet archives are opened, and perhaps not then. Was the note a pure ploy, one last gasp in Stalin's campaign to keep West Germany out of NATO? Or was there an opportunity, the last and then the lost one, to begin a serious negotiation about Germany's future?

Looking at the sequence of events, in Chapter 5, suggests the interaction of stakes on the two sides. For both sides, and especially for the United States and its allies, now including the West German government, any opportunities that were lost depended on risks neither West nor East was prepared to take. Trying for a unified Germany on one's own side risked that it might wind up on the other. And so both settled for an outcome that was neither's first-best but not a bad second-best for both, a divided Germany in a divided Europe.

7

Stalin's German problem, like the one that confronted his successors, was both West and East Germany; East Germany was no doubt nearly as large in his calculations as the Federal Republic was in Washington's, and the tracks of East Berlin's influence in Moscow are visible through the years. Moscow's decision in the 1970s to open new relations with West Germany required it to manage a change of East German leaders. Most stunningly, when Gorbachev determined on reform in his country, he felt compelled to turn eastern Europe loose. He was no doubt as surprised as anyone at how fast the break-up occurred and how soon it overwhelmed East Germany, symbol and tangible benefit of the Great Patriotic War against Hitler.

IMAGINING THE FUTURE

One way to conjure possible futures for Europe is by analogy. Analogies have the virtue of stretching our thinking by forcing us to answer in which particulars the future resembles a particular past; comparing several analogies may then suggest new possibilities. Europe's future, one analogizes, is like this or that period in the past. But which analogy is appropriate?

Is it post-World War I, a combination of a weak Russia and an unstable eastern Europe, with a greater chance this time that the dominant power will be Germany—stretching the analogy further, a Germany that might be tempted to do a new deal with Russia like that of the 1920s? Stretching too far distorts, but it will suggest a question, about the importance of America's engagement in Europe, and a caution, about expecting too much of international architecture—the League of Nations then, pan-European structures like the Conference on Security and Cooperation in Europe (CSCE), also called the Helsinki Final Act, now.

Or does the better analogy for the future Europe come from the nineteenth century: either the original Concert of Europe, major powers not far divided by ideology and joined in commitments to restraint and self-restraint in a loose continental system; or what brought the Concert a-cropper—distance from the cataclysm that had impelled the original cooperation and the waning of agreement on the status quo in new strains over new issues, all infused by the passions of domestic politics?

Or is this Europe after Germany's second unification like that after its first in 1871—one power rising, then and now Germany; one empire disintegrating, then Austria-Hungary, now the Soviet Union; and the United States now perhaps a little like Russia then, its role in Europe uncertain? If the Rapallo agreement of the 1920s between two weakened states, Germany and Russia, is a tortured analogy for the years ahead, what about Russo-German relations after 1871, when Germany was on the rise and Russia struggling to recover from its defeat in Crimea?

The hints from these analogies help call attention to what is distinctive now, the subject of Chapter 6. One difference from Europe's pre–Cold War past is the presence of nuclear weapons. A second is the form of interdependence among western Europe's states. If the abstracted logic of strategy is not decisive, it is incisive, a starting point for asking "if not, then why?" For forty years, the logic has pointed to nuclear weapons for the Federal Republic. If dependence on America in turn anguished Germans (and other Europeans) because they might be abandoned and terrified them because they might be involved in nuclear war against their will, nuclear independence would have provided deterrence on the cheap.

The logic remains for a unified Germany. The threat has abated, but the Soviet Union or Russia will continue to have nuclear weapons, and so some German deterrent would be simple prudence. The nuclear logic also holds for other European states, perhaps especially those in eastern Europe for whom threats from neighbors is neither an abstraction nor an artifact of the past.

West Germany did not go nuclear during the last forty years because politics both muted the need and negated the possibility. Most likely, unified Germany will not go nuclear in the future. If it does not, it will be because new political arrangements also succeed in raising the cost or minimizing the need of any nuclear decision in new circumstances. Imagining the shape of such arrangements is answering the "why" part of "if not, then why?"

An answer to "why?" is the second distinctive feature of Europe at present. Surely the nations of western Europe are past fighting with each other; war has ceased to be a question of costs and benefits but rather has become almost literally unthinkable. The new "interdependence" is economic and cultural, but its novelty can be overstated, for in those respects western Europeans a hundred years ago, or seventy, were also interdependent without using the word. They were each other's prime trading partners, and their elites were familiar, sometimes family.

Rather, the more striking change is interdependence as institutionalized through the EC. Europeans grouse about the supranational authority of the EC, but they recognize its necessity. A "United States of Europe" is not in the cards, but existing institutions provide visible incentive for cooperation, along with ways to settle disputes. Extending that institutional framework eastward within Europe will be slow, but eastern Europeans will still desire admission to Europe's "club," the EC, and so have some incentive to avoid the erratic politics or conflict with neighbors that would make them unfit members.

In the back of many minds, especially in Europe, is a fair-weather future for Europe, the starting point for Chapter 7. Traditional security concerns recede and economics come to the fore, with the EC eventually becoming the organizing framework for Europe. Meanwhile, NATO gracefully declines while all-European collective security arrangements, based on the Conference on Security and Cooperation in Europe (CSCE), become Europe's residual insurance policy. How long the transition takes will depend on the weather—faster if the weather holds fair, slower if clouds appear.

Yet this vision has its own deficiencies. No one who has worked on CSCE issues in the government could either dismiss CSCE or be too enthusiastic about it. The CSCE has the advantage of including as "European" both the United States (and Canada) and the Soviet Union. The corresponding disadvantage is that it also includes over thirty other states, including some small ones not above playing the spoiler on Europe's grand stage where unanimity is the operating principle. CSCE can be the basis for many things: smaller "groupings of the willing" can negotiate arms control or attempt to resolve interstate disputes in Europe beneath a broad CSCE umbrella.

In the end, though, like all insurance policies, collective security systems work best when they are not desperately needed—the lesson of the League of Nations. They are hard put to cope with determined, powerful upsetters of the system; for such threats, there is no alternative to deterrence by accumulating power. For now, such a rogue is not visible on the horizon.

Unified Germany, the focus of Chapter 7, will not necessarily be the agreeable creature Europe has known as the Federal Republic. With unification, "little Germany" will come to an end. The country begins from an introverted base but will become more assertive, perhaps less tactful in pursuing its interests, and history suggests it may miscalculate those stakes, in Europe's east above all. But it strains the imagination, and the time horizon of this book, to imagine a Germany whose power threatened Europe, let alone one tempted to go nuclear.

Germany's explicitness about its interests will be uncomfortable for Germany's allies, but it will carry advantages as well, for with its emergence will come responsibility: no more will Germany be able to deny being a great power, saying "we're just a trading nation," a kind of European Japan, or pleading that it is too hostage to Soviet power in Europe to take responsibility beyond. There will be a gradual ending to the paradox—a country whose citizens wait patiently at empty street crossings for the little green man to appear on the signal, but whose government could not control chemical exports to Qadafy's Libya or Saddam Hussein's Iraq.

What happens to the Soviet Union is anyone's guess. On one hand, the threat that held NATO together—a massive Soviet attack on western Europe through eastern Europe—seems over. On the other, some state on existing Soviet territory, whether Russia or the Duchy of Muscovy, will remain Europe's largest military power, and not all of the thousands of nuclear weapons will go away. Most imaginings of the Soviet empire's disintegration include the possibility of violence, but that violence, while perhaps awful for the territory of the Soviet Union and adjacent regions, would not necessarily threaten the broader peace of Europe.

Yet if 1989 taught the world anything, it was the danger of constricting our vision of the future by believing we understood what moved politics in Europe. Almost anything is possible in Europe east of Germany. Some of the possibilities include the spillover of violence from Soviet territory into eastern, even western Europe. Although betting on hopes makes sense, so does hedging against fears: hoping that a western Europe past fighting can gradually stretch its community of peace eastward while sustaining some deterrence, most conveniently through NATO, during a transition that may not be brief.

If Europe judges some American military engagement *in* Europe to be in its continuing interest, then two nations will have to share the judgment, Germany and America. If more than token American forces remain in Europe, they will have to be in Germany. With unification, those troops cease to be tainted by the image of occupation and German dependence. At the same time, however, as the Soviet troops depart, taking with them the symbol of the threat, Germans will ask why foreign troops should be harbored at all. If there is no threat, aren't they still occupiers despite the end of the Cold War?

THE FUTURE OF AMERICA'S ENGAGEMENT

Questions arise for the United States as well. Will Americans be prepared to keep forces in Europe when the American claim to predominance in the European security order has diminished? The security reasons for doing so may be compelling, but compelling arguments do not always win political debates. Americans will continue to be tempted to say "we've won, so let's go home." Perhaps a future historian will be impressed by the American military engagement in Europe as a half-century interlude, not as an enduring change in Europe's configuration.

Whether the troops stay or go, the security anchor to America's engagement will weigh less. That anchor, with its troops, commands, and NATO meetings, was the principal mission of the U.S. army and the principal business for American diplomacy; it exerted a correspondingly lavish claim on presidential attention. If America is to stay as engaged, it will have to be on a new basis. The economic connections will not disappear, nor the tourists and students, whatever the exchange rate; nor will the profusion of cultural symbols, like jeans or music, that Americans see as theirs but which others probably perceive as international. But those will not provide the basis for a political engagement akin to that entailed in reconstructing western Europe and then containing the Soviet Union over the last forty years.

No such comparable project is now at hand. For instance, reconstructing eastern Europe and the Soviet Union is a tempting candidate. However, aside from the technical reasons why eastern Europe, let alone the Soviet Union, is not postwar western Europe, Europe's east seems destined to be Europe's responsibility, for better or worse. The United States, having convinced itself it is poor, has also convinced itself that talk alone can rebuild eastern Europe. A grand new bargain over issues beyond Europe seems an unpromising venture on which to hang the future of the trans-Atlantic connection, while the time is not yet ripe for a dramatic initiative to manage the global economy, one that in any case would be trilateral, involving Japan.

Might this not be the time for seeking to avoid new trans-Atlantic projects, rather than for seeking them? This approach would not be disengagement, let alone isolationism in whatever "neo" incarnation. American troops would remain in Europe in some numbers. The approach would try to make facts into virtues, letting nature take its course, but thinking of the course as one to welcome rather than bemoan. It would mean limiting the claims we make on our European partners and, in so doing, on ourselves. It would mean trying to invest particular policies with less political capital, and so to run less risk that every particular incident will become a litmus test of cooperation and every failed test an occasion for handwringing or recrimination.

Such a tack would rest on the assumptions that security threats are not pressing, but domestic business is—for both the United States and Europe. America will confront no shortage of international problems, but no mortal threats of the sort that animated it for the last forty years. The Soviet Union (or Russia), its threat to the United States overstated in the past, may be underestimated now, but it does not pose a direct threat to territorial integrity, sovereignty, or political institutions—not for western Europe and surely not for the United States. The same seems to be the case for threats from beyond Europe, the Gulf war of 1990–91 notwithstanding.

The names of the more serious "threats"—competitiveness and Japan—call attention to the judgment on which the alternative approach rests: if the world will allow the United States to avoid grand new trans-Atlantic projects, American interests will require it. America's pressing business now lies at home, not abroad; the tails of those problems stretch across borders, but their roots are at home. For instance, no amount of beating on Japan to open its markets, however appropriate, will help American industry as much as competing better with Japanese products in the United States. If America's urgent business is at home, the same is the case for Europe.

This call to demand and expect less is a far cry from the staple of trans-Atlantic rhetoric over the last two generations, and a very different choice from the one America made in the years after World War II. It can be criticized as an invitation to those who want to disengage, even newly isolate, America, not refocus its energies at home. The criticism is apt. Yet, the question is whether it will be wise to try to sustain, in general, the level of American internationalism of the Cold War and, in particular, the intensity of the American engagement in Europe. It is better to recognize the ending of a mortal conflict as a momentous change, and to try to refocus energies accordingly.

Dividing Germany

JUST AS the postwar order ended in Germany, so it also began there. It ended the day the Berlin Wall was punched open, November 9, 1989; or perhaps earlier in the summer the day communist Hungary decided it had more to gain from capitalist West Germany than it had to fear from Moscow and so let roll the "freedom trains" carrying East Germans to new lives in West Germany. In those weeks the division of Germany ended, in important psychological and political ways if not yet in all formal ones, and with it, so ended the postwar order in Europe.

Germans, East Germans in particular, were the main actors in bringing down the old order. They surprised everyone at how quickly their candlelight vigils in the streets of Berlin and Leipzig and Dresden revealed that the regime's means of control, overwhelming on paper, were in fact discredited, and almost empty. The speed left East Germany with not much by way of leaders, political structures, or visions of the future, and it left the rest of us to wonder how we could have been so misled in our assessments of the old regime's economic health and political control.

Those East Germans did owe a large debt to Mikhail Gorbachev, who made reform the order of the day in eastern Europe and, at the critical moment, told the East German regime it could not count on Soviet support—far from it, if it repressed its opponents by force as China had done at the beginning of the summer. He would condone no Tiananmen Square blood running in the streets of East Germany. Helmut Kohl's West German government finished what the East German people had begun; it supplied the vision and the leaders and the structure.

The contrast between Germans' role in ending and in shaping the postwar order in Europe could hardly be sharper. In 1980–90 Germans were in the driver's seat. In 1946–48, their country devastated and its Nazi experiment disgraced, they had been an object, not an actor in the decisions that created Europe's dependence and America's military engagement.

As soon as they could believe Germany might lose World War II, the men in London, Washington—and Moscow—set their minds to Germany's future role in Europe. Their first actions set in motion the division of Germany, even if they did not quite intend it that way or even realize it was happening. Sooner than they realized, provisional decisions created enduring facts; each hesitant, reluctant step changed the calculations of risk about the next.

The construction of the postwar order in Europe began and ended with the division of Germany. The first steps were halting and half inadvertent, intended less as decisions than as interim solutions to practical problems. Not so five years later when the division was ratified by integrating West Germany into NATO: then the decision was conscious, its implications for the European order acknowledged and accepted, including by Germans although not without second thoughts. That final step finished what was begun with the North Atlantic Treaty and the dispatch of American troops to Europe—the security order in Europe—and ratified the American military engagement on the European continent.

Planning for Postwar Germany

As the tide of battle turned toward the allies, planning for what to do with Germany circulated in Washington and London. On the American side the argument remained mostly at the working level, for President Franklin D. Roosevelt sought to defer decisions about Europe's future politics while fighting its present war. And so the arguing produced confused and sometimes conflicting policy results. Yet that arguing is still of more than historical interest, for it reflected differing notions not only of why the war occurred but also of how to prevent the next one—how to structure a peaceful Europe.

How again to deal with a vanquished Germany turned on assessments of what had gone wrong after World War I.[1] There was common ground in Washington on two points—that surrender this time around should be unconditional, not permitting a defeated Germany to bargain for its terms, and that the victors at Versailles had been deeply mistaken in pressing enormous reparations claims on Germany. If the economic effect of those claims had not been virtually to guarantee upheaval in postwar Germany—on that issue there was argument—they surely had been bound to become a lightning rod for German grievances and a poisoner of Germany's relations with its neighbors. Beyond these two points of agreement, however, assessments varied and with them, prescriptions.

For those, in the state department and elsewhere, who traced Germany's slide toward fascism and war directly to the Versailles peace treaty of 1919, the prescription for this time around was relative moderation. The 1919 treaty had explicitly contravened its own central tenet, self-determination, in the case of defeated Germany, depriving that country of a tenth of its population and a seventh of its territory—Alsace-Lorraine and the Saar in the west, Danzig and the Danzig corridor (West Prussia) in the east, cutting off East Prussia from the rest of Germany and so virtually guaranteeing that German-Polish relations would be an open sore.

Then, Germany had been excluded from the League of Nations, branded with the guilt for having caused the war, limited in its arms and armed forces, and compelled to pay enormous reparations. Moreover, the Ruhr had been demilitarized and temporarily occupied, an occupation France later used to compel German payment of reparations.[2] This time, in the view of those who argued for a moderate peace, Germany would be demilitarized and denazified but with controls kept, in the words of a 1943 state department committee, "to the minimum in number and in severity which will be compatible with security" and intended to foster "a minimum of bitterness" from the German people.[3]

As time passed, the more any official had come to worry by war's end about the future shadow of Soviet power in Europe, the more attractive dealing moderately with Germany became and the less was the temptation to consign Germany forever to vacuum. This argument ran intriguingly parallel to that of those among the victors who had lost the debate in 1919, like Winston Churchill, who had argued then not for punishing Germany but for quickly rehabilitating it as a bulwark against Bolshevik Russia.

By contrast, for Treasury Secretary Henry Morgenthau, Versailles had gone both too far and not far enough. He and others—a group which sometimes seemed to include the president, influenced by his schooldays in Germany and service as assistant secretary of the navy after World War I—saw Germany as by nature aggressive. Versailles had done nothing about that; worse, by compelling reparations, it had encouraged Germany to rebuild its industrial base—ostensibly for reparations but ultimately for war.

Morgenthau's plans, in various forms, called for dismantling Germany's remaining heavy industry and flooding its coal mines, making Germany into a country primarily agricultural and pastoral in nature. If the Ruhr, he put it to an aide, were "stripped of its machinery, the mines flooded—dynamited—wrecked—it would make [the Germans] impotent to wage future wars." As to the people, "why the hell should I worry about what happens to their people? . . . They have asked for it." Reeducating young people was imperative, a task that might mean the need, he confided to his diary, "to transplant them out of Germany to some place in Central Africa." The plan would insure that Germany could not turn its industrial might to aggressive purposes.[4]

It is perhaps a mark of wartime passions and the preoccupation with victory on the part of officials at the top of the American government that these strange ideas, whose implementation seems in retrospect implausible, had a running. The influence of these ideas reached a peak in September 1944 when, attending the Quebec Conference at Roosevelt's special invitation, Morgenthau managed to get the president and British Prime Minister Winston Churchill to initial a document incorporating his plan.

The ensuing flap leaked to the public, and Roosevelt privately admitted to Secretary of War Henry Stimson that he had signed the document without much thought. Yet some of Morgenthau's ideas for "planned chaos" were incorporated into the original occupation directive issued to the American army as it fought across western

Europe—JCS 1067.[5] The incorporation is puzzling, for Stimson's department thus approved what he himself strongly opposed.

In 1944, however, a German collapse seemed possible, and General Dwight D. Eisenhower, the supreme allied commander, urgently needed some guidance, never mind the content. To an American military that was about to have the task of running Germany, JCS 1067 probably did not seem as much Morgenthauism as it does in retrospect. Against the military's task the directive had its appeal, because it enhanced the military's authority while offering to let it avoid too deep an involvement in German civil affairs, or responsibility for restoring the German economy should a collapse occur—both prospects that filled senior officers with dread.

Dividing Germany was an obvious compromise between those who sought a generous peace and those who would have dismantled German power. For those who thought Versailles had not gone far enough, it went further; if Germany were inherently warlike, its tradition would be displaced and its power divided. For those who saw reparations claims as the villain of the interwar period, division offered a way to divide responsibility and thus diminish claims this time around. For those who feared a power vacuum in the center of Europe, several states, perhaps in loose confederation, held promise of avoiding it.

The problems with partition were, however, also evident. Division would hardly be attractive to the victors if it only gave vanquished Germany a permanent grievance and with it a permanent focal point for renewed nationalism. In that sense it risked becoming the second war's version of reparations. Creating a host of small states would prevent the revival of German military force, but would such a confederation be viable? Might a Germany divided into thirds produce three relatively strong states and so a stable structure?

Stalin had mentioned partition to Britain's foreign secretary, Anthony Eden, in 1941, along with the idea of moving both the Soviet Union's and Poland's borders westward at the expense of German territory. A variety of partition plans circulated within official Washington. One done in the state department during 1942, for instance, proposed three states, in the south, the northeast, and northwest.[6]

If the underlying problem was German militarism, then partition was a solution more feasible than "planned chaos." A divided Germany would be two steps from aggression, reuniting and rearming, but a united Germany would be but one. On the other hand, the problem with partition as a solution was that it would create a grievance, alienating Germans from the peace settlement and estranging them from the society of peaceable nations.

President Roosevelt spoke favorably, if tentatively, of partition, and he brought up the subject with Stalin and Churchill at Teheran in 1943, there mentioning a five-part division of Germany and linking it to proposed zones of occupation. Both then and at Yalta in 1945, however, the three leaders discussed but sidestepped the issue, referring it in a formless way to the European Advisory Commission (EAC) in London—the group they had created to make recommendations about postwar issues.

At Yalta the question of division was overshadowed by the argument over reparations. Neither the United States nor Britain expected reparations, but the Soviet Union did (and occupied countries sought "restitution")—to the tune of $20 billion for Moscow, half to be delivered no matter what the course of postwar Germany's economy. Roosevelt and Churchill expressed worry over the possibility of disorder, even starvation, in the industrialized western sectors where food was scarce. The two did not accept Stalin's $20 billion claim, but Roosevelt did, over Churchill's objection, agree to use it as the basis for subsequent conversation.

DIVISION IN FACT

In the end American decisionmaking about occupation zones was haphazard. The original idea for the EAC had been Stalin's, and Roosevelt remained loathe to make postwar commitments before the end of the war; moreover, official Washington, remembering 1919, feared an isolationist backlash if the war's endgame appeared to be decided in secret in London. And so in late 1943 when the state department circulated a plan for pie-shaped zones giving all three powers access to Berlin, the U.S. military countered that occupation zones were strictly military matters, to depend on deployments at the end of the war.

Early in 1944 the British put before the EAC their own plan, much like what ensued in fact, for a Russian zone in the east, an American in the southwest and a British in the northwest, with Berlin under tripartite administration but deep inside the Soviet zone. The Soviets quickly indicated their approval.[7] Caught off guard, the American military's Civil Affairs Division (CAD) responded with its own plan, one of wartime planning's curiosities. The plan gave the Americans a huge zone in the northwest bordering on Berlin, and the British and Soviets smaller zones to the southwest and east, respectively, the border between them not entirely defined. Moreover, the plan pushed eastward the eastern boundary of the Soviet zone, one Moscow and London had already agreed upon.[8]

It turned out that, in a hurry, CAD had simply appropriated a map Roosevelt had casually drawn in a meeting with the joint chiefs of staff in November 1943.[9] The president, tickled by the mischief he had set loose, authorized his representative to the EAC to accept the boundaries already agreed upon by Moscow and London. He still, however, did not like the assignment of the southwest to the United States, apparently with fears of his own about postwar politics, in this case a revolution in France that would cut off U.S. lines of communication.

Churchill, though, held firm, and the president was persuaded by his military advisors that existing troop deployments would make it easy to occupy the southwest. Intriguingly in light of subsequent events, the president did insist that Britain concede two enclaves in their zone, at the ports of Bremen and Bremerhaven.[10] The American military then negotiated detailed rights of access to the U.S. zone. Ironically, though, the war department continued to resist doing the same with the Soviets for Berlin; that was a purely military matter to be worked out during the invasion.

When the allies' occupation forces moved into their agreed positions, partition became a fact, and the "big three" began to lose interest in long-range plans for making it formal. Churchill put it bluntly

only six weeks after Yalta: "I hardly like to consider dismember-
ment until my doubts about Russia's intentions have been cleared
away."[11] The postwar struggle for Germany was beginning. At the
same time, the first decisive step in dividing Germany had been
taken by creating very different occupation regimes on the backs of
very different occupying armies.

When Roosevelt died, Truman inherited plans and discussions
but no decisions. His occupation directive, JCS 1067/8, signed in
May 1945, stitched together separate departmental perspectives and
so provided the military governor, General Lucius Clay, little clear
guidance. The entire range of German issues—from relations among
occupation zones to partition and reparations—was on the agenda
when the big three reconvened in Potsdam in late July 1945, this
time with Truman representing the United States.

Potsdam seemed to signify the intention to keep Germany unified
but in fact laid the basis for dividing it. Again, reparations dominated the discussion. Stalin fell away from his fixed figure for reparations in return for provisional acceptance by Truman and Churchill
of the Oder-Neisse line as Germany's eastern border. Instead, the
final agreement spelled out a formula for the Soviet Union to take
industrial goods from its zone and receive them from the western
ones. The country was to "be treated as a single economic unit,"
with centralized agencies operating from the Allied Control Council
in Berlin overseeing the exchange of reparations from the western
sectors for food from the eastern.

The avowed aim of the economic policy was to maintain a standard of living throughout Germany "not exceeding the average of
the standards of living of European countries," excluding Britain
and the Soviet Union.[12] The intention was to balance punishment
with viability: on the one hand, Germans should not be better off
than other Europeans, not now and not for some time to come; on
the other, keeping the nation in poverty would risk the need for
large subsidies from the victors in the short run and eventually limit
the recovery in the rest of Europe. The vehicle for striking the balance was an agreed "level of industry," which implied setting ceil-
ings (or floors) on many different lines of production. Needless to

say, the fact of Germany's hardening division cut across all these considerations.

At Potsdam, a superficial unity among the big three was undermined by the so-called first charge principle, ironically included at American insistence. One of the Truman administration's inheritances was the American belief that U.S. taxpayers had financed German World War I reparations payments (albeit indirectly, when Germany reneged on reparations to Britain and France, and the two, in turn, fell short in repaying their war debts to the United States). To avoid a repetition, Truman insisted, over Stalin's reluctance, that the "first charge" on the German economy go for necessary imports, not reparations.

The effect of the principle was to divide administration by giving the military governors control over the flow of goods from their respective zones. In July 1945, Truman authorized the U.S. military "to assume procurement and initial financing responsibilities" for imports into the American zone "whether or not an agreed program is formulated and carried out by the Control Council."[13] The ambivalence of American policy continued; under the pressure of circumstance, the United States rhetorically supported but practically weakened central authority.

The awkward presence of France made western policy even more complicated. In form a victor but in fact the victim of German occupation, France's immediate preoccupation was economic, assuring that its own recovery did not lag behind Germany's, but its enduring one was political—its status as a great power and its stature in relation to its neighbor and historic enemy, Germany. In reclaiming its earlier status, it found support from the United States and Britain, which at Yalta had secured an occupation zone for France.

However, France's second aim, keeping its perennial rival weak, was more problematic. Morgenthauism was not relegated to the political fringe in France. Nor were memories of Versailles and its aftermath, when the grand promises, like the League of Nations, were found wanting as America turned away, and France was left alone to seek its own security in relation to its powerful neighbor. This time around, France sought a long occupation of Germany, along with measures to deprive it of the industrial riches in the Rhineland, the Saar, and the Ruhr—the last to be separated from Germany if possible, subjected to international control if not.

Truman's response to France's immediate economic problem, coal shipments from Germany, was a directive, issued in the midst of the Potsdam conference in July 1945, authorizing the American occupation authority to "make available for export out of the production of the coal mines in Western Germany a minimum of 10 million tones of coal during 1945, and a further 15 million tons by the end of April, 1946."[14] The directive's goals quickly turned out to be wildly unrealistic; they meant asking the American army occupiers not only to secure a minimum standard of living, provide reparations to the Soviet Union, and finance needed imports, but also to export enough coal to promote France's own recovery. Well less than half the stipulated coal exports were actually delivered—a constant source of French complaints.

The larger nest of issues—from who would control German industrial territory to how it would be controlled and how Germany's economy could benefit Europe, France in particular—turned on control of the Ruhr, which because of its importance was tantamount to control of the western Germany economy as a whole. The official American position, that the Ruhr should remain German but might be placed under some international control, covered disagreements that ran through other issues as well.

For Clay and his fellow occupation officials charged with running Germany, economic recovery was of paramount importance. To that end, they favored noninterference in the Ruhr and suspected French motives. By contrast, others in the American government were inclined to sympathize with French fears about the long-term security implications of who controlled the Ruhr, or to feel that, tactically, an international authority might be used to hasten French acceptance of Germany's rehabilitation more broadly, or both. As the Cold War's imminence impelled Americans to seek Germany's full presence in western defenses, interest in using the Ruhr as a lever on French policy grew.

The eventual compromise was the International Agreement on the Ruhr, negotiated in 1948 and agreed to in 1949.[15] As it turned out, the agreement was largely overtaken by events as the onset of the Cold War shifted attention, in Washington especially, from controlling Germany to enlisting it. The agreement's failure did, however, drive French leaders, Robert Schuman in particular, to contemplate more venturesome ways of solving their historic problem, living side-by-side with Germany. In this way the Ruhr agreement prefigured the real beginning of European integration in 1950, the European Coal and Steel Community (ECSC).

In 1946, France's preoccupation with Germany was all the clearer because it was the one thing on which all its political parties could agree. Its postwar politics revolved around a volatile coalition of communists, socialists, and Catholics, with the communists securing nearly a third of the votes and holding key government portfolios including defense. French politics became still more confused when General Charles de Gaulle—the wartime hero still smarting from what he regarded as condescending treatment by his allies, symbolized by his exclusion from Potsdam—resigned the provisional presidency in early 1946 to build his own political party.

Western policy became hostage to French instability; western leaders had to look over their shoulders at the French reaction to their German policy. France, unrepresented at Potsdam, did not regard itself as bound by the agreements; fearing German power, it continued to veto the arrangements for central German authority. But when Clay, who plainly found the French every bit as troublesome as the Soviets, requested that the Truman administration put pressure on Paris to be more cooperative in implementing the Potsdam accords, he was usually put off politely: Washington feared that the French government would collapse under pressure, bringing the communists to power.

Throughout 1946 the four powers were at loggerheads, and the practical facts of Germany's division increased apace. With the "economic unit" of Potsdam a dead letter, Moscow had consolidated its hold on its eastern zone, creating a ruling party through the forced fusion of the social democrats and communists into the Socialist Unity Party (SED in its German initials). Absent an agreement on centralized agencies, the Soviet Union had withheld grain shipments to the western sectors and, in April 1946, refused to implement a common import-export plan that would have eased the food shortages in the western zones.

James Byrnes, Truman's secretary of state, tried to force the issue by proposing a four-power treaty to disarm Germany for a twenty-five year period. The proposal, made at the end of April 1946, received no formal Soviet response until July, when the Soviet foreign minister, V. M. Molotov, rejected it. Molotov's response parried the idea, again with reparations as the ostensible reason, by saying that Germany's demilitarization could not be assured until reparations had been completed.

In the interim, the United States took a significant step of its own. On May 2 Clay ordered an end to the dismantling of German plants in the U.S. zone and to shipments of reparations to the Soviets until Potsdam's arrangements for economic unity were established. Clay's action is susceptible to various interpretations, which it has received, with political motives to suit the inclinations of the interpreter.

It is probably fairest, however, to see the decision, while dramatic in retrospect, as a piece of Clay's business. His mission was not the grand politics of postwar Europe, though his actions bore on that future, and his report to Washington soon after his decision outlined a political structure for Germany. Rather, his immediate task was the practical one of feeding Germans and making their economy self-supporting. Contrary to the assumptions of occupation,

> after one year . . . zones represent air-tight territories with almost no free exchange of commodities, persons, and ideas . . . no one unit can be regarded as self-supporting, although [the] British and Russian could become so. . . . As it now stands, economic integration is becoming less each day.[16]

Clay had been compelled to seek congressional appropriations in aid of the German economy. In the circumstance, stopping the immediate drain was logical. If the premises of his mission were wrong, then that fact should be acknowledged quickly. So Clay implicitly argued in his report, which also proposed for the first time integrating the British and American zones if all else failed.

Britain's financial problems in its own zone paralleled America's; the cost of importing food was a particular drain for a Britain that was endeavoring to rebuild and a Labour government that was trying to construct a welfare state. Accordingly, after Molotov's rejection of the Byrnes treaty, Ernest Bevin, the British foreign secretary, informed the other allies that Britain would be compelled to "organize the British zone" and "to produce for export in order to reduce the burden on the British taxpayer."[17]

To salvage the fact, or at least the façade, of four-power occupation, Byrnes immediately proposed that the other powers merge their zones with the American. Only the British did so, after considerable hesitation, and the two nations began working out arrangements for Bizonia, as the federation was to be called. Byrnes articulated the shift in American policy at a speech in Stuttgart in September 1946:

> If complete unification cannot be secured, we shall do everything in our power to secure maximum possible reunification . . . it is the view of the American Government that the German people through Germany, under proper safeguards, should now be given the primary responsibility for the running of their own affairs.[18]

As significantly, Byrnes announced the turnaround in U.S. occupation policy. American troops had been scheduled to remain in Germany for some two years; now, Byrnes announced, they would remain in Germany "for a long period. . . . We are staying here. As long as there is an occupation army in Germany, American armed forces will be part of that occupation army."[19] Against its inclinations, and without quite realizing it at the time, the United States was edging toward a long-term engagement in Europe.

DEBATING PARTITION

Interestingly, George Kennan, the author of the famous "long telegram" from Moscow in February 1946 and of the Mr. X article in *Foreign Affairs* the next year, the person generally considered the originator of the containment policy, was himself pessimistic about the prospects for a unified Germany. In a sequel to his long telegram, written from Moscow in March, several months before Byrnes moved toward Bizonia, Kennan reckoned that Moscow was happy to have several months after Potsdam for stock-taking. While the centralized agencies could be useful to the Soviet Union as a means of advancing its control of Germany, that time was not necessarily at hand. Thus, Moscow would not oppose the agencies in principle but for the moment would be happy to have the French "run interference for them."

His assessment amounted to a nifty prediction. Because he doubted that the agencies would be effective "in averting the final communization of Germany," there were two alternatives: try to keep Germany unified but risking its vulnerability; or

> carry to its logical conclusion the process of partition which was begun in the East and . . . endeavor to rescue [the] Western Zones of Germany by walling them off against Eastern penetration and integrating them into an international pattern of Western Europe rather than into a united Germany.[20]

The argument over dividing Germany then makes fascinating reading now after the country has reunified. By 1947, keeping Germany pastoral was plainly unworkable; this kind of "industrial disarmament"—in the description of John Foster Dulles, the presumptive secretary of state in a Republican administration after the 1948 presidential elections—condemned the allies at best to perpetual occupation and charity.[21] Moreover, the postwar Strategic Bombing Survey had revealed that while bombing Germany had destroyed its cities, the bombs had scarcely reduced its industrial potential. As Eugene V. Rostow put it in 1947: "German industry today has the capacity to support a German army within a few months, and German economic life on the old scale within a few years."[22]

For Dulles the conclusion was not that Germany should be divided, but rather that its unification ought to be paralleled by that of Europe as a whole—language that could have come from the mouths of German leaders Helmut Kohl and Hans-Dietrich Genscher as they sought to reassure their partners about German

unification in 1990. Dulles accepted that Germany as a single economic unit would, left to its own devices, naturally become a more
centralized state. To avoid that progression, the agreement to place
Germany's industrial heartland, the Ruhr, under a form of joint control would "make it possible to develop the industrial potential of
Western Germany in the interest of the economic life of Western
Europe, including Germany, and do so without making Germany
the master of Europe."[23]

Rostow, then young and out of government but later undersecretary of state in the Johnson administration and arms control negotiator under Reagan, regarded a unified Germany within a western
European federation as nearly as bad as one holding the balance
between East and West. As to the second:

> the Russians are much better equipped than we are to play the game
> in Germany. As in 1939 they would have the support of powerful
> groups of nationalist Germans. The Soviets could offer the Germans
> prizes . . . Silesia and East Prussia [the territories given to Poland at
> Yalta], for example. Instead of a capitalist Germany facing East we
> might find a National Communist Germany backed by a neutral Rus-
> sia facing West.

On the other hand, even a post-Potsdam Germany was, for Rostow,
too big to federate in a European union; the danger of domination
was too great whether or not the Soviet Union saw German federation as a hostile act. Given Germany's industrial potential, its permanent disarmament was "inherently unworkable."[24] If disarmament
was impossible and unity destabilizing, that left only division. Rostow's conclusion was that Germany should be divided into three or
four states within a European union.

THE MOSCOW CONFERENCE

Whatever these American arguments, and despite the fact that they
were not yet resolved, the Moscow foreign ministers meeting ratified
the incipient division of Germany that events during 1946 had created. Byrnes left the state department in January 1947. He had

wanted to leave government service for some time; Truman, who regarded him as too slow in recognizing the shift to the right in American politics and not always scrupulous in keeping the president informed of his activities, was happy enough to grant his wish.

Byrnes was replaced by George C. Marshall, the war's "silent hero." Marshall retreated to his office for his first weeks to read into the job. Germany was at the top of the agenda and Moscow his first mission.

Planning for Bizonia was not yet complete, and the step itself was still regarded as transitional, not final. The Moscow meeting was thus more open in prospect than it appears in retrospect, a fact reflected in the briefing papers prepared for it.[25] Indeed, the Report of the Secretary's Policy Committee on Germany labeled partition "a solution incompatible with the objective of a neutral Germany." Would a neutral Germany incline toward the West? The paper was tentative: such a Germany would be a potential western ally but would also try to play East against West. In that game Moscow would have advantages, most obvious among them the control of Germany's eastern borders on which Rostow had focused.

As earlier, the host of issues came down to two—unification and reparations. In retrospect, an agreement on them was not impossible. The American briefing papers for the meeting contemplated a federal Germany with considerable autonomy for the *Länder* (or states) as a safeguard against manipulation from the East. Those same papers cited hints that Moscow might again reaffirm the unity of Germany's economy provided it received reparations from current production. On the last score, there was evidence at hand to suggest that Germany would be able to pay: the Strategic Bombing Survey and more specific estimates by the Federal Reserve and the Office of Strategic Services indicated that Germany would be able to pay between $2.5 and $3.5 billion annually.[26]

That, however, was not how American policymakers saw matters at the time. To them, Germany was prostrate and dependent, not a surprising view; it was hard to see beyond the unusual circumstance of defeat and the artificial condition of division. There was also the imperative of looking over their shoulders at Congress: so long as the United States was providing aid to Germany, *any* plan for German reparations out of current production was bound to evoke the interwar image of American taxpayers indirectly footing the bill for reparations.

More to the point, events in Europe's southeast weighed heavily on the discussions in Moscow about its center, Germany. While Marshall prepared for his meetings, Britain conveyed, in two notes received by the state department on February 21, 1947, the disturbing, though not entirely surprising, news that it would be unable to maintain its positions in Greece and Turkey, aiding the Greek monarchy in its civil war against communists and modernizing the Turkish army.[27]

After a flurry of initial decisions to fill the gap—the beginning of the line of policy known first as Point 4, then as the Truman doctrine—Marshall left southeastern Europe to his deputy, Dean Acheson. He did so with the instruction that Acheson should take what action he deemed necessary without regard to Marshall's mission in Moscow, an instruction, as Acheson put it in his memoirs, that amounted to a "commanding officer in a forward and exposed spot [calling] down his own artillery fire upon his own position to block an enemy advance."[28]

While retrospective, Acheson's language is nonetheless suggestive, for it is the language of containment, not of negotiation. Marshall made two stops en route to Moscow, in Paris and Berlin. In Paris he met with French president Vincent Auriol and heard an earful about coal; as earlier, the words were economic but their subject was political: German power. France was receiving only half its requirements of German coal, a situation that, if continued, would mean France would lag behind Bizonia in reconstructing. On the other hand, Marshall's French interlocutors suggested, if France received guarantees about German coal shipments, it "would find it possible to go along with the United States views on other German problems."[29]

In Berlin Marshall conferred with Clay, his political advisor, Robert Murphy, and with Dulles, who had been invited to come with the secretary. The men reviewed but did not change the basic American position. Clay, his mind fixed on his job of feeding Germans, again suggested a thorough stock-taking of Germany's economic potential before reaching any sweeping political decisions.

Dulles, having prepared a memorandum for the meeting, sought to broaden the conversation to high policy. He emphasized themes he had touched on in his New York speech before leaving, holding to the idea of a unified Germany but worrying about its implications—it would have "an enormous bargaining power" in any event, and could become "independent of both East and West"; but there was also the risk, at worst, that it would be subject to "political penetration" by the Soviet Union. As a safeguard, he again proposed that "the European settlement should seek primarily to solidify and strengthen Western Europe."[30]

Whatever agreement might have been possible, the Moscow meetings went according to Potsdam's form. Molotov, following Byrnes's lead at Potsdam, proposed a package, much as the United States had expected he would: there could be no unification without reparations. As the foreign minister put it on March 19:

> If . . . we all agree that the realization of the economic unity of Germany, far from preventing the payment of reparation, would certainly include the solution of the reparations problem, it should not be very difficult to reach agreement about other things. The main point is to decide the problem of reparations at the same time as deciding that of the economic unity of Germany.[31]

In substance, there was, in Marshall's words, "much in common in the four views."[32] Clay's remarks at the meetings underscored the link between reparations and division: how the former came out would be decisive in "fixing American influence in Germany at the Elbe [the eastern border of the western sectors] rather than along the Oder-Neisse [the eastern border of the Soviet sector]," hence "the United States should not take an adamant stand without a study of the availability of reparations from current production which would show the costs unwarranted."[33]

If the United States and its allies had been willing to consider reparations from current German production, the elements of a compromise were at hand: some of Moscow's original claim had been fulfilled, and Molotov at Potsdam had offered a reduction of $2 billion. Moreover, Moscow might have been willing to compromise on other differences, such as control over the Ruhr, where Moscow wanted a role, or the form of German government, where it opposed federalism. So Molotov indicated more than once. At the same time, however, he played into western concerns by continuing to reiterate the Soviet $10 billion claim when Germany's ability to pay from current industrial production was manifestly hypothetical.

By the spring of 1947 there was little disposition for compromise left on the part of the United States, or, for that matter, Britain or France. Marshall had little room for maneuver and was little inclined to use what he had. Congress seemed determined to cut the amount of civil relief provided to Germany, and the war department, in return, assured Congress that food subsidies could be eliminated within three years of implementing Bizonia. Any scheme for paying Moscow reparations from current production was bound to look to Congress, even if not to the administration, as indirect payment by American taxpayers.

In a luncheon with Bevin on March 22, Marshall spoke of "the political impossibility of securing agreement by an American Congress to a course of action which involved the indirect payment of reparations," and so he "had opposed this with the view that the Soviet demand for some form of reparations out of current production during the next two years would be implacable."[34]

The American reluctance, however, did not derive primarily from money. Given that Soviet behavior, in eastern Europe but also in Germany, was regarded by Americans as duplicitous at the least, seeking venturesome compromises seemed too risky to contemplate. The safer course was to hold firm. If American influence to the Oder-Neisse would thus be sacrificed, at least that to the Elbe could be consolidated. The risk-averse course was perhaps the more inviting because unification was not unambiguously so. Division, and thus a firm western hold on the western zones, could limit opportunities for Soviet meddling. And there was still the question, articulated outside government by Rostow, of whether a reunited Germany would be too powerful.

Georges Bidault, the French foreign minister, was the only clear winner at Moscow, and the conference was pivotal for French policy. For France as for the Soviet Union, the first issue was financial—in France's case coal shipments from Germany. Yet coal shipments were only a piece of the real issue—France's postwar station in relation to Germany—and a divided Germany could be seen as a first-best for France, not a second-best. It was still more attractive because of what the Soviet Union opposed but the United States and Britain conceded—French control of the Saar.

Bidault left Moscow with promises of more coal (in a three-power agreement of April 19), the clear prospect of controlling the Saar, and the hazier one of a divided Germany—success all around. The combination of Soviet hostility to and Anglo-American support for French claims was a turning point in French policy, one confirmed when the communists were expelled from the French coalition, even if over price controls and not foreign policy, in the spring and summer of 1947.

En route home Marshall stopped again in Berlin. He agreed that Clay should move ahead quickly with Bizonia. The conference and its aftermath meant, as one member of the delegation wrote immediately afterward, that American troops would be in Germany for the indefinite future.[35] If seeking a first-best, a unified Germany firmly part of a western confederation, looked impossible or too risky, the United States could have a second-best, such an arrangement for the western part of a divided Germany. But the price would be continuing American engagement.

GERMANY'S FUTURE, AND EUROPE'S

Had the Moscow meetings succeeded in producing a provisional German government and a commitment to currency reform throughout the four zones, both the immediate and the more distant future might have turned out very differently.[36] A provisional government would have had a life of its own, perhaps susceptible to the blandishments Rostow feared since its overriding goal would have been reunification. On the other hand, most of its members would not have been communists.

Molotov himself suggested that such a government could have considerable elbowroom, on the model of what transpired in Austria or Japan:

> The Allies must not assume direct moral responsibility for everything that takes place in Germany. Appropriate responsibility should be borne by a German government endowed with the necessary powers.
>
> The situation in this respect can be explained by citing the example of Japan. We know that Japan has it own Government although supreme power rests with the Allied occupation authorities. We could cite other examples as well.[37]

He also suggested that Germans themselves should decide in a vote whether to have a centralized or a federal government.

What actually happened in the western sectors after June 1948 is clear testimony to what a four-power currency reform for all of Germany might have accomplished if it had been decided on at Moscow. The assessments of Rostow and others would have been proven right: Germany's underlying economic dynamism would have been apparent, and American (and British) food subsidies quickly could have been exchanged for raw material inputs. In fact, industrial production in West Germany jumped by 60 percent after the currency reform and reached prewar levels by 1950. Faced with a choice between reparations and partition, a provisional government would have opted for reparations.

Had they tried hard to break the logjam at Moscow, American negotiators would have held two advantages: control over the flow of reparations and the threat of partition. Neither of those advantages would have been unalloyed; the flow of reparations would have entailed opportunities for Soviet influence in the western sectors, for example, and the threat of partition would have been a difficult trump to play. But there was the opportunity to keep a unified Germany in play had the United States and its allies been willing to try.

By early 1947, however, they were not willing, or they reckoned the risks of trying to be too high. Kennan regarded the chances for Soviet-American cooperation over Germany as "pipe-dreams."[38] The year 1946 had been decisive. The disillusion bred of Soviet disregard for the Yalta agreements on eastern Europe was high. Kennan had sent his famous "long telegram" from Moscow at the end of February 1946, and in March Winston Churchill, speaking in Fulton, Missouri, with President Truman at his side, evoked the image of an "iron curtain" that had descended in Europe. In November the Republicans took control of both the House and the Senate, with a swing of over a hundred seats in the House.

Events in eastern Europe seemed to have validated the prevailing view that "you couldn't do business with Stalin." For Acheson, it was a "mistake to believe you can sit down with the Russians and solve questions." Kennan's long telegram was optimistic about thwarting the Soviet Union with firmness but not about negotiating with the Kremlin: "Russian rulers sought security . . . only in the patient but deadly struggle for total destruction of rival power, never in compacts and compromises with it."[39]

This view was not unquestioned. Walter Lippmann, the dean of American political commentators, criticized Kennan and containment precisely on the ground where Kennan felt vulnerable, and where he later argued he had been misunderstood—that containment amounted only to holding the line, primarily with military means, and hoping for the best. As Lippmann put it: "For a diplomat to think that rival and unfriendly powers cannot be brought to a settlement is to forget what diplomacy is all about. There would be little for diplomats to do if the world consisted of partners enjoying political intimacy and responding to common appeals."[40] Yet, whatever Kennan came to think of containment as it was developed, by 1947 it seemed the prudent course. Negotiation seemed to have failed; better to try firmness.

In the circumstances, what might have produced another American policy is not easy to conceive. So much would have had to change. Perhaps if Marshall had taken over as secretary sooner, he might have stretched bipartisanship further. Surely the image of Dulles, the presumptive heir apparent, invited along to a critical negotiation by the sitting secretary of state is a potent symbol. It reminds us that not all our memories of past bipartisanship in foreign policy are pure nostalgia. Yet Marshall's was the bipartisanship of the weak, a Democratic administration trying to extract money from a Republican Congress while sharing the presumption that the 1948 elections would sweep it from power, turning heirs apparent into heirs.

Perhaps if Roosevelt had lived much longer, he might have been prepared to run risks his successor could not. He might have continued to believe he could do business with Stalin, or at least to have tried, and remained popular enough to stave off the right in general and the Republicans in the 1946 elections in particular. But there still would have remained the attitudes of America's allies, France in particular. And none of these speculations would have counted for much without more help from Moscow.

If Germany's postwar history had been different, so would Europe's (and, no doubt, the world's). To say that is only to underscore the importance of Germany as both cause and effect of the ensuing order. Would a unifying Germany in the late 1940s have made for faster or slower European integration? The hypothetical is too far from reality, with too many moving pieces, to be sure of the answer. It might have been faster because a unified Germany would have provided even greater impetus for France and the others to find a way to tie it in; on the other hand it might have been slower because a Germany in the process of unifying would have remained the central preoccupation, especially of itself.

In that puzzle there are echoes of the Europe of the 1990s and beyond, now that Germany is unified. In the 1940s, though, what intervened was the Soviet threat. Attention in Washington and London, if not in Paris, turned from economics to security, from whether Moscow might prevent the economic integration of Germany to whether it might overwhelm western Europe with the shadow of its military power if not overrun it by force of arms.

Creating Dependence

The argument still rages over the extent to which the turn from cooperation to hostility among the wartime partners was inevitable. In any event the turn came, and with it ended the hopes for great power entente, or even world federalism, embodied in the United Nations. Those hopes reemerged only with the fall of the Berlin Wall, and then in more modest form.

Yet despite the turn, the kind of European dependence on the United States that was enshrined in the NATO alliance was not the initial conception on either side of the Atlantic. During 1946 and 1947, while the recent victors in a hot war swung ambiguously toward a cold one, western Europe stirred to organize its own defense, with the United States as a residual guarantor. Europe was to defend itself; so officials thought in both Europe and the United States. America would not abandon Europe as it had after the previous war, but it would return home, its engagement in Europe remaining only that of a backstop and ultimate guarantor of security.

Instead, though, Europe's dependence ensued under the imminent threat of the Cold War becoming another hot one and in the presence of nuclear weapons. In opting against self-defense and for a structural alliance with the United States, Europe bought deterrence on the cheap through nuclear weapons. The nations of western Europe reacquired all the attributes of sovereignty save the most important—responsibility for their own defense.

As Europeans first stirred to organize security arrangements, their minds stayed on the last war, so recently at hand. Germany, though divided and occupied, was still the enemy, so labeled in the Anglo-French Treaty of Dunkirk in 1947. It became an ally only by stages. Once the other Europeans reached out for America's protection, Germany's western sectors became allies in fact, for Europe's protector was also Germany's occupier. Once western Germany had become a democracy and once Europe had turned to the Soviet threat, the Federal Republic could hardly be excluded from full alliance membership.

Indeed, with America in Europe and in Germany, NATO membership provided both German territory as a buffer against Soviet attack and some constraint on West German action. The next step, though, was harder still to take, especially for France. If Germany were a full member, with American and other allied troops on its soil, it would have to be defended; if it were to be defended, how better than with German troops? But that meant not only circumventing the demilitarization to which Germany had been subjected at war's end. If France's concerns over *its* former enemy were to be met, they could be met only at the price of a deepened American military engagement.

And so for the United States, the counterpart to Europe's dependence was an American military engagement that was tantamount to a permanent one. That state of affairs was new for the United States, and it ran against the republic's historical tradition. Despite the Soviet threat, the engagement had to be choked down by the body politic in stages, and in the end it was still officially advertised as temporary, until such time as Europe could again resume responsibility for its own defense.

The British Initiative

For both America and Europe the turning point came in the first months of 1948. If precise timing is required, a series of secret meetings held at the Pentagon the last week of March is as good as any. No American leader in 1945 or 1946 or even 1947 had in mind a military alliance linking the United States to western Europe. George Washington's admonition against entangling alliances rang in their ears despite the wartime collaboration. They were prepared to fight off a retreat toward the isolation of the interwar period, to make of the United States a backstop for Europe. But they expected that to be hard enough.

The Marshall Plan fit their intentions. Set in motion by Secretary Marshall's speech at Harvard in June 1947, it reflected the primacy of economic reconstruction. It was American help given to Europeans who could use it. They had the technical expertise and the organization. The United States would help them get on their feet. Just as America had gotten into Europe before the war with Lend-Lease, it would get out of it with something similar—American aid to a European initiative.

Yet less than two years after Marshall's speech, the United States was engaged in a permanent military alliance with Europe. The primary reason for the dramatic change was the obvious one, Soviet misbehavior. Moscow had refused to withdraw its troops from the Iranian region of Azerbaijan in March 1946; two months later civil war broke out in Greece; and by 1947 communist governments had taken power in Poland, Hungary, and Romania.

In February 1948 a communist coup succeeded in Czechoslovakia, while communist agitation was on the rise in France and Italy. Czechoslovakia was a special blow. Its government was led by two patriots, Eduard Beneš and Jan Masaryk, tainted neither by collaboration with the Nazis nor hostility to the Soviet Union. If a democratic middle ground could exist anywhere, it was Czechoslovakia, the eastern European state with a prewar democracy. The communists in the government proclaimed emergency powers, and on March 10 the pajama-clad body of Masaryk, the foreign minister, was found dead in the courtyard below his apartment—ostensibly a suicide but probably a murder.

In March the American government whipped itself into near hysteria when the American high commissioner in Germany, General Lucius Clay, cabled his warning that war with Russia "may come with dramatic suddenness"—a warning carefully leaked all over Washington, not least on Capitol Hill.[1] Belgian foreign minister and later NATO secretary-general Paul-Henri Spaak, one of many who were later called fathers of the European-American alliance, recorded in his memoirs that the title "belongs to Stalin."[2]

If Stalin was the father of NATO, its midwife was the British foreign secretary, Ernest Bevin, who gets as much credit for the shift in American policy as any American. Marshall's words in June 1947 had been just what he was waiting to hear. As he described it several months later at the National Press Club in Washington:

I assure you, gentlemen, that it was like a lifeline to a sinking man. It seemed to bring hope where there was none. The generosity of it was beyond my belief. It expressed a mutual thing. It said, "Try and help yourselves and we will try to see what we can do. Try and do the thing collectively, and we will see what we can put into the pool."[3]

Yet at the same time as Bevin heard Marshall speak of economic assistance, his own thinking was turning from economics to security. What motivated his turn was the impasse among the victorious four powers over a peace agreement. By the spring of 1947 he had ceased to hope for success and had determined not to let the string of vetoes concerning Germany by Stalin's foreign minister, Molotov, paralyze the three western nations.

Wartime collaboration was breaking down. The postwar security order, Bevin concluded, would have to be based on something else. By September he was confiding to a French colleague that the division of the continent was all but inevitable, and that "it therefore became necessary to attempt to organize the Western states into a coherent unity. The time had now come for a return to the political plane."[4]

The pretense of four-power cooperation in the Council of Foreign Ministers ended entirely in London in mid-December 1947, and Bevin turned in earnest to new security arrangements. He met in London on the seventeenth with the French foreign minister, Georges Bidault, and said the time had come to create "some sort of federation in Western Europe, preferably of an unwritten flexible kind." To the Frenchman he also confided that London and Paris would have to "advise Washington while letting the Americans say and think that it was they who were acting."[5]

Meeting with Marshall that same night, he outlined the same ideas, again in general terms. Bevin knew his listener and so was cautious. There was no mention of formal alliance; rather this would be "an understanding backed by power, money and resolute action"—a kind of spiritual federation.[6] Marshall seemed to agree in principle but sent John Hickerson, the state department's director of European affairs, to the foreign office the next day for more specifics. Hickerson learned that Bevin envisioned "two security arrangements, one a small tight circle included a treaty engagement between the UK, the Benelux countries and France. Surrounding that, a larger circle with somewhat lesser commitments but still commitments in treaty form bringing in the U.S. and Canada also."[7]

The foreign secretary's vagueness probably reflected the state of his own thinking, mixed with some discretion for the benefit of the Americans. The reference to "spiritual federation" was especially elusive; it confused Bevin's own foreign office. He developed his ideas further over the next month, first in papers put before his cabinet colleagues on January 8, 1948, then in a cable to his ambassadors in Washington, Paris, and Ottawa, for them to inform the respective governments.[8]

The Marshall Plan was welcome, but "progress in the economic field will not in itself suffice to call a halt to the Russian threat." What was needed was a "Western democratic system" comprising, in addition to Britain, "Scandinavia, the Low Countries, France, Italy, Greece and possibly Portugal. As soon as circumstances permit, we should, of course, wish also to include Spain and Germany without whom no Western system can be complete." Still no talk of "alliance," and Bevin's direct reference to the American role was suitably cautious. But it was the skeleton of an alliance, and, to boot, an alliance that would include the enemy-about-to-become-friend, Germany—all this less than three years after the armistice.

In his message to Bidault, Bevin went one step further. He suggested an approach to the Benelux countries—Belgium, the Netherlands, and Luxembourg—offering them an arrangement similar to the Anglo-French Treaty of Dunkirk, signed the previous year. Bidault readily agreed, having earlier suggested to Bevin a joint approach to Belgium, and the offer was made on January 20. But the Dunkirk treaty had been shaped for the last war, not the next: it was explicitly aimed at aggression from Germany.

No doubt, Bevin, the ex-wagon driver and trade union leader, with no lack of savvy for all his lack of formal education, was primarily a practical politician beset with a grave problem—the Soviet Union. He was never one to defer action for want of a detailed plan. As he had confided to Marshall in London:

There is no chance that the Soviet Union will deal with the West on any reasonable terms in the foreseeable future. The salvation of the West depends on the formation of some form of union, formal or informal in character, in Western Europe backed by the United States and the Dominions—such a mobilization of moral and material force as will inspire confidence and energy within and respect elsewhere.[9]

He put the point with high drama in mid-February, after the coup in Czechoslovakia, opening an emergency meeting with the American ambassador, Lewis W. Douglas:

We are now in a crucial period of six to eight weeks which will decide the future of Europe. I have no fear of the future provided we get through it. But I am really anxious lest the period immediately before us should turn out to be the last chance for saving the West.[10]

If, in retrospect, it seems tolerably clear that Stalin's actions were improvised opportunism, not preinvasion calculation, it is hard to fault European or American leaders at the time for fearing the worst. The balance of military force in Europe had tilted sharply toward the Soviet Union, perhaps by several to one. The American presence, three and a half million soldiers at war's end, was only 200,000 two years later, and those were configured for occupation duty, not stopping an invasion. The epigram attributed to Robert Lovett, Marshall's undersecretary of state, was overstated but not by much, even as its pithiness was characteristic: "All the Russians need to get to the Channel is shoes."[11]

Wartime British planning for the postwar era had inclined toward the conclusion that, whatever the success of the United Nations, Britain's interests would require association with a western European security grouping, in turn cooperating with the Commonwealth and especially the United States.[12] The planning contemplated two alternative forms of such a security system. One, which dominated British policy until early 1948, was a series of bilateral treaties along the lines of the Treaty of Dunkirk. The other, a multilateral pact, was the one toward which Bevin now turned.

Bevin took his ideas public in a speech to Parliament on January

22, 1948. Marshall's formal response was favorable if guarded, and the general American reaction was also favorable. Congress was just beginning hearings on the Marshall Plan, formally the European Recovery Program (ERP), and so was attentive to indications of Europe's will. Senator Arthur Vandenberg, the Republican chairman of the Senate Foreign Relations Committee and the symbol of bipartisanship in foreign affairs, called it "a terrific speech—one of the most helpful things we have heard from Europe."[13]

Encouraged, Bevin took the next step. Through his ambassador in Washington, Lord Inverchapel, he proposed Anglo-American talks looking to a defense agreement that might reinforce the efforts of the five European powers. Inverchapel saw not Marshall but his undersecretary, Robert Lovett. What he got from Lovett was caution. Bevin proposed, Lovett said, nothing less than a military alliance. When Inverchapel mentioned the need for a general commitment to go to war in the case of aggression, he thought he saw Lovett shrink back physically.

Lovett cataloged the reasons for caution, especially including Congress. What Lovett said, diplomatically, was that Congress might be diverted from its consideration of ERP by talk of a security pact. What he no doubt meant was that Congress would have to digest ERP before it could even think about choking down more. A few days later, on February 2, Lovett was even more discouraging, politely declining the secret bilateral talks Bevin had proposed.[14] Sure of agreement, Bevin had dispatched his personal representative, Gladwyn Jebb, who arrived on the second, only to turn around and go home.

DEBATING THE AMERICAN ROLE

Behind Lovett's caution lay an emerging American debate, one reflected most clearly within a single building, the state department. The department's Europeanists, especially John D. Hickerson, the director of the office of European affairs, and his deputy for western Europe, Theodore C. Achilles, had come to the conclusion that a security pact was necessary and that the United States should participate. In a January memorandum to Marshall commenting on Bevin's initiative, Hickerson had written that while the

> objective is magnificent, his first step (extension of the Dunkirk Pact against German aggression) is highly dubious. In my opinion a European Pact modelled on the treaty of Rio de Janeiro is the best answer to the security problem for Western Europe. For such a pact to be really effective, the United States would have to adhere. I believe that this country could and should adhere to such a treaty. . . .[15]

A few days later, Hickerson spelled out the advantages of the Rio formula for Inverchapel:

> automatic action [though not specifically military action] against aggression whether from without or within was provided. . . . conceived in these terms the European defense system would not seem specifically directed against the Soviets and might make it easier of acceptance by states whose geographical position rendered them more vulnerable to Soviet pressure, such as Sweden. . . . it would be even possible for the Soviet Union to join the arrangement without detracting from the protection which it would give to its other members.[16]

By contrast, the department's two main Sovietologists, Charles E. ("Chip") Bohlen, the counselor, and George Kennan, then director of the policy planning staff, held to the idea of a European arrangement backed by an American guarantee. Writing to Marshall at the same time as Hickerson, Kennan also applauded the Bevin initiative, and he, too, expressed misgivings about extending the Dunkirk framework. But his reasons were different:

> Military union should not be the starting point. It should flow from the political, economic and spiritual union—not vice versa. . . . People in Europe should not bother their heads too much in the initial stage about our relationship to this concept; if they develop it and make it work, there will be no real question as to our long-term relationship to it, even with respect to the military guarantee. This will flow logically from the circumstances.[17]

Kennan's 1946 "long telegram" earned him the reputation as the author of containment, but he himself became more and more skeptical of the policies pursued in containment's name. In his memoirs he wrote that "the greatest mystery of my own role in Washington in those years . . . was why so much attention was paid in certain instances . . . to what I had to say, and so little in others." Neither he nor Bohlen believed an actual Soviet invasion was imminent. He likened the situation to walking calmly through a garden containing "a dog with very big teeth"; the "baring of fangs" he regarded as calculated to intimidate Europe into staying aloof from the Marshall Plan.[18]

Less fixed on the Soviet threat, he was more preoccupied with the long-term course of European politics. For him the threat was more the demoralization of Europe's states, reflected in communist success in Italy and France, than the Soviet Union. The formal trans-Atlantic commitment that Hickerson and others thought was necessary to reassure western Europe, Kennan feared would only militarize Europe's integration. That, in his view, would only make the German problem harder, freeze the United States and the Soviet Union into hostility, thus fixing the division of Europe, and distract Europe's attentions and resources from their primary political and economic tasks.

He spelled out these ideas in internal memorandums, then later in his memoirs. The clearest version at the time was a paper written in the autumn of 1948, when a formal alliance seemed inevitable but its precise form was still open. Preoccupation with Soviet pressure

> is already widespread, both in Europe and in this country. It is regrettable; because it addresses itself to what is not the main danger. . . .
> the need for military alliances and rearmament on the part of the western Europeans is primarily a *subjective* one, arising in their own minds as a result of their failure to understand correctly their own position. Their best and most hopeful course of action, if they are to save themselves from communist pressures, remains the struggle for economic recovery and internal political stability.

Compared to this, intensive rearmament constitutes an uneconomic and regrettable diversion of effort.[19]

If there was to be an alliance, then it should be as limited as possible. It would be a mistake to "raise for every country in Europe the question: to belong or not to belong." To do so "would make it impossible for any of the satellite countries even to contemplate anything in the nature of a gradual withdrawal from Russian domination, since any move in that direction would take on the aspect of a provocative military move." Kennan had his eyes on the United States as well as Europe, in ways that evoke more recent American debates. He feared that if an alliance was not an empty gesture, it would mean that the United States would become "further over-extended, politically and militarily . . . concerning the increasing discrepancy between our commitments and our military resources."[20]

Most intriguingly, Kennan seemed to have in mind global architecture like that of the interwar period, only this time with confederal arrangements in place in Europe to manage German power. The United States would be more committed to Europe than before the war but would not be tied down by formal alliance: "our policy is still directed . . . toward the eventual peaceful withdrawal of both the United States and the U.S.S.R. from the heart of Europe, and accordingly toward the encouragement of the growth of a third force which can absorb and take over the territory between the two."[21] This was the logic of the Marshall Plan, European recovery leading to the construction of a new Europe. But in the winter and spring of 1948 it was giving way to another logic, that of a permanent American engagement, including the military, in Europe. And Kennan was falling off that train of logic.

THE PENTAGON TALKS

In security more so than economics, the initiative was the Europeans', Bevin's in particular. Washington was hardly indifferent in either area—after all, the United States had provided $10 billion in economic aid before the Marshall Plan. For all of Stalin's menace, however, venturing into security arrangements in early 1948 risked cutting across the economic business then before Congress. It also ran against the echoes of "no entangling alliances" still ringing in Washingtonians' ears, echoes reflected in the state department's internal debate.

And so the Europeans were entreating the Americans as they organized themselves. The Benelux countries rejected the bilateral Dunkirk framework, seeking instead a broader self-defense pact under the UN Charter, and their rejection gave Bevin another opportunity to press Washington for its view. As the five western European powers negotiated the Brussels treaty, their diplomats pressed their American counterparts for support and "eventual military guarantees."[22]

On March 17, 1948, the Brussels treaty was signed. Less pointed at Germany than the Dunkirk treaty, it mentioned the threat of German aggression only in its preamble, and it was both collective security (not bilateral guarantees) and European self-help, the two connected in the treaty's title as "collective self-defense, for a period of fifty years."[23] At almost the hour of the signing, President Truman applauded the act in terms that encouraged the Europeans:

> I am sure that the determination of the free countries of Europe to protect themselves will be matched by an equal determination on our part to help them do so. The recent developments in Europe present this nation with fundamental issues of vital importance. I believe we have reached a point at which the position of the United States should be made unmistakably clear.[24]

Bevin and Bidault immediately picked up on the Truman message and a simultaneous one by Marshall, cabling to Marshall on behalf of their Brussels colleagues with a proposal for talks with the United States at once.[25]

In fact, Marshall had already agreed to secret bilateral Anglo-American talks, touched off by events not in Europe's center but its periphery, Scandinavia. On March 11 the British embassy in Washington had passed the state department an *aide-mémoire* reporting

Norway's fears that it would be under pressure from Moscow to negotiate a bilateral friendship and mutual defense treaty along the lines of the Finnish-Soviet pact then nearing conclusion. Marshall agreed to bilateral talks on the twelfth, probably after discussing the idea briefly with Truman that morning at the edges of a cabinet meeting.

Bevin's part in the Brussels cable was thus something of a cover. Washington was concerned about including the French for security reasons, and Bevin did not mind the exclusion, for his *aide-mémoire* had contemplated a set of overlapping security arrangements; the restricted talks would focus on the North Atlantic area. His Brussels cable did, however, betoken his intention to broaden the discussions as soon as possible, and he did pass a quiet word of the upcoming talks to the new French premier, Robert Schuman, who was in Brussels for the treaty signing.

The exclusion of the French on security grounds is a nice irony, for Donald Maclean, then a rising British diplomat but later discovered to have been a Soviet spy, sat in not only on the trilateral talks but also the subsequent negotiation of a North Atlantic treaty until he was promoted in August. Until Soviet archives are open we will not know what he told his handlers, but his presence meant that Stalin had access to both the blueprint for the western alliance and, more important, the list of materials needed to construct the political basis for it.

The most straightforward interpretation, and probably the correct one, is that whatever Maclean reported, Stalin discounted, perhaps even thought a trap. After all, this was the same Stalin who in 1941 had acquired (but disbelieved as British disinformation) as good intelligence of an impending invasion as any nation ever possessed. No doubt if he saw or believed any of Maclean's take, he simply paused a moment, then proceeded with his chosen course.

Yet because much, though not all, of Stalin's behavior was *so* convenient for the builders of the Atlantic alliance, a clever conspiracy theorist is tempted to harbor the hypothesis that Stalin *wanted* the alliance to succeed. The very day the trilateral talks ended, April 1, 1948, the Soviets first halted British and French military trains to

Berlin—the run-up to the first Berlin crisis, and welcome material for the alliance-builders.

This bizarre hypothesis requires equally bizarre, or at least clever, inferences about Stalin's motives. If his convenient actions were calculated, he would have had to fear he was overreaching, that he might not get his first-best, dominance over all Europe, or even his second-best, an allied or friendly socialist Germany. Then, he *might* have preferred some structure in western Europe—and an American military engagement—to a state of unpredictability in which Germany would loom large. It is probably safest to conclude that Stalin discounted Maclean or, more likely, did not believe his actions had much effect on western deliberation. But since he was careful in calibrating the timing of his actions at other points in the formative postwar years, it remains tempting to see his lack of cunning this time as ambivalence over whether he wanted Germany divided or not, America in or out of Europe.

The trilateral talks—the United States and Britain had agreed to include Canada, which had special ties to both, and the Canadians had quickly agreed—were conducted in strictest secrecy in the bowels of the Pentagon. They were chaired by Douglas, the American ambassador to London, and included diplomats and military men from each of the three countries. They lasted but eleven days.

On the American side, who they did not include was as important as who they did. Those who remained skeptical of moving beyond American guarantees to a European security system, most notably Bohlen and Kennan, were absent, Kennan away on a trip to the Far East, represented by a junior. Their exclusion made immediate consensus easier on the American side at the cost—as the secret British history of the talks put it, speaking specifically of Bohlen—of nourishing "his hostility, which he reserved to exercise with great effect at a later stage."[26]

The question of the American Congress came up again and again in the talks. On the first day, the British participants argued forcefully that the Brussels arrangement required a firm U.S. commitment to aid with military force in the event of any aggression in

Europe. The Americans responded by emphasizing the president's March 17 statement demonstrating clear support. Going further would require congressional approval, no matter whether the commitment was given as an executive promise or in a treaty, and the Senate had not yet been approached.[27]

Or, as the British foreign office summary of the meetings records:

> At the final meeting the Americans entered a warning that it was by no means certain that the idea of a pact would in fact be approved by higher authorities concerned. Hickerson said that some presidential declaration might in practice be all that the Americans would be able to offer. Much would depend on whether some fresh Soviet action maintained the present tense atmosphere. If complete calm prevailed, it would be much more difficult to sell the idea of a pact to the senatorial leaders.[28]

The minutes of the last meeting set out the daisy-chain of approvals required: first by Undersecretary Lovett, then by Secretary Marshall, then to the NSC, then by James Forrestal, the secretary of defense, then the president, then a few members of Congress, especially including Vandenberg.

The Americans first argued for simply extending the Brussels treaty, but the British, Jebb having consulted Bevin during the negotiations, responded with the case for a broader Atlantic pact. The Benelux countries might not want the Scandinavians to join Brussels, and the latter, especially Norway, might not wish to; moreover, associating the United States and Canada with the Brussels treaty would be awkward because of the treaty's economic provisions.

By the second meeting, the group was drifting toward a mutual defense agreement, the Americans pointing out that whatever emergency assurances the United States might offer, if those were to be sustained, eventually Washington would require reciprocal commitments by allies. Hickerson and Douglas repeated over and over that this was a working level meeting, hence no commitments made by anyone were binding; the task was "one of determining objectively upon a possible best course of action."[29]

Yet beneath this analytic blandness, Hickerson and Douglas were trying to stretch the writ of the president's March 17 speech in order to commit the United States to a military pact, if not an alliance. They had the previous year's Rio treaty as an opening wedge. It had the benefits of being both automatic and nondiscriminating: an attack on any signatory was an attack on all, whether the aggressor was outside or inside the pact. It did, however, provide the escape hatch that American constitutional procedures required: military responses were not explicitly mentioned, and each of the parties was to "determine the immediate measures which it may individually take."[30]

Moreover, there was no mention of U.S. military assistance during peacetime, a controversial inclusion in the subsequent North Atlantic Treaty. If the Rio pact was an opening wedge for an Atlantic security pact, a handy precedent, it was no more than that, for Rio seemed to Americans more a formalization of the Monroe Doctrine than a mutual security alliance.

The emerging conclusions were put on paper, primarily by Jebb and Hickerson, then discussed at the last session on April 1. The paper amounted to nothing less than a blueprint for an alliance:[31]

> Thirteen nations—Britain, France, Canada, Belgium, Luxembourg, the Netherlands, Norway, Sweden, Denmark, Iceland, Ireland, Portugal, and Italy—would be sounded out secretly, then invited by the president of the United States to negotiate a mutual security treaty.
>
> Meanwhile, the president would declare, unilaterally, that the United States would regard any attack on a Brussels treaty signatory as an attack on itself and act accordingly.
>
> Such a pledge would also be extended to any new adherents to the Brussels treaty—specifically, Norway, Sweden, Denmark, and Iceland—and Italy would be approached after its 1948 elections, a pivotal struggle between the communists and Christian Democrats.
>
> The United States and Britain would jointly declare that they would countenance no attack on the political independence or territorial integrity of Greece, Turkey, or Iran.

When circumstances permitted, Germany (or its three western zones), Austria (or its three western zones), and Spain should be invited to join both the Brussels treaty and the North Atlantic pact.

FROM TALKS TO ALLIANCE

Truman administration officials were looking over their shoulders at Congress, and beyond it to the American public, during the trilateral talks; they did so still more during negotiation of the North Atlantic Treaty itself. In both instances the question sharpened around the form of pledge or commitment the United States would make. Hickerson, for instance, warned the negotiating group in Washington on August 12 that the treaty

> would constitute one of the most far-reaching changes in our foreign policy in U.S. history. Therefore, it is necessary before concluding such an arrangement to insure that the treaty would meet with Congressional approval. Acrimonious debate over the Treaty or serious objections to certain of its provisions by leaders in Congress would actually serve to jeopardize the security of Western Europe.[32]

Yet if Truman officials looked over their shoulders at members of Congress, they did not actually consult them much, at least not formally. The contrast to the practices of our own times is as marked in one direction as Marshall taking his would-be Republican successor, Dulles, with him to Moscow was in the other. Bringing senators who would have to ratify a treaty into the negotiating process, a matter of course now, was not a practice then. The presidential election impended, an election that both the administration itself and its opponents expected Mr. Truman to lose. With a change of administration in the offing, the Truman team may have felt little desire to consult and the Congress little need to be consulted.

The Senate leadership was not shown the critical negotiating result, the so-called Washington Paper of September 1948, until February 1949, after the election. In the interim, once the Truman administration was reinstalled and under pressure from the Europeans, the weaker commitments in the Washington Paper were strengthened. The task of selling them fell to Dean Acheson, appointed secretary of state at the beginning of Truman's second term, after Marshall's illness.

Acheson found himself in a position that was unfamiliar then but not later: he negotiated with the allies on behalf of the United States and with the Senate on behalf of the allies. He succeeded with the Senate, which approved the North Atlantic Treaty on July 21 by a vote of eighty-two to thirteen. As earlier and later in constructing the alliance, Stalin helped; the Berlin blockade, from July to September 1948, bracketed the main treaty negotiations and was still a fresh memory by the time of the Senate debate.

Yet if the ratification showed how far American opinion as reflected in the Senate had moved, it also demonstrated the limits of the change. What the Senate regarded itself as approving was political reassurance, the logical extension of the Marshall Plan, not the means of balancing military power on the continent of Europe. It was a kind of Monroe Doctrine extended to Europe but with the United States receiving reciprocal pledges from the nations thus protected. As Acheson put it, the treaty would help to "promote full economic recovery through removing the drag of insecurity." Vandenberg agreed. What impressed him was the "notification to Mr. Stalin which puts him in exactly the contrary position to that which Mr. Hitler was in, because Mr. Hitler saw us with a Neutrality Act. Mr. Stalin now sees us with a pact of cooperative action."[33]

The treaty was ratified with the emphasis on European self-help that had been set out in the Vandenberg resolution and embodied in Article 3 of the treaty, which stipulated that "the Parties, separately and jointly, by means of continuous and effective self-help and mutual aid, will maintain and develop their individual and collective capacity to resist armed attack." As Acheson put it to the senators in executive session, Article 3 was to "ensure that nobody is getting a meal ticket from anybody else so far as their capacity to resist is concerned."[34] Trans-Atlantic arguments over who was getting "meal tickets"—later called "burden-sharing"—were thus built into the structure of the alliance from day one.

Most strikingly in view of what came only a year later, administration officials repeated over and over again that there was neither commitment nor plan to send U.S. troops to Europe beyond the two divisions already there for occupation duties. The reassurance was most striking, and later most embarrassing in Acheson's interrogation by Senator Hickenlooper (R, Iowa):

> I am interested in getting the answers as to whether or not we are expected to supply . . . very substantial numbers—of troops and troop organizations, of American troops, to implement the land power of Western Europe prior to aggression.
>
> Is that contemplated under article 3, where we agree to maintain and develop the collective capacity to resist? In other words, are we going to be expected to send substantial numbers of troops over there as a more or less permanent contribution to the development of these countries' capacity to resist?

Acheson's answer was short, sweet, and unequivocal: "The answer to that question, Senator, is a clear and absolute 'no.'"[35]

Much of the Senate's attention and its arguing concerned the nature of the American pledge, and the resulting ratification was accompanied by safeguards aplenty for congressional prerogatives in war-making. For executive officials, however, getting congressional approval for military assistance to the Europeans was nearly as important as the treaty; for some of the allies, France especially, which was still as worried about Germany as it was about Russia, it was more so.

The debate over assistance turned the self-help argument on its head, for now the issue was whether American assistance to the allies was implied by the treaty, and returned, ultimately, to the nature of the American engagement. Both Vandenberg and Senator Robert Taft (R, Ohio), "Mr. Republican" and a man already running for his party's 1952 presidential nomination, opposed an effort by the United States to balance Soviet military force in Europe. Vandenberg, like Kennan, did not think it was necessary to do so and did not regard the treaty as requiring the effort; Taft, by contrast, did so regard the treaty and therefore opposed that portion of it.

EUROPEAN ROLES

For many of us Americans born after the war, even those of us who have managed European issues inside the U.S. government, the role of Britain in creating this dependence is harder to fathom than it would be for an American who had lived through the war. For us, Europe has more and more meant Germany over the last three decades, and until 1989 Germany meant West Germany, the Federal Republic. If the issue was economic, the EC in Brussels also demanded attention.

For us, the Anglo-American special relationship retains a tug. But it is a tug of sentiment more than strategy. British diplomats in Washington are active and informed, often better so about our deliberations around town than we are.[36] Given their access and our more-or-less shared language, they are welcome discussion partners. For us, and still more so for political leaders, they are also welcome company in a strange world.

In 1948, however, Britain was a world power, Europe's leading power even as it occupied a position somewhat apart from Europe, while Germany's three western sectors had not yet been permitted to declare a government. Britain's lead as the only real European victor was plain; and its position across the channel meant its guarantees had some of the external character of America's.

Moreover, American planning for the postwar era had presumed that Britain would resume something like its prewar role; that was true of security and economics alike. In both areas, postwar arrangements would be multilateral, global if possible, but the Anglo-American tie would be pivotal. The large emergency loan the United States made to Britain, $3.75 billion in July 1946, was intended precisely to enable that country once again to become a bulwark of the international economic order.

It took time, perhaps until the Greek-Turkish crisis of early 1947, for official Washington to realize that its premise was mistaken, that Britain was not up to the task. It then took additional time, but less, to reach the conclusion that perhaps Britain *plus* western Europe together might play that part—the premise of the Marshall Plan.

In the security realm, the "superpowers," in William Fox's title which coined the term, were originally three, not two—America, Russia, *and* Britain.[37] The wartime premise was that wartime cooperation would continue into the postwar period, and the security order would be based on that tripartite cooperation, in and around the United Nations. As the looming Cold War dashed that presumption, there still remained traces in the American debate of the feeling that NATO should not interfere with U.S. security obligations under the UN Charter. And there remained more than traces of the assumption that Britain would be the principal American interlocutor.

Canada's role is an interesting footnote to this story, for on a smaller scale it, too, was more important than a present-day American would imagine. That importance was mostly a result of wartime collaboration with both Americans and Britons, along with the personal force of some of its leaders, but it also reflected an older conception of Canada's role. Then, Britain was still the mother country. Though it is seldom noticed, Canada made its retreat from Europe a generation ago when it wound down its defense connection; absent that connection, changes in Canada's population and trade, changes not so different from America's, turned it away from Europe. In that there may be indications for the United States as its own security connection to Europe winds down.

This book is ultimately about America's role and American policy, but its subject is Europe. It was not for want of American reluctance about a formal alliance that another form of security order in Europe—an extension of the self-help of the Brussels treaty, for instance—did not arise. Americans were hardly pressing the Europeans to accept an alliance; quite the contrary, they were more the courted than the courtiers.

Britain, in particular, feared that self-help à la the Marshall Plan would only turn out to be a disguise for a return to the disengagement of the interwar period. Moreover, engaging the United States would avoid, or at least defer choices that Britain's politics did not make easy. It would avoid a clear-cut choice between the special relationship with the United States, plus considerable freedom of action globally, on the one hand, and commitment to a continental coalition on the other. If Britain were to associate with "frogs" and "wogs," not to mention "Huns," at least it would be in the framework of continued Anglo-American comity. With luck, American engagement would save British resources, deferring hard choices about more and more expensive overseas military commitments.

These tensions in British policy were apparent throughout early 1948 as Bevin engineered an alliance. On the military side, the British military chiefs convened to consider the implications of Bevin's diplomacy. There was, in particular, the awkward question of a "continental strategy," thus far neglected. These meetings, from January 29 to February 2, produced a split. Field Marshall, later Viscount Montgomery, the army chief, advocated a continental strategy but was opposed by his air and naval colleagues, both of whom argued for the traditional British maritime and air strategy based on small mobile forces for deployment anywhere in the world.[38]

The debate continued on into the spring, with the prime minister, Clement Atlee, inclined toward the traditional view. Only in May, when the chiefs met with the minister of defense, was it agreed that Britain would plan to fight alongside its western European allies. And even so it took Britain as long as the United States, two more years, before the defense committee of the cabinet agreed that Britain would send reinforcements to the continent if the Soviet Union attacked.[39] Thus Bevin was building a security system to which Britain was unprepared to commit much by way of practical help—a fact that probably increased the foreign secretary's interest in engaging the Americans.

Bevin's own department opposed a purely continental pact. A February 1948 memorandum summarized why.[40] First there was the fact that a purely continental coalition could not alone be sure to deter the Soviet Union. Second was the worry, which found echoes in Kennan's arguments on the other side of the ocean, that it would be "unnecessarily provocative to the Russians." The third and fourth arguments were more characteristic of Britain's dilemma. A western union needed to be constructed by stages, and at this point a regional pact would be going too fast.

Finally, the Europeans seemed to the foreign office to be in the damned-if-they-do/damned-if-they-don't position with regard to American opinion that was characteristic of later episodes as well: "We do not wish by concluding a regional pact of this character to encourage the American school of thought which believes that Western security can be sufficiently assured by a Western regional pact without American participation." Too little European initiative, the foreign office argued, would not merit American engagement, but too much might make it seem unnecessary—an argument that fit Britain's convenience.[41]

With Bevin, France had taken the lead in organizing the European response to Marshall's speech, and for it, too, an Atlantic security arrangement was in 1948 if not first-best, then not a bad second-best. If Soviet hostility was making it less and less likely that Germany could be allowed to remain prostrate, then an American engagement could protect France from both Soviet threat and German revival. For France as for Britain, if money could thereby be liberated, colonial burdens could be sustained. With luck, the Americans might even help with those as well.

AMERICAN POLITICS, GERMAN FIRST-THOUGHTS

On the part of the United States, there is the intriguing question of whether the half-way solution Kennan and others envisioned was possible given American politics—another teaser from the past hanging over the future. Kennan feared that the United States would not be consistent enough to play the central role in a Western system. In hindsight it was, though not always easily or gracefully.

What now seems more relevant is the opposite question: was the United States up to playing the aloof but interested power-balancer that Kennan imagined? Put crudely, was the United States capable of participating usefully in a structure it did not run? William L. Clayton, the undersecretary of state for economic affairs, writing in a memorandum to Marshall in May 1947 after his trip to Europe, made a strong case for U.S. assistance. The United States had "grossly underestimated the destruction to the European economy by the war. . . . Without further prompt and substantial aid from the United States, economic, social and political disintegration will overwhelm Europe."[42]

Clayton's urgency was one of the streams that fed into the secretary's "Marshall Plan" speech the next month. Clayton thought the Europeans would establish some sort of federation to manage recovery but stressed—directly contrary to Kennan—that *the United States must run this* show."[43] His specific point of departure was the shambles of earlier relief distribution efforts, but his broader implication was suggestive: while the United States would benefit from the aid, its economy immediately, sustaining political support for the program would be perilous without a visible American lead.

Germans were at first bystanders to these debates about their future, only later actors. But they were hardly disinterested at any stage. Reconstructing their views is problematic because the constraints of occupation diminished the record of those views. However, it takes little sleuthing to recognize that, given their recent experience, many Germans had had enough of the nation-state or were tempted by some broader European framework that might subsume it. Nor, too, is it a surprise that few of those, in the words of one Swiss observer, "consciously postulated the dependence on one of the victor powers as an alternative."[44]

In these circumstances, the idea of Europe as a "third force" exerted a powerful attraction as a strategic vision: only if history permitted such a force could Germany be reunited and in possession of some freedom for maneuver. The strategic vision of a third force was intertwined with the ideological notion of a "third way" between capitalism and communism. Only some mediation of the emerging East-West conflict could permit Germany to be reunified, and only some societal path between capitalism and socialism would permit such a mediation.

The specific motives of these "third forcers" varied.[45] For the social democrat Richard Löwenthal, the primary aim was the political construction of a Europe between the two emerging superpowers. For Jakob Kaiser, the chairman of the Christian Democratic Union (CDU) in the Soviet occupation zone, the primary business at hand was somehow achieving German unity and forestalling the sovietization of the eastern zone. Others were motivated by the fear of a new war, while still others harbored hopes of incorporating the best features of the two systems, or of setting conditions for a revival of Christianity, or some other such lofty purpose.

For all, however, the imperative was creating a third power-center in Europe, one justified by sustaining a liberal order in contrast to the two superpowers. They depended on the presumption that the Soviet Union was not bent on dominating all of Europe, or on imposing totalitarian social systems everywhere, and hence was not necessarily an implacable opponent of the liberal principles they cherished. Organizing the three western zones of Germany into an Atlantic alliance, acceptable in principle only to a minority of Germans, could be justified only if Soviet dominance of eastern Europe, including eastern Germany, was regarded as tantamount to permanent; it would become necessary only if Soviet expansion westward was a real threat.

The suspicion that the threat was real distinguished Konrad Adenauer from the third forcers. He acknowledged the need to reassure Germany's neighbors, especially France, and he accepted that a broader framework might mitigate the effects of Germany's defeat. He was also prepared to contemplate the idea of a mediating influence. But the main point was protection. As early as October 1945 he called the "division in Eastern Europe, the Russian area, and Western Europe a matter of fact."[46] And he came early to the conclusion that the western European democracies would not be strong enough alone to resist Soviet pressure.

As he put it in March 1946, "Europe could only be saved with the help of the USA."[47] Thus the idea of a federated Europe was, for him, inseparable from a tight link to America, and he supported every proposal for a larger American presence in western Europe.

Adenauer shared the fear of a Europe dominated by Russia, an "Asian power," as he put it, with his future social democratic opponent, Kurt Schumacher. Unlike Adenauer, a Rhineland Catholic who, while a German patriot, regarded Germany east of the Elbe almost as foreign terrain, Schumacher had neither an emotional tug toward the west nor a desire to see capitalism in Europe reinvigorated through America's agency.

The two men agreed that reconstruction in western Europe could become a "magnet" for the East. For Adenauer, however, the magnetic field was Europe, not just a truncated Germany. For him, a unification policy nationally conceived and nationally executed had no chance. Schumacher's eyes, by contrast, stayed fixed on German unification, and he hoped the economic vitality of the western zones might produce the magnet for drawing in eastern Germany.

But for Schumacher there could be no compromise with totalitarian communism bent on dominating Europe; Kaiser's temptations to mediation were empty dangerousness. And so from the time of his opposition to the forced fusion, in Soviet occupied Germany, of the Social Democratic and German Communist Parties, Schumacher was if anything a more forceful advocate of integrating western Germany into a western Europe bound to the United States than was Adenauer.

That this Europe ran counter to his ultimate goals both for Europe and, more painfully still, Germany, was not lost on him: opting for this western Europe meant acceding to the division of Germany between east and west. Schumacher thus held back from drawing the consequences of his advocacy just as this western Europe was coming to fruition, in the winter of 1947–48.

Whether another course of European construction, and American relation to it, was possible is unknowable. History admits no reruns. We cannot know whether the Soviet Union would have taken the lack of a military alliance as weakness and pressed its advantage. That debate rages still. Nor can we know whether the western Europeans themselves would have taken a more standoffish American posture as lack of interest and thus thrown in the towel, or as healthy respect for their nationhood and thus redoubled efforts at integrating their own defenses.

With Stalin in the Kremlin, the course America took seems, in retrospect, the risk-averse one. It is so even if it played some part in confirming Soviet hostility and the division of Europe—and of Germany as well. It is what the Europeans sought; it provided breathing space against a threat that looked real enough to many Europeans as well as many Americans.

Moreover, in the 1950s World War II was a fresh memory, near at hand, while Stalin, for all his threat, had not attacked and did not. In those circumstances, ceding sovereignty to a distant America in the realm of defense did not seem just a technical necessity in view of the looming Soviet threat and the need to construct nuclear deterrence. It also suppressed the knotty question of who would have nuclear weapons and why, and who not and why not. If Stalin induced the western Europeans to cooperate with each other more than they might otherwise have, the American connection, for all its price in sovereignty, made that cooperation easier.

Integrating Germany, Engaging America

On the basis of recommendations of the Joint Chiefs of Staff, concurred in by the Secretaries of State and Defense, I have today approved substantial increases in the strength of the United States forces to be stationed in Western Europe in the interest of the defense of that area. . . . A basic element in the implementation of this decision is the degree to which our friends match our actions in this regard. Firm programs for the development of their forces will be expected to keep full step with the dispatch of additional United States forces to Europe.[1]

The words were President Harry Truman's. He spoke on September 9, 1950, ten weeks after North Korean troops had poured across the border into South Korea. The effect of his announcement is difficult to overstate. American forces in Europe were to be converted from occupiers of Germany into deterrers of the Soviet Union. While their dispatch was not regarded as permanent—indeed it was advertised as temporary—logically, so long as the Soviet threat continued, so should the presence of additional troops.

The decision was part of a complicated bargain with America's European allies, especially France, over rearming western Germany. The German element of the bargain was, for Europe, at least as important as the decision to send American troops across the Atlantic in significant numbers.

The troop decision prepared the ground for the announcement that General Dwight D. Eisenhower, the wartime commander and war hero, would be the alliance's supreme commander and would also take charge of U.S. forces. The American engagement was complete and so, save for the final integration of West Germany, was the alliance. What was not yet complete was the engagement of the American body politic as represented by Congress.

EYEING GERMAN TROOPS

The division of Germany, set at Moscow in the spring of 1947, hardened through the fears of 1948 and the creation of NATO. However, just as Soviet misbehavior at critical moments—the pressure on Norway, then the Czechoslovakian coup in 1948, for instance—had been powerful arguments for western action, so the relative lack of such misbehavior was an implicit ground for inaction. The fears of 1948 waned as the line against communism held in France and Italy, and the urgency of converting NATO from a security pact into a military organization diminished apace.

The lessened sense of immediate threat gave play to differences over the role of western Germany. For the United States, which sought a strong Europe but whose politics still argued for a weak American role, if Europe were to be defended, it should be defended by European soldiers. If the threat could not be met with the forces at hand, then incorporating Germans into Europe's defense was only logical. For France, at the other extreme, Europe should be defended without Germany, and that required a clear American participation, the more the better.

As usual the British were somewhere in between France and the United States. Their immediate concern over Germany was less than France's, but their disinclination to integrate in a European continental coalition was much greater; that much was plain in Britain's internal debate over its postwar role. Bevin had tugged the military along with him in his alliance diplomacy. But ensuring British freedom of action was still a rallying cry for the military, the political establishment and, not least, the public beyond them.

The logic to arming West Germany had been discussed in Washington as early as 1947, but it took the explosion of the first Soviet atomic bomb in the autumn of 1949 and then the outbreak of war in Korea to convert discussions into planning. Planning within NATO—the so-called Strategic Concept approved in December 1949 or the Medium Term Defense Plan of April 1950—inevitably meant some discussion of what to do about Germany. However, in the summer of 1950 there was no NATO military organization, and western forces consisted only of American and British occupation forces in Germany, plus poorly armed Benelux and French forces scattered throughout western Europe, the bulk of the French army tied down in Indochina. The concern over western weakness had been sharpened by the Soviet creation, beginning in late 1947, of highly trained *Volkspolizei*, or peoples' police, in East Germany, a force that eventually came to number 50,000.

Lucius Clay, now out of government, spoke publicly of arming Germany in November 1949, and at the same time the U.S. army began studying the question. In April 1950, NSC-68 circulated in Washington. The historic document, drafted primarily by Paul Nitze, Kennan's successor as head of state's policy planning staff, called for a more active pursuit of containment: given the "sharp disparity between our actual military strength and our commitments . . . our military strength is becoming dangerously inadequate," and it was thus necessary to undertake a rapid and sustained buildup. The American defense budget, $15 billion in 1950, leapt to $50 billion by 1953 as the police action in Korea became a full-fledged war.

NSC-68 put in lucid prose the military emphasis to containment that Kennan later came to regret, feeling he had been misunderstood. The document did not call for German rearmament directly but did suggest that the United States make "separate arrangements with Japan, Western Germany, and Austria which would enlist the energies and resources of these countries in support of the free world."[2]

At the end of April 1950, the American high commissioner for Germany, John J. McCloy, cabled Henry Byroade, the state department director of German affairs. McCloy's message was that constraints on German industry should be lifted and West Germany brought into the West's defenses. His argument was that Germany could only be stable if it were successful and treated as an equal:

> Germany must be brought into [the] Western community (through a North Atlantic Union or by other means) as rapidly as possible. And it is folly to think of bringing her in as permanent second-class mem-

ber. The real problem of US policy in Europe seems to me therefore to be that of finding [a] way to foster [the] right kind of Germany and to have that Germany accepted by other Western powers, and indeed by [the] whole democratic world, as an equal partner.[3]

On the other hand, the state department, and especially its secretary, Acheson, felt that rearming Germany was a game not yet worth the candle. Paris sought to exclude Germany from NATO, permanently if possible, and whatever military advantage accrued from German divisions would be offset if their entry unraveled NATO and alienated France. Accordingly, Acheson told both the Congress and the public, as he put it in April 1950, that "the United States has firm international commitments, both for German disarmament and against German rearmament, and there is no change in this position."[4]

West Germany's demilitarization had been stipulated the previous November in the Petersberg Agreement between the three western high commissioners and the new government of the Federal Republic, led by Konrad Adenauer. The terms were categorical: "The Federal Government further declares its earnest determination to maintain the demilitarization of the Federal territory and to endeavor by all means in its power to prevent the recreation of armed forces of any kind."[5]

Categorical words notwithstanding, the Washington debate sharpened over the spring and summer of 1950. In April the joint chiefs of staff approved the army study, which called for incorporating German divisions under national command into NATO, and in May they pressed to raise the subject at NATO's North Atlantic Council meeting in London. Acheson objected and did not raise rearmament.

In June the National Security Council considered NSC-71, which characterized the chiefs as "firmly of the opinion that, from the military point of view, the appropriate and early rearming of Western Germany is of fundamental importance to the defense of Western Europe against the USSR." However, President Truman recorded his own view, with characteristic terseness, in a note to Acheson, that the chiefs' recommendation was "decidedly militaristic and in my opinion not realistic with present conditions."[6]

The British also were turning toward the question of German rearmament. Viscount Montgomery, the newly appointed commander of the Brussels treaty organization, the Western European Union, expressed the view as early as the spring of 1948 that no defense of Europe on the Rhine, much less the Elbe, could be accomplished without German forces. In March 1950 Conservative leaders Winston Churchill and Anthony Eden, now in the opposition, said much the same thing in Parliament.

The Labour prime minister, Clement Atlee, criticized their view as irresponsible, but he too was feeling the pressure of circumstances, both internal and external. The same month the Tories spoke out, British troops were called out to quell a riot that developed over the closing of a steel plant in Germany, and the Labour government turned toward some form of armed German constabulary. The British chiefs favored rearmament in some form, and in May Atlee confided in a letter to Bevin: "I think it unlikely that Germany will settle down without some armed forces. One must consider the tradition of the German state."[7]

What little sentiment there was in France in favor of rearming Germany was confined to military circles. It depended on taking a gloomier view of both the Soviet threat and French capacity than was characteristic of Paris. If France could not, for economic reasons, sustain a large military buildup, then a rearmed Germany, and not France, would at least become the front line against any possible Soviet aggression—more a third-best than a second.

West Germany, now the Federal Republic, was becoming an actor; it was no longer merely the well-pondered object of decisions by others. Adenauer, now the chancellor, confided to his diary in late 1949 that "rearmament might be the way to gaining full sovereignty for the Federal Republic." Indeed, in reconstructing the factors that determined his view, sovereignty came first, security against Soviet action in eastern Germany second, and a European federation third.[8]

THE SHOCK OF KOREA

The Korean invasion brought the argument to a head. It also changed minds, in a way that is not so easy to understand in hindsight. For us, the invasion now appears, at its most menacing, as an indication that the battle lines in Europe had firmed along the division of Germany, and so the military confrontation between East and West had moved to Asia and what later came to be called the Third World. With more reliance on what came later, the invasion can be seen in the light of the split between the Soviet Union and China.

At the time, though, China was only recently "lost," its split with Russia unimagined and communism a monolith. It did not take paranoids, or conspirators, to see the invasion as, at worst, a feint in preparation for an attack in Europe, at best as an indication that weakness invited adventure. As Acheson later wrote of himself: "My conversion to German participation in European defense was quick. The idea that Germany's place in the defense of Europe would be worked out by process of evolution was outmoded. Korea had speeded up evolution."[9] Truman, also a convert, wrote that "any map will show it, and a little arithmetic will prove what the addition of German manpower means to the strength of the joint defense of Europe."[10]

By midsummer 1950 the question about rearmament in Washington was not "whether" but "how." A state department response to the JCS in July put rearmament in the context of both European integration and American influence. Europe was being constructed but "arrangements for a real framework of strength in Western Europe including Germany [have] not been altogether up to the hopes and expectations of the Department of State." For their part, the French were "moving rather rapidly, considering their past traditions and policy." But pushing rearmament risked unhinging Europe's integration, not promoting it.[11]

Moreover, the United States

still was in a position to shape the direction of . . . developments as our prestige in Germany is still great. We can expect this influence to diminish rather rapidly. . . . In this connection, one fact of great significance cannot be overlooked. The truth is that the majority of Germans, and particularly the democratic elements we are supporting, do not today desire to see Germany have armed forces. . . . Under such conditions, to force the German uniform back into the picture would without question act to the disadvantage and disillusionment of those elements in Germany on which we place our hope for the future.[12]

State's concerns, however, represented a rear-guard argument, and planning went forward, with the brittle relations between state and defense only somewhat improved by the fact that Byroade was an active-duty Army colonel seconded to state. As Acheson himself put it: "The question was not whether Germany should be brought into the general defensive plan but rather how this could be done without disrupting anything else that we were doing and without putting Germany into a position to act as the balance of power in Europe."[13] Perhaps, he noted in passing, the answer was some kind of European or North Atlantic army that might subordinate German units under a supranational command.

As the United States moved forward with enormous increases in its defense budget, the logic of burden-sharing built into NATO implied that the Europeans should make counterpart efforts. On July 22, 1950, Acheson told his embassies in Europe that the United States would require, by August 5, the "firmest possible statement from European countries of [the] nature and extent of increased effort, in terms of increases in both forces and military production, they propose to undertake."[14]

A supranational army was the obvious way to square the circle, having German troops without a German army or general staff. McCloy, on the scene in Germany and fearing Europe's demoralization in the wake of Korea, came to favor the idea despite the technical qualms of his military advisor, Col. H. A. Gerhardt. McCloy's August 3 cable to Acheson was a brief for a European army: "the rate of achieving [western European defense] has been far too slow"; national armies will not do, for "even France lacks the capacity, if not the will, to build a national army able to carry the brunt of the defense"; German forces are thus necessary but "re-creating any German national army now or in the foreseeable future . . . would be a tragic mistake. . . . It would undermine much that we have so far achieved in democratizing German society."[15] Gerhardt and McCloy's legal advisor, Robert Bowie, were recalled to Washington for consultation.

August and September 1950 were the critical months not only in Washington but in London, Paris, and Germany as well. Churchill turned Atlee's criticism of rearmament into a needle: "It is now," he said at the end of July, "five months since I raised the question. The Prime Minister called me irresponsible when I did so. . . . Perhaps it is better to be irresponsible and right, than to be responsible and wrong." On August 11, at Churchill's motion, the Council of Europe passed a resolution calling "for the immediate creation under the authority of a European Minister of Defense, of a European army, subject to proper unified democratic control and acting in full co-operation with the U.S.A. and Canada."[16]

On August 17, Adenauer called in the allied high commissioners in Germany to express his concern over signs that the Russians were converting units of the East German *Volkspolizei* into a well-trained army. He asked the allies for more troops of their own and for authority to raise a special West German federal police force of 150,000. At the same time, he brought up the possibility of a German contribution to a European army.

For France, whose army was bleeding in Indochina, America's reluctance, before Korea, to enter into NATO's military arrangements was a particular unhappiness. If Europe was to be defended without German troops—and, given Indochina, without many French either—then an American engagement was the answer. Politically, too, tight trans-Atlantic arrangements could give France status, a clear advantage over Germany as the Federal Republic reacquired economic vigor.

These ideas were spelled out in French memorandums passed to the United States on August 5 and 17. For its part, France would undertake a buildup, constructing fifteen new divisions. At the same time, "the experience of the last two wars," in the first of which "France had at first to carry almost alone the military and financial burden of the war," underscored the need for "unity of command" in peace, something "like the combined chiefs of staff in the last war." Some alliance agency, left vague in the wording, but probably NATO's standing group in Washington, should assume the function of a general staff, not just for Europe but also for "all possible theaters of operation."[17]

Joint command would be supported by procedures for joint budgeting. Interestingly, more than half the August 17 memorandum was devoted to financial arrangements, including a specific plea for support of the French franc lest rearmament breed inflation—"such as the adversaries of the Atlantic Pact are hoping for and predicting"—and thus devaluation. The memorandum was one of the few instances in postwar alliance history when economics and security explicitly crossed. The French did it under duress, and they drew the connection in positive terms, promising to do more in defense if the United States were forthcoming in economics.[18]

By the beginning of August, Truman had approved Acheson's recommendation that the United States move toward rearming Germany through a larger framework, one that would include American forces.[19] Acheson had proposed to the defense department what the British might have called a *vue d'ensemble* and the French *un "package deal"*—American aid contingent on the Europeans doing more, an increase in American divisions in Europe from four to six, and the establishment of an integrated NATO command under an American supreme commander.

What Acheson, however, envisioned as a process whose conclusion, German troops, would be obvious enough, the Pentagon wanted to convert into an immediate package, take it or leave it. He thought that once a joint command was established, "the inevitable logic of mathematics would convince everyone that any plan without Germany was untenable," but "to insist on requiring the inclusion of Germany at the outset would delay and complicate the whole enterprise"—a "murderous" tactic.[20]

But it was a tactic hard to oppose, a package hard to refuse. On military grounds, sending more American troops without arming Germans could be argued as exposing those troops to destruction in the event of an attack. Moreover, what could be clearer evidence for the American Congress that Europe was prepared to share the burden than German troops. McCloy in Germany continued to press for a decision soon, arguing that time was precious and France would "not oppose prompt action within a European army structure." Only David Bruce, the U.S. ambassador in France, continued to argue for a gradual approach, more U.S. and British troops plus a stronger French army preceding German rearmament. For his view he was criticized as having gone native, representing French views with "excessive vigor."[21]

A NATO foreign ministers meeting scheduled for New York on September 12 provided a deadline of sorts. On August 26, Truman directed Acheson and Secretary of Defense Louis Johnson to hammer out joint recommendations. The way Truman posed the questions, after two months of discussions within official Washington and two weeks before major discussions with allies, suggested that the answers were still open, more open than they probably were in fact:

Are we prepared to commit additional United States forces to the defense of Europe;

Are we prepared to support, and in what manner, the concept of a European defense force, including German participation on other than a national basis;

Are we prepared to look forward to the eventuality of a Supreme Commander for the European defense forces;

Are we prepared to consider full United States participation in European defense organs . . .[22]

On September 8, Truman approved the joint Acheson-Johnson recommendation, essentially the Pentagon package in somewhat more subtle wrapping. The United States would commit additional forces as soon as possible, "in order that any doubts of American interest in the defense, rather than the liberation of Europe, will be removed, thus increasing the will of our allies to resist." A European army within the framework of the North Atlantic Treaty would elicit "the maximum contribution from European nations and . . . provide as well a framework in which German contribution of a significant nature could be realized." The two secretaries advocated appointing a supreme commander as soon as possible. And the final item in the package was plain: "we should proceed without delay with the formation of adequate West German units."[23]

The next day Truman made his public announcement. NATO had become a military alliance, and the American occupation had become an engagement. But Truman went public only with the announcement concerning American troops. There was no mention yet of Germans; the package was still under wraps.

THE CONFRONTATION WITH FRANCE

Acheson did not much like the decision but regarded it as the price of the Pentagon's cooperation. France would hardly be surprised when the subject of rearming Germany came up, but still the American decision would be a bombshell when presented to the allies with no explicit consultation in advance—one in the long sequence of such unilateral American decisions stretching from the Marshall Plan itself to the Strategic Defense Initiative in 1983. But the details of the joint recommendation would leak soon; a *Washington Post* story appeared as early as September 9.

Bevin had passed a note directly to Acheson on September 4 covering a paper from his chiefs, the substance of which he also passed to René Pleven, the French prime minister. Bevin's government was "not . . . prepared at present to agree to the re-creation of a German army," a fact the chiefs recognized. Yet they were firmly of the opinion that Europe could not be defended without Germany. Thus they recommended, and Bevin implicitly endorsed, acceding to Adenauer's request of August 17 for federal German police, much on the model of the East German force but perhaps scaled back to some 100,000 volunteers.[24]

Acheson opened the New York meeting of the big three foreign ministers, scheduled around the NATO meeting, then immediately adjourned it for a private talk with Bevin and Robert Schuman, the French foreign minister. There he dropped what came to be known as the "bomb at the Waldorf," the package deal, American reinforcements but only if Europe raised sixty divisions, "ten of which might be German." His auditors, forewarned, were still shocked. Bevin repeated the idea of expanding the German federal police, worrying that the U.S. proposal would give the Germans too much leverage over the allies.

Schuman had been caught between his hopes that the meeting would not raise rearmament and his warnings, from Jean Monnet among others, that the Americans were bent on doing so. "Why on earth are you in such a hurry?" he entreated. Monnet's concern elaborated Bevin's—that raising rearmament would let Germany slip from the context of Schuman's recently proposed Coal and Steel Plan, of which Monnet was the architect, and play off East and West. To Acheson, Schuman portrayed the effect on France of German rearmament; even if he agreed, neither his government nor his parliament would go along. When France itself had rearmed, when a combined NATO staff and supreme commander had been established: only then could France consider German rearmament.[25]

The issue was debated that afternoon before the formal conference, the next morning among the foreign ministers, and the following day, the fourteenth, in a private meeting of the three ministers and their high commissioners. Schuman again repeated that France could not accept German rearmament while France itself desperately needed arms, and that he would veto moves toward rearmament. He could not understand why the United States was in such a hurry on that score, rather than carefully laying the groundwork by first integrating its own forces into NATO. To Acheson, however, that meant that the French "were prepared to accept what we offered, but they were not prepared to accept what we asked."[26]

Acheson tried a compromise of sorts, suggesting an agreement on the "basic principle of the program" along with a "decision to keep German rearmament lagging behind that of the other powers." Schuman saw through the idea to his own politics: the agreement, even if only in principle, would leak and be interpreted "as an irrevocable decision which would result in German units receiving materials which France itself needed and France would be on the same footing as Germany."[27]

The scheduled two-day meeting of NATO foreign ministers followed. Again, rearmament dominated discussion. France was more and more isolated: assurances that Washington would name Eisenhower as supreme commander had brought the British on board, and the United States also picked up support from Italy, Canada, Norway, and the Netherlands. The three ministers again convened in private and again were at loggerheads, as reflected in their communiqué, which recorded them as "fully agreed that the recreation of a German national army would not serve the best interests of Germany or Europe" but also that "the questions raised by the problem of the participation of the German Federal Republic in the common defense of Europe are at present the subject of study and exchange of views."[28]

The three had earlier agreed to return to the issue with their defense ministers, and those meetings began on September 21. On the American side, Truman had again tempted George Marshall into government service, to replace Johnson as secretary of defense; Johnson's brain tumor, ultimately fatal, had caused his behavior to pass, in Acheson's words, "beyond the peculiar to the impossible."[29] Marshall's stature was reassuring to the allies, and his relations with Acheson, his former deputy, made for less sparring between state and defense and so for more disposition to compromise.

However, if new people on the American side made for easier dealings, newcomers on the French side made them more difficult. The French defense minister, Jules Moch, a socialist, was no fellow traveler of communists; as interior minister during 1947 he had used his powers to deal toughly with communist-led labor riots. But he had been active in the wartime resistance, and his son had been tortured by Nazis; rearming Germany was not for him.

Moch's British counterpart, Immanuel Shinwell, "Manny" to his wide circle of friends, a fellow socialist, a North London Jew who had worked his way to the top of the Labour Party, appealed to Moch, arguing on the twenty-third that it would be "fatal not to take advantage of [the] US offer of troops" by rejecting German rearmament in principle. Psychology alone indicated that West Germany had to have a stake in its own defense.[30]

Moch later admitted that American troops were a strong inducement, but at the time he and Schuman continued to repeat that they could not accept rearmament even in principle. Yet they realized they could not reject it out of hand, nor did they try to prevent the topic from arising. The Americans countered that they could not guarantee congressional approval of either U.S. troops or assistance without the prospect of German forces.

Moch offered some hope: while he doubted that his parliament would support German participation in western defense, "there was a chance of getting a 'package' sold to the Parliament," but the package had to "include precise information of what [the] French [could] expect from the United States and how many and at what date U.S. divisions would arrive in Europe." To Moch's question of how many German divisions Washington contemplated, Marshall responded that the answer depended on how many divisions Paris raised.[31]

On the twenty-third the group agreed, at Moch's suggestion, to delay a meeting of the defense ministers, scheduled for October 16, until October 28, "in order," as Acheson put it in his cable for Truman, "to attempt to get favorable French parliamentary action." While Moch "needed much ammunition if he is to sell this package to his Parliament . . . he was willing if the ammunition is forthcoming."[32]

On the twenty-third and after, Acheson suggested, in Moch's words, that "if, in October, the French government notifies us that it is irrevocably opposed to German rearmament, we shall have to reconsider our whole plan and look for another solution."[33] The words were part threat, part recognition of France's veto; they put the monkey on Paris's back but probably were not taken by Schuman and Moch as explicit threat, for Acheson was optimistic about French action. So he told Bevin. Moreover, on the twenty-fifth, in drafting the North Atlantic Council resolution, the Americans agreed to language that indicated the supreme commander would be appointed *before*, not after a European army had been created— the state department position all along.

The resolution, issued on September 26, called for:

> The establishment at the earliest possible date of an integrated force under centralized command and control composed of forces made available by governments for the defense of Western Europe; . . .
>
> The Supreme Commander shall be appointed as soon as there is assurance that national forces will be made available for the integrated force adequate to enable the latter to be reasonably capable of fulfilling its responsibilities.

At French insistence, the resolution indicated there had been no final decision about Germany but did append language indicating the issue had been discussed and that the NATO defense committee had been requested

> to make specific recommendations regarding the method by which . . . Germany could make its most useful contribution to the successful implementation of the plan, bearing in mind the unanimous conclusion of the Council that it would not serve the best interests of Europe or of Germany to bring into being a German national army or a German general staff.[34]

Logic and American Politics

By one train of logic, sending troops and so converting a security pact into a military alliance was the next step in a series that ran back to the Marshall Plan and before. Once the United States had made western Europe's independence and prosperity *its* objective, then it was a question of what means were required. If aid for economic recovery alone would not do, then reassurance in the form of a security guarantee was necessary. If that, too, proved insufficient, then making the military alliance real was the logical next step. This had been Bevin's logic, embraced by Hickerson and ultimately accepted by the Truman administration.

Yet the engagement in Europe was as sharp a break in America's military tradition as the constructing of an alliance had been in its diplomacy. That the engagement became over forty years part of the landscape of American foreign policy obscures how sharp a break it was at the time. Moreover, each previous step had been billed as *the* answer to Europe's plight. So it was with the Marshall Plan, and so Kennan argued and believed. So it had been argued, over Kennan's qualms, about the North Atlantic Treaty.

In retrospect, the previous steps look oversold and probably were—Washington has not changed that much in forty-plus years; ringing affirmations that this or that is *the* solution are still the order of the day. More important, though, events ran faster than conceptions, the late 1940s and early 1950s echoing the late 1980s and early 1990s. When Marshall began assembling his Harvard speech, his approach was almost casual. Neither he nor the men around him then intended to build either a military alliance or an American presence in Europe; none then thought it would be necessary. They cannot easily be faulted for not imagining that each step would not be the last. And so arguments for the next step, arguments whose need was unimagined, were not made.

Still, the debate was slow in coming. At first Truman's announcement was treated merely as part of post-Korea toughness. Republicans who had been criticizing Mr. Truman for not standing up to communism could hardly fail to applaud his action. When it came, though, the debate consumed the Senate almost to the exclusion of all other business for three months, January–March 1951. It was, in effect, a debate about America's engagement in Europe if, as usual in politics, high politics included, it was not as conclusive at the time as it seems in retrospect.

Midterm elections intervened between Truman's announcement and the Senate debate, reducing the Democratic majority in the Senate to two and confirming the shift of the Republican Party's center of gravity away from its liberal, internationalist wing. Dewey's loss of the presidency in 1948 had seemed a loss for "me too-ism"; Republicans were feeling that Truman had reaped all the political benefits from policies they had been crucial in shaping. Bipartisanship was further frayed by Vandenberg's illness, U.S. losses in

Korea, and, on the Truman administration's part, by the rise of Senator Joseph McCarthy and his hunt for "communists" in the administration.

Former president Herbert Hoover prefigured the debate in a radio broadcast in December 1950. While criticized as extreme isolationism, his argument was not so easily dismissed. He did not advocate a return to Fortress America, nor was he indifferent to the communist menace. But he reacted to a line of policy that seemed more and more costly while it was less and less conclusive. Instead, "the foundation of U.S. policy must be to preserve for the world this Western Hemisphere, Gibraltar of Western Civilization."[35]

American defense would give pride of place to air and naval forces "to hold the Atlantic and Pacific Oceans with one frontier on Britain . . . and the other on Japan, Formosa and the Philippines." As for Europe,

> the prime obligation of the defense of Western Continental Europe rests upon the nations of Europe. . . . To warrant our further aid they should show they have spiritual strength and unity to avail themselves of their own resources. But it must be far more than pacts, conferences, paper promises and declarations. Today it must express itself in organized and equipped combat divisions of such large numbers as would create a sure dam against the red flood. And that before we land another man or another dollar on their shores.

The logic was not impeccable—Europe would not be helped until it had proven it did not need it. But Hoover's theme resonated deeply in American history—the flexibility of a maritime strategy over the rigidity of continental commitments; the willingness to sacrifice the old world to save the new.

Hoover foreshadowed the debate, but Senator Robert Taft, "Mr. Republican," the man who wanted to occupy what his party wanted to possess, the presidency, defined it in early January. Strange as it seems today, the "great debate" actually was, if not parliamentary arguing British-style, then at least a time when speeches made on the floor of the Senate still mattered. For Taft, the test of foreign policy was not international but domestic, not its effect on the world but on the United States. From the Marshall Plan onward, the Truman administration had grown progressively more committed to the notion that America's security was inseparable from Europe's. Thus, when one step, standoffish assistance, had seemed insufficient, it was prepared to take the next and the next.

By contrast, Taft feared that the track would have disastrous consequences at home:

> The key to all the problems before this Congress lies in the size of our military budget. That determines the taxes to be levied. It determines the number of boys to be drafted. It is likely to determine whether we can maintain a reasonably free system and the value of the dollar, or whether we are to be weakened or choked by Government controls which inevitably tend to become more arbitrary and unreasonable.[36]

His conclusions were akin to Hoover's—an emphasis on the American homeland and, especially, on air forces as a way to deter attack on it. However, he recognized the American commitments to allies that had been accrued by the Truman administration, and he was not opposed to sending troops to Europe, provided they were token in numbers and temporary in deployment.

The debate was all the sharper because it mixed foreign policy substance with the prerogatives of the two branches. Taft chafed under bipartisanship because he believed it inhibited debate. At the same time he was a staunch defender of the role of Congress. After all, the Senate had assented to the North Atlantic Treaty on certain assumptions. The administration now appeared to be contravening those assumptions—bad consultation if not bad faith. As Taft put it in January: "What is being talked about today is something entirely different from what was being considered when we adopted the Atlantic Pact."

This constitutional dimension was the background that, then as now, often dominated the foreground of policy. For whatever combination of busyness, inattention, and distaste at the prospect of dealing with McCarthy, the Truman administration had not brought the Congress along in its internal debates. It had moved but Congress had not. It later paid a price for its failure. If the constitutional dimension is not emphasized in this discussion, that is not to diminish it. But it is familiar, a sign of how little Washington has changed for all the rosy memories of bipartisanship. It is not that substance and process are both important, they are inseparable.

The constitutional dimension is usually thought of as the executive versus Congress, but that description is no more than shorthand. Then, and more so later, the fault lines of divided American government partly ran along but partly cut across the boundaries of the two branches. Institutional loyalty is one tug, felt by all members but in different degrees—attenuated, for example, for House Republicans once they became a permanent minority. Tugs of substance compete, as does still the pull of party loyalty, especially for congressional leaders if their party holds the presidency: so it was for Senator Tom Connally, the Democratic chairman of the foreign relations committee in 1951.

Indeed, the constitutional question became the first focus of the debate. In early January 1951 Republican senator Kenneth Wherry of Nebraska, a consistent opponent of a growing U.S. role in Europe, proposed a resolution "that no ground forces of the United States should be assigned to duty in the European area for the purposes of the North Atlantic Treaty pending the adoption of a policy with respect thereto by Congress."[37] The tactic was shrewd, for it was hostile in intent but procedural, and so appeared neutral in substance. As such, it was hard to oppose for those members of Congress who approved of the president's policy but not of the way it had been made.

The question of sending American troops to Europe turned on the strategic issue, the role of western Europe in American strategy. However, it also raised one more specific question, how the defense burden would be shared, and one broader one about the nature of America's postwar defense effort.

The congressional argument, that in the Senate especially, paralleled the debates that had been running through officialdom for the previous several years. For instance, Taft's strategic arguments were opposed in the Senate most forcefully by two Democrats, Paul Douglas of Illinois and Connally of Texas, and one Republican, Wayne Morse of Oregon, an articulate maverick, later a Democrat and opponent of the war in Vietnam.

If Taft worried that an American and NATO conventional buildup in Europe would provoke the Russians, his argument, Douglas and Connally pointed out, condemned the United States to perpetual inferiority.[38] In other respects, too, their arguments paralleled those of the drafters of NSC-68: they regarded increased defense spending as necessary, and they saw nuclear and conventional weapons as complements, not alternatives. If present nuclear superiority conceded something to Taft's arguments, conventional forces still needed building up in anticipation of superiority lost.

Taft's critics emphasized America's strategic stakes in western Europe, both its industrial potential and the air bases on its territory that facilitated direct strikes on Soviet territory. The loss of Europe would be a serious blow to the United States; Connally, in particular, stressed that the combined industrial capacity of the Soviet Union plus western Europe would exceed America's by an uncomfortable margin.

Whether the burden was being shared fairly had been part of the debate in 1949, and it was again, just as it was over and over in the next forty years. Then, as later, it was hard to be against the Europeans "doing more," no matter how much they did. Congressional politics also made that exhortation a superficial cluster-point: it protected the flanks of those who supported a large U.S. military engagement in Europe, offered arguments for those who opposed it, and simply made sense for those in the middle who thought the engagement sensible but expensive.

The administration's case was argued in the Senate by Massachusetts senator Henry Cabot Lodge, a man who lacked Vandenberg's stature but who had inherited his leadership of the internationalist Republicans. He pointed out the flaw in Hoover's logic:

> To say that we should not extend any help to Europe until they are completely strong and do not need our help is like telling a sick man that we will not give him his medicine until he has recovered. The test should not be that they are able to carry the load alone, it should be that they are making the greatest effort which they are capable of making.[39]

Lodge agreed that in principle the United States "should not commit a single additional soldier to Europe without an iron-clad agreement that the dispatch of that soldier means an automatic commitment of a very much larger number of European soldiers." Like Europe's defenders in future Congresses, however, he believed the condition was being met. European willingness to rearm was being underestimated; those nations had committed themselves to build sixty divisions to America's ten.

Republican senator Knowland of California, a charter member of the China "lobby," turned Lodge's principle into a fixed criterion—again, the tactic later used by both opponents and defenders of the American military engagement, with the criterion set according to whether the setter wished the Europeans to meet it or fall short. For every six divisions fielded by the Europeans, the United States would dispatch one more until the United States had sent ten. This six-to-one ratio had been suggested by the administration in 1949 when it justified military assistance on the grounds that Europe would spend six dollars for every dollar the United States provided.

There was a certain logic in 1949 and 1951 to the burden-sharing argument, but that logic tarnished over time. Then, if Europe was palpably unprepared to defend itself, the United States still had the option, in principle at any rate, of redrawing its defense perimeter elsewhere, pursuing the maritime strategy outlined by Hoover. Once committed, however, for the United States to threaten to withdraw its troops if Europe did not do more was, logically, only to threaten to cut off its nose to spite its face. Indeed, the more seriously the United States took the Soviet threat, the greater was the spite entailed in any such threat.

To be sure, logic is not always decisive in congressional politics, or any other, but the illogic of burden-sharing threats was not lost on Europeans, who came to see the whole issue as intramural squabbling in the American system. Those Europeans could be roused to take action to meet whatever criterion was being called for, but the action was usually cosmetic and usually intended to be so by the congressional setter of the criterion, who was trying to head off his colleagues less sympathetic to Europe's defense effort.

THE GREAT DEBATE

The debate waxed through the winter of 1950–51. The administration turned from aloofness with regard to Congress to active courtship of it. Truman said he would welcome a resolution supporting his policy, and Connally succeeded in getting the Wherry resolution referred jointly to the foreign relations and armed services committees but without the commitment Wherry sought that it would be reported out quickly.

General Eisenhower was the administration's first weapon. He reported from a fact-finding trip to Europe as though he were a visiting head of state, appearing before five congressional committees and a joint session of the two houses in two days. However, his appearances won few converts, and, in a tacit admission that the votes were not there for a resolution in support of administration policy, the Senate Democratic leadership decided to hold hearings on the troops question.

The hearings, which stretched over twelve days in nineteen sessions, were stage-managed by the Democrats to begin and end with witnesses sympathetic to the administration. The arguments, both constitutional and substantive, were familiar. The unanimity of the military in support of the administration was, however, striking. World War II was a near memory, and the reputation of the military was high. So, too, was the image of their independence from partisan politics, a difference from our own time in which the aura of the military remains but the careers of the joints chiefs as political animals are apparent for all to see.

General Curtis Le May, then the influential head of the Strategic Air Command (later he achieved notoriety for his remark about bombing Vietnam back to the stone age and for his candidacy as George Wallace's running mate), testified for Wherry, the opposition. But he admitted, grudgingly, that he too supported sending troops to Europe. While he favored according air power priority over ground forces, he agreed that the two were complementary, not mutually exclusive—just the argument the administration was seeking to make and the opponents of a continental engagement, like Herbert Hoover, were trying to refute.

When Marshall announced on the first day of hearings that the administration planned on sending four more divisions to Europe, to join the two already there, the debate over substance was all but over. The press and Capitol lobbies had been abuzz with wild rumors of huge numbers, and four was modest by comparison. Taft, after all, was not opposed to sending *any* more troops, and sending four divisions would neither make American forces the bulk of Europe's defense nor denude other U.S. forces for other purposes. If it was not always quite fair to pin the label "isolationist" on those who opposed four more divisions, it was not hard to do so; Dewey so labeled his compatriot Wherry—a demonstration of how divided the Republicans were on the troops issue.

In the final stage of the debate, the closed sessions of the two committees on the wording of a resolution, there was almost no discussion of whether Truman's decision was wise policy or not. The focus of argument was constitutional—in what form to approve the decision and thus with what precedent for future administrations. The leadership's proposal, advanced by Connally and Richard Russell of Georgia, was a sense-of-the-Senate resolution, not binding on the president and not requiring House action. The opponents wanted more, either a concurrent resolution, which would have required House action as well, or better still, a joint resolution, which would then have become law if the president signed it.

However, neither side particularly relished involving the House— another aspect of congressional politics that has not changed—and neither's interests would have been served by a resolution the president might have felt compelled to veto. The arguing then shifted to the wording of the resolution, in particular how it would characterize America's effort by comparison to Europe's, how it would approve Truman's decision, and what it would require of future presidents who sought to deploy troops to Europe.

With regard to relative efforts, the initial draft's "fair" American share and European role "commensurate" with capacity became the understanding that the Europeans would make the "major contribu-

tion to the ground forces under General Eisenhower's command."[40]
The last issue, constraining future presidents, turned out to be the
most contentious. John McClellan, an Arkansas Democrat, proposed
the decisive amendment, one that made clear that while the Senate
supported sending four more divisions, no additional "ground
troops . . . should be sent to Western Europe . . . without further
congressional approval."

The amendment was quickly opposed by the leadership and narrowly defeated, but the losers succeeded in getting a second vote,
and this time the result, again close, went in favor. After one more
argument about burden-sharing, the amended resolution passed,
sixty-nine to twenty-one, with Taft voting in favor. Moreover, two of
the nay-sayers, Ellender of Louisiana and, interestingly in view of his
later opposition to presidential policy in the Vietnam war, Fulbright
of Arkansas, thought the resolution not too weak but too strong a
trespass onto the prerogatives of the president.

Notwithstanding the vote, the great debate left several hostages to
fate; in that sense, it confirmed America's military engagement in
Europe but did not, could not, settle the question once and for all.
The first and most notable hostage was constitutional, not substantive. The engagement was from the start embedded in tussling between the two branches over the role of Congress in dispatching
American forces abroad.

Second, administration witnesses, under pressure, labeled the engagement tentative; so they no doubt believed it was. For instance,
Senator Smith of New Jersey asked Eisenhower the following long
question:

> You did contemplate, I think, when I spoke to you before you left, the
> possibility of starting with a certain level of force, and by degrees that
> could be reduced so far as we were concerned as they took over . . .
> their own defense . . . along the line of our Marshall-plan aid, which
> started rather large and came down to zero. I don't know whether you
> would get to zero in this.

The general's answer was brief: "I don't know whether you would
get to zero but that would be the objective in any planning in which

I took part." Senator Gillette asked Marshall if there was anything magic about the figure of four plus two divisions. Marshall replied: "No, certainly not."[41]

Third, while the final resolution made no mention of precise ratios, the debate leading to it set the burden-sharing issue in a narrowly contingent form: the United States was prepared to do X but only if the Europeans did some multiple of X. Congress did not want to say "no" but feared that saying "yes" was handing the executive a blank check. In this, burden-sharing was directly connected to the constitutional argument. Taft brought the two together in suggesting a one-to-nine ratio of American to European forces and a provision to limit American forces in Europe to no more than 20 percent of all U.S. ground and 10 percent of all U.S. air forces.[42]

FINISHING THE BARGAIN:
THE EUROPEAN DEFENSE COMMUNITY

The American vote left not only hostages to political fates in the United States but one large loose end in Europe—France. France continued to worry at least as much about its former enemy as its new one at the height of the Cold War, but under American prodding it moved to accept what it had opposed before, West German rearmament. Its purpose, however, was tactical, embracing in order to postpone, grand ambition in order to delay. Its instrument was the so-called Pleven plan presented on October 26, 1950, later called the European Defense Community (EDC).

Earlier in 1950, the French had made their grand decision of the postwar period, to tie their fate to Germany's through the Schuman plan for a European Coal and Steel Community (ECSC), the skeleton of the European Community. Yet before ECSC negotiations were complete, the Korean war intervened and with it, the awkwardness of German rearmament. The French response was to hurry completion of the Pleven plan, a defense counterpart to the ECSC. In the end, though, the EDC almost came to soon, not smoothing but spoiling France's turnabout in approach to Germany.

The plan would, the men in Paris reckoned, take years to create—if it could be created at all. A West European force reporting to a West European defense minister under the authority of a West European assembly: the sweep was tantamount to a West European confederation. Moreover, there was to be neither West German national army nor general staff, and German soldiers could number no more than a fifth of the entire force—thus answering the old question about how Germany could be strong enough to impress Moscow but weak enough not to threaten Luxembourg.

Once seized of the prospect of German troops in Europe's defense, however, the American governmental machine was no respecter of French tastes in pace, and a draft agreement for the renamed European Defense Community was ready in May 1952. France signed at month's end but immediately began raising its price for agreement, conditions impelled as much by concerns over Germany as over the Soviet Union. It sought, in particular, a permanent Anglo-American military presence on the continent, along with a pledge to intervene against any EDC member that violated the treaty.

What French politicians had liked as a tactic looked less attractive as a fact, however, and the EDC was voted down in the French national assembly in August 1954. Neither American pledges nor American threats—by Secretary of State John Foster Dulles of an "agonizing reappraisal" of America's commitment to the continent if EDC were voted down—could carry the day.

However, within weeks France accepted the entire package for the Federal Republic—sovereignty, accession to NATO, *and* rearmament. It did so primarily because the United States—and Britain, then still regarded as a junior version of the United States, a counterweight from outside the continent to German power—were finally prepared to provide concrete assurance against the revival of German power that France most feared.

The EDC was a purely continental venture, though backed by American guarantees, and so left France alone with its former enemy. Britain had opted out, fearing the EDC was what Schuman and Monnet hoped it was—like the Coal and Steel Community, another opening wedge toward a federated Europe. Of that Britain wanted none. As British foreign minister Anthony Eden put it to the House of Commons in 1954: it was "part of the intention of the EDC plan as a whole that it should lead to federation" and Britain "would not feel willing to join in a federation of that kind."[43]

Having described the obstacle to Parliament, Eden described in his memoirs how he hit upon the solution, in British fashion, in his Sunday bath: "I preferred to bring Germany into N.A.T.O., under the various safeguards which had been devised for her entry into E.D.C. . . . We would have to devise safeguards which were effective but not blatant."[44] Integrating the Federal Republic into both NATO and the Western European Union (WEU) was nifty sleight of hand: NATO tied in the United States, and the WEU, of which Britain was a member, included, as the EDC had not, a pledge to come to the defense of any member attacked from any quarter.

Moreover, the WEU was a face-saving way for Bonn to accept a clutch of constraints, most notably forswearing nuclear weapons and pledging to integrate its entire armed force into NATO. During the London conference of September and October 1954, Britain promised what it had been unwilling to earlier: it would sustain four divisions on the continent and would not "withdraw those forces against the wishes of the majority."[45]

For its part, the United States joined in two critical commitments. One paralleled Britain's troop commitment:

> The United States will continue to maintain in Europe, including Germany, such units of its armed forces as may be necessary and appropriate to contribute its fair share of the forces needed for the joint defense of the North Atlantic area . . . and will continue to deploy such forces in accordance with agreed North Atlantic strategy.

As important, Washington, along with London and Paris, took on pledges aimed at the former enemy, future ally, the Federal Republic:

> They will regard as a threat to their own peace and safety any recourse to force which . . . threatens the integrity and unity of the Atlantic alliance or its defensive purposes. In the event of any such action, the

three Governments ... will consider the offending government as having forfeited its rights to any guarantee and any military assistance provided for in the North Atlantic Treaty. ... They will act ... with a view to taking other measures which may be appropriate.

For all Stalin's paternity of NATO, it is far from evident that he alone would have been enough to impel the creation of a western European federation including an armed Federal Republic.[46] As late as 1948, when the Cold War boded to become hot, the Brussels pact, signed by Britain, France, and the Benelux countries, still identified Germany explicitly as a potential foe in its preamble. The United States then was more entreated than entreating in the second act of building the postwar order, negotiating NATO itself.

Yet in the final act, integrating Germany, it required an American push to overcome differences within western Europe, most notably France's reluctance. Neither memories of the last war nor fears of Stalin and the possibility of the next one alone seem likely to have sufficed. The Europeans accepted dependence in that most critical attribute of sovereignty, national defense, and so spared themselves the divisiveness of competition in autonomous defense policies. They also, France in particular, solved their "West German" problem sooner than they might, in France's case with the momentous bet, the Schuman plan for the European Coal and Steel Community.

There ensued a remarkable period of stability and renewed prosperity in "Europe," the term soon appropriated by western Europe (eastern Europe referred to as just that, often in conjunction with "and the Soviet Union"). The (western) European Community became a reality; it was less than the European federalists hoped for but more than anyone writing from the perspective of the previous century might have imagined. The question that hovers over the future is whether the conjunction of military dependence and political success was cause and effect or purely coincidence. Would western Europe's politics have been so happy had its nations opted then for self-reliance instead of dependence on the United States? Was the United States Europe's protector, or was its role as a pacifier of western Europe's historic quarrels also important?[47]

Economics and Security

AT WAR'S END, regional arrangements had not been fundamental to the thinking of Americans and their principal interlocutors, the British. The two nations shared the premises that postwar economic arrangements would be global in scope, and Britain would resume something like its prewar role. As those two premises were gradually found wanting, the American emphasis shifted from restoring a global order with Britain as a nearly equal partner, to reconstructing Europe as a temporary expedient, to, finally, accepting that Europe's recovery required Europe's integration, even if Britain opted out.

Throughout, economic and security considerations were entangled, and Germany was pivotal. At the time of the Marshall Plan, too much stress on what became the Cold War was still contentious in Europe and, to a lesser extent, the United States as well. Yet Europeans and Americans alike shared the presumption that rearmament could not come ahead of recovery. Divided by its occupiers and distrusted by its neighbors, Germany was the laggard, not least because France feared its recovery. So the Marshall Plan provided Europe, and France in particular, a broader structure for German recovery just as it also gave the U.S. Congress a broader context for American assistance.

Then and later, no set of security arrangements would have made sense if it had lacked a sound economic base; any measure had to meet the test of economic logic. Given its achievement, "Marshall Plan" became ever after the rallying cry for those who sought rapid economic transformation. After the fall of the Berlin Wall, a plan similar to the Marshall Plan, the solution to western Europe's problems after the world war, was recommended as eastern Europe's answer after the Cold War, and so some detail on how the Marshall Plan worked is worthwhile.

In 1950, when war in Korea reawakened fears of war in Europe, the allies, and not least the French, had to confront sooner choices that were more comfortable to defer. If Germany were to be a full partner in Europe's defenses, it could not be a second-class citizen economically. Incorporating Germany into western Europe's defenses meant, for Germans, accepting division; for Germany's allies it meant ratifying that fact of division.

For France, the choice was epochal: if Germany could not be constrained through occupation, it had to be contained through integration, as a full partner in the European Coal and Steel Community (ECSC). For the United States, accepting ECSC, indeed cheerleading for it, signified plainly what had been implied earlier—that Washington regarded Europe's integration as in its interest even at the price of some economic discrimination against the United States.

THE LOGIC OF THE MARSHALL PLAN

The United States should do whatever it is able to do to assist in the return of normal economic health in the world, without which there can be no political stability and no assured peace. Our policy is directed not against any country or doctrine, but against poverty, desperation and chaos. . . . Any government that is willing to assist in the task of recovery will find full cooperation, I am sure, on the part of the United States Government . . .

It would be neither fitting nor efficacious for this Government to undertake to draw up unilaterally a program designed to place Europe on its feet economically. This is the business of the Europeans. The initiative, I think, must come from Europe. The role of this country should consist of friendly aid in the drafting of the European program and of later support of such a program so in far as it may be practical for us to do so. The program should be a joint one, agreed to by a number, if not all European nations.

The words were George Marshall's at the Harvard commencement in June 1947.[1] Ernest Bevin, the British foreign secretary, described the speech as a "lifeline," but it might equally be considered a hunting license. It said to the Europeans "you have a license to tell us what you want. We are prepared to be generous, but exactly how much will depend on you." By leaving participation open to all, Moscow included, the United States would take what George Kennan called a "calculated risk"—one, however, that virtually no one in Washington in the spring of 1947 expected to lose.

The Marshall Plan was the crowning triumph of postwar American foreign policy, the United States at its best. Its genesis neatly reflected the mix of economic and security purposes. It came up on the economic side of the state department as the solution to problems on those officials' minds: the earlier underestimations of Europe's needs and the failure of earlier aid, especially the large loan to Britain in 1946; the worry that cooperation among the Europeans was ragged; and the reading that their own Congress would quickly have enough of piecemeal aid requests, each advertised as final. If Congress were to be generous in granting assistance, it would have to be for "Europe," not for a series of programs for individual countries.

The idea immediately appealed to those on the political side of the department, especially Kennan and the policy planning staff, for their own reasons. It would strengthen Europe to resist pressure from the Soviet Union and buck up individual nations, especially France and Italy, to fend off internal challenges from communist parties. And, not least, it would put the various "German questions"—from division to economic recovery to rearmament—in a larger European framework. Between Marshall's speech in late spring 1947 and the congressional appropriations of funds the next spring there intervened the crises in Czechoslovakia as well as in Greece and Turkey, all of which added momentum to the political and security drive behind the Marshall Plan.

The plan itself as initially conceived was a finite response to a pressing problem—if Europe was not devastated, some of its cities were, and its economies were disrupted, its capital depleted. What the Marshall Plan offered made economic sense and could be accomplished within the four years planned for it. On that there was broad agreement across Washington officialdom and the press attentive to foreign affairs. In 1947, while assessments of the military implications of the looming Cold War still differed, in Europe but also in the United States, all could agree that healthy economies in Europe were the bulwark of western security. So was increased cooperation among the western Europeans as part of a reconstructed global economy.

What was required was money and incentive. The Europeans, it was assumed, knew what they needed to do; they had been given the hunting license. The Marshall Plan was the preeminent American relation to western Europe. It was *the* policy and meant to be *the* answer; once European economies were back on their feet, Europeans could take care of themselves. For those Americans who, like Kennan, soon came to fret in anticipation of the military dimension winning priority, the urgency of economic reconstruction was all the greater.

Moreover, while the amount of U.S. aid seems grand in light of today's penny-pinching American mood, it did not seem so grand at the time. In the four years of the plan, Congress appropriated over $13 billion. Translated into 1989 dollars, America's total aid to western Europe in the decade between 1946 and 1955 was equivalent to $170 billion. Funding for the first year of the plan amounted to about a percent and a half of American gross national product (GNP), not so large for a country that had just emerged from spending half its GNP on war. Nor does it seem so large in light of later American military spending during the Cold War, which often was reckoned at three percent of GNP or more in defense of Europe.

To its European participants, the aid amounted overall to less than five percent of their GNPs, though exact figures depend on which exchange rates are used in the calculation and are thus somewhat arbitrary. How much the aid helped the Europeans became the subject of subsequent debate. American revisionists, most of them free-marketeers, argue that the United States provided little help, which the Europeans didn't much need anyway, and moreover, accompanied their cash with anti-free market advice that only slowed recovery.[2] Some of these arguments are careless economics: for instance, to say that U.S. dollar inflows were offset by the local currency needed to buy them misconstrues the plan's purpose, which was providing hard currency, dollars, the bottleneck to securing needed imports.

More thoughtful critiques focus on the timing of aid in relation to

Europe's reconstruction, or in other ways question whether American policy made much difference.[3] By 1947 European industrial and agricultural production hovered at less than three-quarters the prewar level, but the aggregate covered lots of variation by country and region. Much of the continent was already on the way to recovery, but Germany was lagging, its territory forcibly divided and so its economy unnaturally fragmented into pieces that were scarcely viable on their own.

The Marshall Plan was relatively simple, though the planning that went into it was not.[4] Its purpose was providing dollars to the European states in order to permit them the imports needed for recovery. The dollar transfers were from government to government, the U.S. Treasury to European central banks, which then sold them to importers in exchange for local currency. Some seventy percent of all Marshall Plan aid was "spent" in the United States, a figure that is both less important than it seems and more so.[5] It was less so because, economically, whether particular subventions of dollars were returned themselves to the United States in sales of exports or freed other hard currency for dollar-denominated imports was of no account.

It was more so because using plan dollars to purchase imports from countries other than the United States—"offshore purchases," as they were labeled at the time—was controversial even in the 1940s. With several exceptions, however, aid was not tied to imports from the United States because, for the most part, it didn't have to be. Most of the hard currency imports the Europeans needed had to come from the United States anyway; the major exception was Middle East oil.

Moreover, in 1947 the United States had a huge balance-of-payments surplus—equal to four percent of its GNP, a percentage, interestingly, identical to West Germany's surplus in 1989 before unification. Its problem was not selling its exports but assuring that its customers, especially in western Europe, had the dollars to buy them—a far cry from the 1980s and 1990s. The few ties that were mandated, in tobacco or shipping, for instance, reflected the influence of specific American sectors with powerful domestic lobbies.

It came as little surprise to economists but some shock to politicians to see what it was the Europeans needed. Members of Congress expected that a Europe rebuilding would require capital goods, but in fact such goods amounted to only slightly more than a tenth of total imports in the plan's first year. The reasons are not hard to find. Most capital goods, like plants or infrastructure, are not imported; one cannot import a canal or a highway. They are constructed locally, with imports providing the factors that cannot or are not yet produced at home. In the case of the Marshall Plan, more than two-thirds of those factors were the "four Fs": food, fuel, feed, and fertilizer.

In the event, Stalin was nearly as important a parent of the Marshall Plan as he later was of NATO. Between Marshall's embracing rhetoric of June 1947 and congressional passage of the plan in the spring of 1948, there intervened the shock of Czechoslovakia. In May 1947 Kennan's first memorandum as head of state's newly created policy planning staff did "not see communist activities as the root of the difficulties of western Europe," and so American "aid to Europe should be directed not to the combatting of communism as such but to the restoration of the economic health and vigor of European society."[6]

By the spring of 1948, however, the Washington rhetoric was all anticommunism and the Marshall Plan all the more popular for it. Moscow, which had declined to participate in the plan itself, then kept eastern Europe out, brutally so in the case of Czechoslovakia. In this atmosphere, the Marshall Plan's first year appropriations passed both houses of Congress by wide majorities. This turn in the backdrop of the plan did, however, validate the concerns of Kennan and others that rearmament would come to interfere with the objective they regarded as paramount, economic recovery.

By 1950, as the Cold War became hot war in Korea, the official U.S. objective did turn from economic reconstruction to defense, and these concerns increased apace. First came the military aid that Europeans had sought as part of NATO. The next year the Marshall Plan's formal name changed from European Recovery Program (ERP) to Mutual Security Program (MSP). Yet, for all the concern, the program probably changed less than its name. It did become more attractive to Congress, which then as now was not fond of seeming to give money to foreigners. Calling the gift "defending the Free World" helped; total aid to Europe, four and a half billion dollars in 1949–50, jumped to over seven billion the next year.[7]

The effect of the turn to security on Europe's economies depended on the fungibility of aid. To the extent that aid now labeled "military" only paid for weapons the Europeans would have imported with hard currency anyway, the aid was aid and what it was called was of no account. To the extent that Europeans' arms were twisted to use dollars in buying foreign weapons that they would not otherwise have procured, the result was to diminish the assistance to their economic recovery, and the effect depended on the magnitude of the arm-twisting by comparison to the increase in aid levels. No doubt there was some diversion to military purchases, but since the Marshall Plan's Paris managers were interested in getting dollars into European hands, they were suitably creative: in one case, France was permitted to spend ERP aid importing weapons from itself, via its deployments in southeast Asia!

Managing the Plan, and Incorporating Germany

There was only one donor of funds, the United States, so coordination, hard enough at the time, looks easy in hindsight. Congress was as unenthusiastic about giving the state department responsibility for the program as state was to take it, so a separate Economic Cooperation Agency (ECA) was established. Its director was Paul G. Hoffman, president of Studebaker Corporation, whose appointment, like the creation of a separate agency, betokened a businesslike approach to aiding Europe. In Europe the program was run from Paris by W. Averell Harriman, earlier Truman's secretary of commerce, ambassador to Moscow, and chairman of a critical planning committee for the Marshall Plan, later a Vietnam peace negotiator and confidant of Democratic presidents.

In parallel, the participating European nations created a permanent Organization for European Economic Cooperation (OEEC). Germany, still under occupation, was not represented when the western European foreign ministers signed the OEEC protocol in 1948, but thereafter its three western zones did participate under the guidance of the British and American military governors—the first chance postwar Germans had to participate in any international undertaking, even indirectly. The Bristish and American zones were represented by Bizonia, which had been created by the merger of the two zones in early 1947.

Once the Federal Republic had come into being in 1949, Adenauer seized the Marshall Plan's opportunity in both money and equality. He appointed to the cabinet a special deputy chancellor with responsibility for the Marshall Plan, a practice that soon became the norm for participating countries. German technicians dispatched to Paris easily joined the interchange among colleagues from European nations who shared both a common purpose, restoring markets, and much of a common culture, Turkey perhaps excepted. The European representatives pored over each other's plans, and in the process they learned a good deal about their neighbors' economies.

The conditions were the same for all the countries—to the benefit of Germany, the former enemy, and the occasional annoyance of Britain, which wondered what had become of the "special relationship." In the plan's second year, the United States insisted that the OEEC allocate the U.S. aid by country. That did not occur for the nations could not agree, and the United States became the decider of last resort. Yet given the level of exchange in Paris, when the United States made the final decisions, those choices neither came as a surprise nor were contentious.

The Marshall Plan was suffused with American hopes and tinged with American self-righteousness, the hopes shared by many Europeans: if Europe could not become a United States of Europe, at least it could remake itself in America's federal image. American enthusiasm for free trade was at a peak; free-traders felt vindicated by the Depression, and the United States emerged from the war with nearly half the world's GNP and a still larger share of its industrial production. Accordingly, most of the time Americans urged Europeans toward free markets at home and liberal trading abroad.

The pressure did not always succeed, nor were the sides of any given argument always divided by the Atlantic Ocean. There was a host of bright American ideas, not all of them free-marketeer—from a customs union in the summer of 1947 to proposals to build a stronger OEEC than could be achieved, from coordinating investment plans, which on the whole did not succeed, to trade liberalizations that mostly did. But there were many grand European initiatives as well, most of which also did not pan out.

At the Marshall Plan's Paris headquarters, noble aspirations ceded pride of place to the urgent practical task of restoring national economies. In the process, the Americans tolerated, sometimes encouraged, a good deal of central planning—national lists of and arguments for particular imports—though with enough flexibility to change as circumstances required. Ludwig Erhard, the architect of the West German *Wirtschaftswunder* or economic miracle, and later chancellor, underscored that the free-marketeers were not all Americans when he later described how he had circumvented a plan for food rationing simply by coming to the office on a weekend to destroy the plans. Presto: with no rationing, prices did their work, and the queues for food disappeared.[8]

The ECA's emphasis on what came to be called integration among the western Europeans was bound to mean some economic discrimination against the United States; after all the point of any customs union is to increase trade among members, which inevitably would divert some trade from nonmembers. Then and later, Europe's integration might be seen by Americans as to their benefit, but the benefits, political and economic, were indirect, while the immediate cost in specific trade was direct.

Washington's subterranean debate on this question was all but over by 1949. America's economic preeminence made any costs modest, and the more Europe turned toward the Cold War, the more pleasantly unity of any sort among the Europeans rang in U.S. ears, those on Capitol Hill especially. Hoffman publicly voiced the American approach in the autumn of 1949, calling for "a far-reaching program to build in Western Europe a more dynamic, expanding economy which will promise steady improvement in the conditions of life for all its people: This, I believe, means nothing less than an integration of the Western European economy."[9] The word "integration" was put in Hoffman's mouth because it sounded weaker than "unification" and was a little vague. But Hoffman referred to "the creation of a single European market," the avowed EC in its Single European Act of 1986, and he supported integration among subgroups of countries if need be. "Little Europes" were better than none at all, and might in time become bigger.

In the Marshall Plan's second year the United States sponsored the European Payments Union (EPU). Remarkably from the perspective of the 1990s, the Marshall Plan had been uninterested in exchange rates. Letting national exchange rates float was simply not an option; everyone was opposed to the idea even if they could no longer remember quite why. No doubt, Bretton Woods in 1944 had settled the question: Europe, like the rest of the world, would aim for currencies convertible at fixed rates; the rates could be changed if need be, but the need had to be real and the occasions infrequent.

The EPU was a stopgap designed to stimulate trade within Europe by creating an OEEC-wide clearinghouse. Rather than settling national accounts bilaterally, the countries would settle, through the EPU, their net position with the group as a whole. The ECA had promoted the plan as a way station en route to global convertiblity. And so it turned out to be. Yet the latent tension between succoring Europe and sustaining markets open to the United States became plainer when Europe moved from priming the pump of national economic reconstruction to beginning to shape an integrated European marketplace—the European Coal and Steel Community.

Europe Stepping Out

The United States had been more than a bystander in the OEEC, for the body reflected the insistence that Europe organize to make use of American aid and that it free up trade to help itself. But the OEEC, operating on the basis of unanimous consent, lacked the authority to produce an integrated European recovery program. What it had done was reconstruct national economies behind tariff walls, transport differentials, import quotas, and other barriers. There remained no shortage of uneconomic mines and steel mills.

Successive attempts to eliminate tariffs on broad categories of products had gone as far as the low-tariff countries were prepared to go without compensating reductions in tariffs by the others. Attempts at smaller customs unions, like the Benelux countries or France and Italy, had no better than a mixed record; in fact, smaller unions offered fewer possibilities for compensating reductions and thus made the adjustments required by cuts more difficult.

And so by 1950 thinking turned to a very different and radical approach, not an effort to negotiate a broad customs union among a few countries but instead to address a few sectors among all of them: the Schuman plan for creating a single European coal and steel community.

The immediate problem in 1950 was France's, and it was as much political as economic: if West German troops were necessary to defend Europe, then how could France ensure that the defenders would not again become threateners? And if Germany could not be prevented from recovering economically—or, put positively, if Europe, including France, could not be economically strong while Germany was weak—then how could France ensure that Germany's recovery would be to France's advantage, not its detriment? The two questions were two sides of the same coin. So were the responses. In the military area, the response was the Pleven plan, whose logic the French ultimately decided they could not accept.

In economics the response was the Schuman plan, which preceded the outbreak of war in Korea and thus the urgency of planning for a European army. Named for French foreign minister Robert Schuman, it was the creation of Schuman's countryman, Jean Monnet. The two men came to the same project by different paths. Monnet was an Anglophile and Atlanticist by temperament; he had done business all over the world and spent the war in London, where he inspired Churchill's proposal for an Anglo-French union. He was brought to the question of Germany by necessity.

In contrast, Schuman's life was Franco-German reconciliation, and this moment was once in a lifetime. The son of a Lorraine family, he had studied at three German universities before taking a doctorate from Strasbourg. He had been drafted into the German army during World War I, and only at war's end, in 1919 when he was thirty-three, did he become a French citizen.

The plan was as bold a stroke in its way as the Pleven plan and, unlike the once-for-all of Pleven, was one whose incremental logic might make it self-reinforcing, not self-defeating. If Germany could not be beaten, then better to join it in ways that offered hopes of making its capacity for aggression in Europe a thing of the past. As Schuman put it to a British audience in 1953:

> Why should we have recourse to this idea, to this new-fangled supranational institution? . . . I will tell you quite simply that it is to enable Germany to accept restrictions on her own sovereignty. . . . And if we wish to make Germany accept these restrictions, we must set her an example . . . we cannot retain for ourselves more power in the sector concerned than Germany will have. . . . It will mean identical renunciation on both sides and in the most delicate matters, such as the army and the production of coal and steel, products essential to the preparation for war and the formulation of policy.[10]

The choice of coal and steel was Monnet's, preeminently political and explicitly with war on his mind. More modernized industries might have been easier in economic terms, presenting fewer technical problems and holding out more receptive managers and unions. Moreover, in 1950 before the Korean war, Europe faced what it had in the 1930s—a steel glut, not a shortage—so the prospect of allocating contraction in those sectors was a less appealing joint venture than sharing expansion in some others. But coal and steel were the sinews of war-making.

By 1950, the German economic miracle was in the offing, and it was apparent that, deprived of its most important farmlands in the lost territories of the east and crowded with refugees, postwar West Germany, still more than prewar Germany, would have to find its future as an industrial state. Once the Korean war began to add to the global demand for steel, it took no seers in France or anywhere else to recognize that limits on German steel production could not be sustained indefinitely; the Ruhr Authority would be too limited as a vehicle for controlling German economic might. Germany could not be a military partner and an economic vassal.

Schuman's logic was explicitly a faith in what came to be called "interdependence." As he put it in his proposal, released May 9, 1950:

> Because Europe was not united, we have had war. A United Europe will not be achieved all at once, nor in a single framework: It will be formed by concrete measures which first of all create a solidarity in fact. The uniting of the European nations requires that the age-old opposition between France and Germany be culminated. The action to be taken must first of all concern France and Germany. . . . This proposal will create the first concrete foundation for a European federation which is so indispensable for the preservation of peace.[11]

Writing in the *Times* of London at the same time he used similarly explicit language: "the solidarity in production thus established will make it plain that any war between France and Germany becomes not merely unthinkable but actually impossible."[12]

Germany quickly agreed. The country had been, by necessity, a latecomer to the Marshall Plan; this was a chance to be a full partner from the start. Schuman's idea matched the preconceptions of Adenauer, the Francophile. It also fit nicely with his tactical needs, for it offered a way out from under the international controls on the Ruhr that had been imposed in 1949. To boot, since the Saar would have to be part of the coal and steel community, the unsettled dispute with France about who owned the territory would at least be softened.

Adenauer, like most of his countrymen, had not liked the idea of the Ruhr Authority but had agreed with Erhard's view that international control would be an improvement on control by Britain, in whose occupation zone the Ruhr lay. More important, Adenauer feared that if he "refused to send representatives [to the Ruhr Authority] it would amount to 'obstruction' which in turn would lead to a stiffening of Allied attitudes." Those "significant considerations of foreign policy," plus the Ruhr's urgent need for aid, had argued for accepting the Ruhr Authority.[13]

Now, Schuman's idea for building an integrated Europe might also make German rearmament and its entry into NATO go down more easily in Adenauer's domestic politics despite opposition from the Social Democratic Party (SPD). Kurt Schumacher, the SPD leader, who had earlier opposed the Ruhr Authority as a clever device to make the Ruhr unsafe for socialism, called the Schuman plan economic nonsense and, echoing his fellow socialists in Britain, argued against appropriating the word "Europe" for a small corner that was dominated by the four Ks in German—capitalism, clericalism, conservatism, and cartels.[14]

Toward a Little Europe

The coal and steel community marked the beginning of the Franco-German partnership as the engine of European integration; at the same time, however, it signaled the parting of the ways between France and Britain. It became a plan for a little Europe, though it was not intended as such. While the two countries had plainly disagreed earlier in the postwar period, not least over Germany, those disagreements had been contained, however uneasily, within the broad shape of three-power policy. But this was a European quarrel, with the United States as an interested and partisan bystander. Britain and France went in separate directions.

Marshall and his colleagues had taken pains in 1947 to assure that their initiative fit London's inclinations, and Bevin had eagerly grasped the offer. In 1950 as later, though, Britain sought a wider but thinner Europe. As the American ambassador in London, Lewis Douglas, put it: "Why did the British undertake to challenge French leadership? On the one hand they were not prepared to join in the Schuman proposal, and, on the other, they were not prepared to pay the consequences for not joining."[15]

The idea of creating an authority to control western Europe's coal and steel startled everyone, including Schuman's own diplomats. Concentrating on his own politics, Schuman gave pride of place to secrecy over consultation, so the plan came as a surprise to Bevin and the British. Worse, Acheson had been in Paris the weekend before May 9, so, turning around the usual postwar pattern of suspicion by France of collusion among the Anglo-Saxons, Bevin suspected Franco-American connivance.

Recovering from an operation, Bevin was grumpy and growling. His first public reactions to the plan were supportive but noncommittal. Monnet and several colleagues then spent a week in London. Their British interlocutors, at first tempted to dismiss the whole idea of a coal and steel community as a bit of Gallic flair, gradually realized that the French were serious, and not least about committing to principles before sitting down at the negotiating table to work out details.

On May 25 Bevin received the French text, agreed to by Bonn. The signatory governments, it said, "are resolved to carry out a common action aiming at peace, European solidarity and economic and social progress by pooling their coal and steel production and by the institution of a new higher authority whose decisions will bind" them—in short, agreeing to the principle of a higher authority in advance of negotiating its details.[16]

Bevin sent a note to Paris proposing that, instead of a full-scale international conference, the French hold talks with Germany, talks in which the British "would like to participate . . . from the outset with the hope that obtaining a clearer picture of how the scheme would operate in detail they might be able to participate in it."[17] That suggestion, participation with no commitment in advance to the idea, was unacceptable to France. France similarly rebuffed a British proposal for a ministerial meeting at which the Schuman proposal might be discussed, again with no precommitments.

The divergence came to a head on June 3 in a battle of communiqués. The British released their proposal, already rejected by Paris, for a ministerial meeting to review the French approach to the idea, in process if not substance. France and its five partners—the Benelux countries and Italy having agreed to the text as well as Germany—released their own communiqué, committing themselves to "negotiations . . . clearly guided by an agreement . . . on the fundamental objectives to be attained," as the French note to London had put it.[18]

Thereafter London sounded friendly to the Schuman proposal, including in comments to Parliament by the prime minister, Clement Atlee. But the two countries had parted company. Britain and France took different paths after 1950 for many reasons, but surely Germany was important among them. France was obliged to share the neighborhood with Germany. Once it became clear that Germany could not be kept down, then joining up with Germany offered a way of keeping up. Not so for Britain, which in 1950 was a world power, Europe's leading power even as it was not quite of Europe. Its lead as the only real European victor was plain; and its position of but not in Europe meant it had both possibilities and interests with some of the external character of America's. Or so it then seemed.

Thus, in opting out of the Schuman plan, Britain cited familiar reasons: its Commonwealth obligations were incompatible with full participation, just as they had been with a full role in the OEEC, and its planned economy could not quickly make the required adjustment; some in the governing Labour Party, like their coreligionists among German social democrats, were not above railing against the plan as a plot, one both capitalist and continental—two strikes against for the British socialists.

But the bottom line for both Tories and Labourites was sovereignty. Neither party was prepared to relinquish control of basic economic activities to a European authority. Labour might construe doing so as conceding the welfare state to the capitalists, while conservatives, like Margaret Thatcher forty years later, might fear that Monnet's language of a European "third force" smacked of statism or socialism or worse. But they both knew what they didn't like. The Tories were more than happy to score political points over Labour's failure to win as much as a seat at the negotiating table, but once seated, their answer to the question of a supranational authority would have been the same. As Churchill put it in Parliament: "why not be there to give the answer?"[19]

Moreover, the genius of the plan was, for both parties in Britain, its fatal flaw. It was not an end but the opening to a much broader economic and political integration. If it worked, it could be expanded; it could be self-reinforcing. But that looked, to Britain, like a slippery slope. Whatever the prospects of a compromise over coal and steel, no important part of the British body politic argued for setting off down that slope.

CREATING EUROPE'S INSTITUTIONS— WITH AN AMERICAN PUSH

The plan finally agreed upon among the six—France, West Germany, Italy, Belgium, the Netherlands, and Luxembourg—was, as Britain feared, the embryo of a federal Europe. That was precisely what it was intended to be by its architects. Most important, the members ceded national authority to a supranational body, initially the high authority of the coal and steel community for just those products, later the European commission for a broader and broader range of matters.

The authority, like the commission after it, was appointed by member governments but not meant thereafter to be directly responsible to them. It was to oversee the abolition of all tariffs and other trade restrictions, like national subsidies, in coal and steel. Likewise, it was to harmonize rates and conditions of transport among the members. Finally, during a five-year transition period it was given discretion—including money, later called structural adjustment funds—to relocate and retrain those workers hurt by the transition, a precedent for later expansions of the community.

The treaty also established three other European institutions—an assembly, later renamed the European parliament, the council of ministers, and a high court of justice to hear complaints about the high authority's actions. The assembly was a response to criticism that Monnet and Schuman were proposing a high authority beyond the reach of democratic control. They were more than sensitive to the criticism, they embraced it, for a European assembly would be one step further down the road to a federal Europe that was not simply the creature of national governments.

Perhaps sensing that, other participating governments, especially

Belgium and the Netherlands, wanted more than a yearly assessment of the community by the assembly; they wanted the high authority to be subject to some review by some body representing national governments. The French, as was to be expected, were sensitive to anything that might strike at the supranational character of the ECSC. The resultant was a council of ministers, composed of government representatives, not an executive but a board of directors between the authority and national capitals.

The various national arguments over the treaty and its implementation set a pattern that, no surprise, was repeated in subsequent expansions of Europe's integration. German industry accepted the plan as a trade for equality; the German trade unions came along, but the social democrats stayed in harsh opposition. The French right, including de Gaulle's supporters, remained hostile to the plan as too much cession of sovereignty. And those industries that feared losing in the competition, especially Belgian coal and Italian steel, fought a rear-guard action and eventually won protection from the full effects of a common market during the transition period.

Just a few days after negotiations over the treaty began, North Korean troops streamed over the border into South Korea. Rearmament began on both sides of the Atlantic, and if expectations of demand for steel outran actual demand, orders did turn up. Fears of steel glut receded. The coal and steel community was being negotiated just as its ostensible purpose was disappearing. On balance, though, the increased demand for steel probably made the negotiations easier: deciding how to share new exports is easier than allocating reduced production. Moreover, history's imprint on the steel industry was that increased capacity today was excess capacity tomorrow.

The more important effect of Korea, however, was on Germany. Almost overnight, the American objective turned from reconstructing Europe to defending the West. Both Germany's production and its soldiers became more urgent. What had been ideas for reintegrating Germany and so reducing its second-class status became proposals for getting German soldiers quickly onto NATO's front line. It was said more often, especially in the United States, that Germany was indispensable to western security. The turning point came in New York in September 1950, when Acheson dropped his bomb, the proposal for ten German divisions.

Schuman had remained implacably opposed to German rearmament, surely so until the ECSC was in place, but it took no great foresight to predict that as Germany's value increased, its negotiating position would harden. As the state department desk officer for Germany, Henry Byroade, put it in September 1950, in a cable to John McCloy, the American high commissioner in Germany, the "German attitude [was] less cooperative recently as they felt their position strengthened by [the] apparent eagerness of [the] Allies to sue for German military support."[20] After all, no matter how much of a Europeanist Adenauer was, his eye was fixed on West German sovereignty, not European federation.

Paris responded by hurrying to completion the Pleven plan for a European army, including Germans, and by insisting that France would accept German rearmament only after the Schuman plan had been signed. But American actions, and particularly McCloy's, were nearly as important. Their subject was the German steel cartel for the Ruhr. German industrialists began to go public with their reticence about ECSC: if the purpose was sharing markets, wouldn't a cartel like that before the war serve as well as a supranational authority?

From the beginning of occupation, the United States had sought to break up cartels and other concentrations in German industry. Few Germans shared this enthusiasm—those on the left were more interested in who owned industry than how concentrated it was—and the ECSC sharpened the issue, for to German opponents the community smacked of a French plot to break up Germany's coal and steel industry. American pursuit of its anti-concentration objective had waxed and waned. Now, Korea seemed to offer Germany a chance to slip away entirely.

French insistence kept the United States on the hook, but the American intervention was direct, and during the first months of 1951 the most important strands of negotiation were in McCloy's hands, placed there in part at Monnet's urging. McCloy sought agreement among the governments in Paris and Bonn, and their respective industries, including those in the Ruhr.[21] By March 1951 the main lines of an agreement were in hand. Both Germany's steel industry and its coal sales organization were to be broken up, though the French did not get their desired cap on the production of any single German firm, and limits were set on how much coal production a steel company could own.

The United States had put pressure on Germany before, most notably the year before when Germany's growing deficit had precipitated a crisis in the EPU, and it continued to do so. Acheson had confided to his British and French counterparts when he was in London in May 1950, though, that he saw occupation as a waning opportunity to reshape Germany.[22]

For its part, Adenauer's government had come under domestic criticism for being America's lackey. That said, however, in this instance he probably did not mind the American pressure all that much—just as other allies at other times regarded a little pressure from friends as nearly as useful as a little help. The U.S. attitude increased his leverage with his own industry and, more to the point, put pressure on his opposition, for while the SPD was unyielding in its opposition to ECSC, its labor union compatriots were tempted by the community's supranationalism and its promise of an escape from the restrictions of occupation.

In the context of occupation, any pressure over economics had a broader implication given that the occupiers were astride West Germany's path to full sovereignty. In this instance, the connection between economics and security was intimate: Germany's geography made it attractive as a military ally, but, equally, its forward position made it vulnerable, hence increasing its own need for protection. It was seeking security assurances from its allies, America especially, as it was bargaining over ECSC. McCloy's arm-twisting over cartels apparently did not include any direct references to American troops or military assistance to Germany, but he hardly needed to mention them directly. If European governments, Germany's included, later came to see U.S. threats to withdraw troops or military protection from Europe as an intramural squabble between the American branches of government, that was not yet the case.

On March 19, 1951, the participating governments initialed the treaty, and two weeks later Germany was notified it could produce steel in excess of the occupation ceiling—thus implementing a September 1950 agreement held in abeyance until the Schuman plan was in place.

AMERICAN RESPONSES

The coal and steel community set the pattern for the American response to European integration. In that regard, both McCloy's concern about cartels and his activism in support of agreement were cases in point. "Community" in the eyes of proponents was "cartel" to opponents. It strains current imaginations to hearken back to 1950 when America was a low-cost producer of not just coal but steel. Coal from eastern American coalfields could be shipped to Europe and undersell local products, while European steel exporters risked being shut out of Asian and Latin American markets by lower-cost American producers.

The concern that the ECSC would limit competition and protect marginal producers ran through early American reactions. Monnet and his colleagues took pains to refute it. In a memorandum sent to Washington on May 12, 1950, he argued not only that the ECSC was different in purpose from a cartel, not protecting the position of existing producers but broadening markets and improving efficiency, the method was also different, not price-fixing in secret but decision making in public.[23]

There had been proposals aplenty in the 1920s for uniting Europe, comprising varied mixes of economics and politics in both purpose and strategy. Then, as after World War II, keeping pace with America was one purpose, holding Russia at bay another; integrating French ore and German steel would intertwine their fates, reducing the risk of a German-Russian rapprochement.[24] The European steel cartel, formed in 1926, reflected both lofty aspirations toward integration and narrower economic concerns. It protected national markets for steel in Europe and gave the central authority substantial control over exports, dividing production and setting prices and terms of export. It broke down with the Depression but was reconstituted in 1933, this time with the United States and Poland as members.

In the case of ECSC the United States judged integration to be in its interest even at the cost of some specific coal or steel exports. In 1950, with the Soviet threat pressing and the U.S. economy preeminent, the choice was not hard. It had been foreshadowed by Hoffman's speech the previous autumn. The costs were recognized but so were the economic benefits: a larger European market was also one in which American firms could do business. In later years the choice was harder but the answer was the same.

Interestingly though, Arthur Vandenberg, the Republican pillar of bipartisanship, had confided to his diary as early as June 1949: "The Soviets know they have lost the cold war in Europe." But he added: "the economic stabilization of Western Europe (in particular of Western Germany) pours a flood of new competitive commodities into the world's market. . . . We are winning the cold war [but] we are losing the long-range economic war."[25]

The assessment made by Douglas, the American ambassador in London, in June 1950 is more representative of the government view:

> We must recognize that authority may be compelled to erect tariffs around these industries or take other steps to protect them. This is risk we must take, even though it may appear prejudicial to us. We would be quite inconsistent, if, on the one hand, we urged Europe to increase productivity, expand production, close the dollar gap, and integrate the European market, and on the other took offense if they did.[26]

The political point was put more sharply by John Foster Dulles, the Republican secretary of state-in-waiting, then serving as a consultant to Acheson and a symbol of bipartisanship in foreign policy. His initial reaction to the plan, on May 10, was

> that the conception is brilliantly creative and could go far to solve the most dangerous problem of our time, namely the relationship of Ger-

many's industrial power to France and the West. This proposal is along [the] line which Secretary Marshall and I thought about in Moscow in 1947 but which we did not believe the French would ever accept.[27]

American officials in later years were not always so effusive in their descriptions of economic integration in Europe, but they all reached the same conclusion: a more unified market in Europe made good politics for the United States and ultimately good economics as well, for the benefits of a larger market would outweigh the specific losses of particular exports. The conclusion held true despite the plain fact that Europe was not integrating as a favor to the rest of the world. It was doing it for itself. Between 1958 and 1962, for instance, trade between the United States and the European Community increased by 50 percent but that between the EC partners doubled.

The United States was an eager advocate of British entry into the EC in the early 1960s. It was so even as its actions along the security track—the Skybolt affair, culminating in the decision to sell Britain the technology for Polaris nuclear missile-carrying submarines—gave French president Charles de Gaulle a pretext for crying collusion among the Anglo-Saxons and so declaring Britain inadmissible to Europe.[28] The United States also supported the next expansions, to Greece, Spain, Portugal, though they were accompanied by disputes over agricultural exports diverted from the United States to the EC.

The judgment about the EC's 1992 program for a single European market was similar. At first, 1992 was more identified in the public mind as the anniversary of America's discovery than a milestone in Europe's construction. Then, ignorance quickly ceded place to concern: Europe would be "fortress Europe" defending the ramparts against American intrusions. By the 1990s, though, most larger American businesses reckoned 1992 good for them, a tent that might be a trifle harder to enter but one that would be larger once inside. And the U.S. government supported 1992 for familiar political reasons, not that it had much choice.

Additional evidence for American support of Europe's integration are the dogs that did not bark, or at least not very loudly. At first blush, the United States and its European allies seem to have argued constantly over economic issues, trade for example. Yet on second glance, all things considered, the arguments seem contained, almost stylized, never over much money and mostly for the benefit of domestic political audiences on both sides of the Atlantic. The successive expansions of the EC produced fresh issues about which to argue but did not change the pattern of the argument.

After 1960 most of those arguments were over agriculture, the effects of the EC's Common Agricultural Policy (CAP). CAP was a natural target, too visible and too tempting to overlook, its subsidies seeming a clear violation of GATT rules. Even so, the amounts of money at stake usually were trivial. The so-called chicken war of the 1960s was a battle over chicken feed, with the United States never threatening retaliation against more than $50 million in EC trade. The dispute over beef hormones in the late 1980s involved $100 million in trade—out of total U.S. exports to the EC of over $60 billion.

ECONOMICS ABSENT SECURITY

Yet security and economics were inseparable in those first postwar years, and Europe's dependence on American military strength endured well beyond those first years. Will the ending of the Cold War mean the fading of American influence over economics as well? And even if Europe's dependence in security has not implied American leverage over economics, has the military tie still been a security blanket, one that has smothered specific arguments, especially those over economics? If the Soviet threat that has preoccupied leaders and given them arguments for containing their politics is less visible, will arguments over economics be more so?

To be sure, the fact that the United States has been the ultimate military guarantor of Europe has entitled it to a commensurate say on defense issues; if that say has often been less than Americans hoped for, it has just as often been more than Europeans desired. Yet the tracks of broader influence—on economic issues, for instance—deriving from America's military engagement are hard to see.

That is so partly because economic and security issues have mostly been handled along separate tracks. American threats to diminish its defense role if Europe were not generous over trade or other economic questions have been seldom made and not very credible when present, explicitly or, more often, implicitly through congressional pressure on the executive branch. They have seemed to all and sundry, and especially to Europeans, the proverbial threat to cut off one's nose—not out of the question but not rational either.[29] They have been more an irritant than a tactic, and probably have done the United States as much harm as good.

Along the way the United States usually got something of what it wanted. But then it was most often the *demandeur*; that was especially true until the 1980s. It also felt itself the aggrieved party, particularly over agriculture. And even so, it seldom got close to all of what it wanted.

Logically, influence deriving from the trans-Atlantic defense connection could have run in either direction, deference by the weak to the strong because they needed the strong, or by the strong to the weak because the strong had to hold the coalition together. Or the two directions might combine. Like Indian princes under British rule, when the strong (United States) cared a lot, it usually would get its way, but in more normal circumstances the weak (Europe) could exact a continuing price for their allegiance. The safest conclusion is that, however America's influence in the security realm is reckoned, the leverage over economics provided by a few American generals—or even many American nuclear warheads—has been modest.

If the influence from security to economics could run either from the weaker to the stronger or vice versa, perhaps it has, inducing both the United States and its European partners to restrain their economic feudings lest the fabric of strategic cooperation be torn.

There is surely something to this argument, though compelling evidence for it is hard to adduce. Europe's postwar economic arrangements and its security connection to the United States were both established in the shadow of the Soviet Union. There was incentive for the allies to hang together lest they hang separately. For reasons more strategic than economic, the United States accepted a more closed European economy than it might have liked—the strength of the weak again. The security tie bound the United States.

The first inter-allied economic dispute of the post–Cold War era, over reforming agriculture in GATT's Uruguay Round at the end of 1990, suggested that the tie might now be less binding for both America and Europe. Official Washington presumed it had an implicit bargain: unwavering American support for German unification would be reciprocated by German pressure on its EC partners, notably France, to reform agriculture. But it did not happen, and German officialdom seemed surprised by the expectation. German vision, fixed inward, extended no further than reassuring its EC partners that Germany would remain loyal.

The original deal implicit in the 1957 Treaty of Rome that initiated the EC gave Germany more open markets for its efficient industry in return for paying a disproportionate share of the EC budget, much of which went to inefficient French agriculture. But as France's industry improved enough so that its industrialists began to like open markets, German farmers became attached to the benefits of markets closed to non-Europeans through CAP. In 1990, given the uncertain politics of a unifying Germany, the German government saw no reason to alienate yet another constituency.

America's transformation from munificent to ordinary in its economic relations with western Europe is arresting; over five decades it has gone from the Marshall Plan to beef hormone or pasta wars. It takes no Marxist bent, no assumption that economics determines politics, to notice that the change roughly paralleled the economic shrinkage of the United States in relation to its allies—in income, exports, and productivity. Nor is the change necessarily unhappy, let alone evil. It simply is. And if it partly reflects unwise American policies at home, it also reflects the success of wise ones abroad, the

Marshall Plan and spirited support for early European integration above all.

Moreover, the transformation has been gradual, and much of its effect has long since become customary. There seems little reason to believe the process of adjusting cannot continue. The United States will continue to acquiesce in accretions to Europe's integration, less now because it is fired with grand hopes for Europe's integration or grand fears of discord in the North Atlantic security community than because it simply does not have much choice and because it recognizes that, in the end, expansion will be good for the American economy.

The waning tug of the security imperative surely will have its effect on economics. But the waning itself is likely to be more gradual than it seemed in the rush of 1989–90, and the effect moderate. If there is dramatic change in the pattern of economic interaction, it seems less likely to ensue from the waning of old security threats than the arising of new economic shocks.

For instance, European monetary union, when it comes, might be seen by many Americans as a hostile act directed at them even as those in official Washington who favored fiscal discipline welcomed the pressure, much as Adenauer and his colleagues did not always mind in private U.S. pressure they objected to in public. Or a global collapse might transpire, triggered by some twenty-first-century equivalent of the oil shocks, first driving America and Europe apart, then perhaps impelling them to creative new cooperation in concert with Japan.

Moscow's German Problem

AT CHARLES DE GAULLE's press conference on the twentieth anniversary of Yalta, February 4, 1965, he spoke of the German problem as "above all the European problem," of the German anguish "created by its own uncertainty about its boundaries, its unity, its political system, its international role, so that the more its destiny remains undetermined, the more disturbing it always appears to the whole continent." A resolution of "the German anomalies" could not come, he warned, before radical change in Russia, which "must evolve in such a way that it sees its future not in totalitarian constraint at home and abroad, but through progress accomplished in common by free men and by a free people . . . the nations it has made satellites must be able to play their role in a renewed Europe." Any settlement of the German problem "would necessarily imply a settlement of its borders and of its armaments in agreement with all its neighbors."[1]

De Gaulle's logic was not at odds with what was coming to be prevailing orthodoxy in the West—a German settlement would follow, not precede a broader unfreezing of the European order—but he perhaps recognized more clearly than most that the unfreezing would hinge on dramatic change in the Soviet Union itself. Any policy of gradually improving relations—called *detente* in French or *Annäherung* in German—would be too little to permit a German settlement until the Soviet Union came or was forced to see its interests in eastern Europe as radically different.

We know less of Moscow's deliberations than those of the western capitals, but questions about Germany have been at least as central, perhaps more so. Soviet leaders have no doubt often been unsure and have improvised, just as western leaders have responded at each step to the conditions of the moment. The postwar history leaves room for argument over whether Stalin and his successors really sought to divide the United States from its European partners or to push America's forces out of Europe.

Indeed, that probably is the wrong way to pose the issue; Stalin himself may not have been able to give a "yes" or "no" answer. It depended. If he could have had the Germany he sought, perhaps the answer would have been "yes." But when he came to see that he could not, the answer changed. When confronted with the risk of a Germany, and a Europe, that was his third- or fourth-best, the second-best solution of an American engagement looked better.

THE MARCH NOTE

The Soviet Union had continued to argue for a four-power conference on the status of Germany, and it pursued the idea in a number of ways, including through initiatives by the East German government. Then, in March 1952, Moscow changed its tack. On the tenth it sent identical notes to France, Britain, and the United States. Their substance was not much different from what the Soviet Union had proposed earlier, but they were more specific and freer of polemic. The notes set out the outline of a peace treaty to end World War II. The four wartime powers would undertake the "most rapid formation of a general German government," thus ending Germany's partition.[2]

Foreign troops and foreign bases on German soil would be liquidated within a year of the treaty. The German government would pledge to observe the borders drawn at Potsdam, the Oder-Neisse line, and "not to enter into any coalitions or military alliances whatsoever directed against any power which took part with its armed forces in the war against Germany"—a none-too-subtle reference to NATO.

Otherwise, Germany was not to be constrained. It could have "national land, air and sea forces essential for the defense of the country" and the capacity to produce "war materials and equipment, the quantity and types of which must be the amount necessary for the armed forces" permitted by the treaty. It would be subject to "no limitations whatsoever . . . regarding the development of a peaceful economy."

The allies' initial response, conveyed in identical American, British, and French notes on March 25, stalled, trying to put the ball back in Moscow's court. A peace treaty was possible only *after* free elections nationwide in Germany and the formation of a free all-German government. Moreover, permitting German national armed forces but constraining Germany's freedom to enter alliances, "would be a step backwards."

A month later Moscow followed up with another note, this one proposing that the four powers "discuss without delay the question of conducting free all-German elections."[3] The note seemed to open a crack of future possibility by suggesting that the four powers might form a commission to verify whether conditions existed for such all-German elections.

In the end the three allies responded to the notes as an effort to divide them and to derail plans to rearm West Germany. They did not reject Stalin outright but repeated the arguments made in the March 25 note in another on May 13. The May note applauded Soviet support for free elections but parried the Soviet suggestion of a four-power election commission, arguing instead for a UN investigation to see if conditions for election existed.

Whether Stalin's notes were more than propaganda, his intentions more than tactical, remains an intriguing historical puzzle. If dividing the allies and playing on disagreement in the Federal Republic was his purpose, he had some success. Acheson called the gambit "old and obvious" but said it appealed to "timid and wishful thinkers—in France, those who feared a reunited and strong Germany and hoped for a 'matured' and 'satisfied' Soviet Union; in Germany, those who grasped at a chance of reunification, however slim, and hoped for security without the cost and risk of alliance with Western Europe and America."[4]

The idea of a national German army did tempt some in the Federal Republic. As Herbert Wehner, then a young SPD parliamentarian, later the party's grand old man, put it carefully in a Bundestag debate: he could not agree that because the western powers were disinclined to concede Germany a national army but insisted instead on a European one, the idea of a national army should be regarded as out of bounds.[5]

Nor were all the reactions to the March note negative in the United States. One portrayed the consequences of failing to pursue the note in stark terms, intriguing in retrospect for their error:

> the first six months of 1952 will go down in history as the period during which the United States lost control over the future of Europe and, specifically, over the future of Germany. . . . Once rearmed and fully sovereign, the Bonn Republic will pursue one very simple objective: It will seek the reunification of East and West Germany and the recapture of its lost provinces. . . . It may drag the Western alliance into a war with Russia—which is what both France and Russia fear.[6]

By the more customary line of positive reaction, Stalin had proposed what the West had sought—a united, free, neutral, and demilitarized Germany. To spurn it for fear that such a Germany might somehow be subverted into the Soviet orbit was to betray a lack of confidence and to misread the strategic context: Germany was not Czechoslovakia; 1952 was not 1947.

By this argument, it was the prospect of West German militarization that had induced the Soviet leadership to rethink its German policy. Since Acheson's first call for German participation in Europe's defense, in his September 1950 "bomb," Soviet policy on Germany had become more forthcoming as West German rearmament neared, less so when the prospect receded. Now, perhaps, Stalin had calculated that a Germany reunified on western terms was less bad than a rearmed West Germany integrated into NATO. If he was bluffing, the way to find out was to call the bluff, not forbear from doing so for fear he might be serious about his offer.

The awkwardness with this line of argument was that Stalin had not proposed precisely what the four western powers had said they sought. He had added one hooker—that a unified Germany could be remilitarized; however reasonable that might have been for some Germans, it was bound to be opposed by France. So Stalin knew.

And so those in the western countries who wanted to see if Stalin was bluffing had to argue both that Stalin's basic change of heart was sincere *and* that his language on rearmament was purely a tactic designed to outbid NATO—they will let you have an army only under their control, but we will let you have one with no strings—what Acheson called "golden apple" tactics.[7]

The West's insistence on free elections first, in which the Adenauer government in Bonn eagerly concurred, had the benefit of putting Moscow's feet to the fire, but it also asked the Soviet Union to pay a concrete price, the loss of East Germany, while its return was still in the future. That sequencing in the West's policy owed to suspicions that, as earlier in eastern Europe, Soviet agreement to election provisions would seem watertight in print but turn out to be porous in fact. The alternative would have been to bargain directly with Moscow over the price of the desired outcome—the withdrawal of Soviet troops from East Germany and the dismantling of the communist system there.

AN OPPORTUNITY LOST?

In any event, the March note was the last real Soviet proposal for a unified Germany. It is plain enough what Stalin's first-best was, a unified Germany in the Soviet orbit. But if he could not have that— and no doubt his reading of history was enough to suggest he could not, and that it might be overreaching to try—then the argument turns on what he regarded as second-best: a divided Germany, whose eastern part was communized and under his control but whose western part was rearmed and integrated into NATO, or a unified Germany that was part of the West even if its military forces were limited and nonaligned.

To be fair to Stalin, if what the three western powers said they favored, a unified but demilitarized Germany, had ever been in the cards, it no longer was by 1952. The idea of a completely demilitarized Germany in the middle of a divided Europe strains the imagination too far. Demilitarization was bound to be relative, which could be taken to be the understanding about Germany's military forces reflected in Stalin's note.

Surely, Stalin and his colleagues were improvising within the outlines of their broad goals. To that extent, imagining his calculations as a mirror image of those in the western capitals is appropriate enough. The safest interpretation is the most conventional one: that Stalin's operational objective was to head off the imminent militarization of the Federal Republic if he could and at the lowest price possible. Throwing in a recognition that a unified but neutral Germany would require armed forces would be unacceptable to France but might tempt Germans, hence divide the western allies.

At a minimum, he might induce a pause in the western plans, and that might in turn stimulate Germans to reevaluate their intentions. If, somehow, the western powers accepted his note, there would be plenty to negotiate, and Stalin's subsequent positions would have turned on how close or distant a rearmed West Germany seemed, and how far the likely outcome in Germany was from Stalin's first-best.

Seen from Moscow, the events of the previous two years could have been fairly read as a determined western attempt to bring Bonn into NATO's military fold no matter what.[8] It would hardly be surprising if Stalin, still more so than western leaders, discounted the effects of his own actions on the other side. And so he too floated one last proposal before settling for his risk-averse option: if he could not get all of Germany, he could get a firm hold on his half.

His own reported remarks to fellow communists in Yugoslavia provide some corroboration for this reconstruction of his calculations. In June 1946 he talked about the possibility that all of Germany would become "ours." But in January 1948 he told the same group: "The 'Westerners' are going to turn West Germany into their own state, and we're going to turn East Germany into ours."[9]

It was not quite that Moscow and the West were trapped into a cycle of escalating mistrust, though there was enough of that. Rather, Stalin was about the reap the fruits of his own previous actions. Overreaching had produced western reaction, perhaps over-reaction. And so by 1952 what disposition there had been in the West for risk-taking over Germany had disappeared, not least in the Federal Republic itself.

In the immediate aftermath of World War II, German thinkers had searched for ways out of their awful predicament: Nazi horrors had discredited the idea of the German state, but neither division nor dependence on the war's victors was appealing. Their gropings went in many directions but clustered around the idea of a third force in Europe, one in which German power could be subsumed even as German unity was sustained, perhaps a force mediating between capitalism and communism but surely one mediating between East and West.

But these hopes depended on another, that the Soviet Union was not a mortal threat which sought domination of all Europe. If it did, as events in 1947 and 1948 seemed to validate, then integrating the Federal Republic with the West was imperative; dreams of mediation or a third force would have to wait. Germans were left instead to hope, however vaguely, that an attractive state in Germany's west would ultimately lure the country's eastern half into the free world. So long as that residual hope seemed all that was possible, Adenauer's policy was not very controversial. Germans of different political persuasions could focus on the hope, suppress the harder questions of when, not to mention how, and get on with building their state.

However, when Adenauer refused to be drawn into exploring what Stalin might have meant with his March note, the social democrats began to diverge from his policy. "Missed opportunity" became the watchword, seriously exploring the chances of a deal the practical alternative. For his part, though, Adenauer had carefully crafted a basis of domestic support for his commitment to alignment with the western powers, including NATO. To suggest now that the policy might have been mistaken, still more to start down a risky new road, was almost beyond contemplating. And so in the aftermath of the March note affair, the Federal Republic signed the so-called

Bonn treaties, which spelled out its link to the European Defense Community (EDC), in May 1952. By the following autumn Moscow stopped answering western notes about Germany.

SEEKING TO SQUARE THE CIRCLE

If mutual risk-aversion before Stalin's death in 1953 is understandable, the curious next several years are less so. This was also the period in which Romania's foreign policy began to slip away from subservience to Moscow. It ended with the establishment of diplomatic relations between the Soviet Union and the Federal Republic, accompanied by strange noises, overtures perhaps, from Soviet leader Nikita Khrushchev. In between, Austria's occupation ended with a unified and western but neutral Austria in 1955, suggestive of some venturesomeness in the Kremlin despite the plain fact that Austria was not, and is not, Germany.

The preoccupying Soviet business at hand was domestic, the internal struggle for power. Malenkov first elbowed aside, then dismissed Beria; in turn, he and Khrushchev then contended for power, with Bulganin and Molotov as lesser claimants. Khrushchev did not gain full ascendancy until 1957 or so. It is possible, even probable, that Germany was a currency in these power struggles. That much was suggested more than once. For instance, after Stalin died, his ultimate successor, Khrushchev, accused his immediate successors, Malenkov and Beria, of plotting to sell out East Germany.

In that sense 1953–55 looks more like 1991 than 1990: in 1990 Gorbachev was, if anything, more able to take risks over Germany because of his domestic preoccupations; the latter distracted attention. They were, moreover, *his* troubles; a power struggle impended but was not yet on. By 1991 it was, and "who lost Germany" was implicitly a currency within it. In 1953–55, tampering with Stalin's legacy might have seemed to offer too many hostages to internal rivals. It would have seemed all the more so to the extent that risk-taking appeared more likely to worsen Stalin's legacy than to improve upon it—a prospect made vivid by the anti-Soviet riots that broke out in East Berlin in June 1953.

And so when the German question opened once more in the summer of 1954, Moscow played it according to Stalinist form and no further. When the EDC failed in the French parliament, the Bonn treaties were supplanted by the Paris treaties as the vehicle for West German rearmament and its accession to the Western European Union and NATO. Moscow reopened unification as an issue only to say it would close it if Bonn signed the Paris treaties. Adenauer was pressed by the SPD chairman, Erich Ollenhauer, to try negotiating with Moscow; March 1952 had been an opportunity lost.

But Moscow did not really offer anything new. In response to his internal critics, Adenauer pointed to the proposals the western powers had made. Moscow had not accepted Bonn's view of unification, and so the Soviet prescription for West Germany amounted to non-alignment. If Bonn delayed in signing the Paris treaties, it risked "sitting herself, without friends, between two chairs."[10] There was again no disposition for risk-taking in the West, including West Germany, and no real incentive for it in Moscow's approach.

The January 1954 meeting of the big-four foreign ministers in Berlin was a case in point. Called in response to Adenauer's initiative, a sign of Germany passing from object to actor, it featured a western proposal for free German elections—the "Eden plan," named for the British foreign minister, later Churchill's successor as prime minister. The four powers would draft an election law for a united Germany, taking into account existing West and East German provisions. The all-German government would then decide whether or not "to put into force, with respect to unified Germany, international agreements concluded after May 8, 1945"—those on everyone's mind were the Bonn treaties, for the EDC was not yet dead in the French parliament.[11]

Molotov responded mildly at first but then made two objections from which he never budged. The first was a return to the Soviet proposals for forming an all-German government before elections; holding elections first, with Germany still under four-power control, he argued, was to show distrust of the Germans. More to the point, he argued over and over against all efforts to persuade him otherwise, that a unified Germany would be constrained to enter the EDC.

The Federal German Bundestag approved the treaties in February 1955 by a roughly two-to-one majority, rejecting an SPD proposal to defer action pending another round of negotiations with Moscow. Three months later Moscow assembled its allies, including East Germany, into the Warsaw Pact, in evident retaliation for West Germany's accession to NATO. Europe's postwar military architecture was complete, and so was the Cold War order.

But for one curious and seemingly isolated episode, the period of turbulence in the Soviet leadership ended with no change in German policy. In January 1955 Moscow sought to influence the Bundestag debate over the treaties by floating an offer to normalize relations with Bonn. The offer lapsed with the vote but was revived in June, and Adenauer made his historic journey to Moscow in September to establish diplomatic relations.

While there, Khrushchev three times made what amounted to pleas for help, hence perhaps for a special Soviet-West German connection. As Adenauer recalled in his memoirs, Khrushchev rambled about the difficulties facing the Soviet Union, China in particular: "We can resolve these problems. But it is very hard. And so I ask you, help us, help us get ready for Red China! And for the Americans . . ." Adenauer refused to be drawn into the conversation, regarding it as disloyal in any case and perhaps as the rantings of an erratic leader.[12]

When Khrushchev had come to Geneva in the summer of 1955 for his first summit with the West, and only his second venture in foreign policy, he and Bulganin indeed had cast odd shadows in their ill-fitting suits, Khrushchev elaborately deferring to Bulganin but commanding his delegation in a way plain for all to see. In his memoirs he recorded his anxiety about the meeting and also betrayed his defensiveness over Germany, perhaps the legacy of the power struggle. For him, when the westerners talked of reunification, their meaning was clear:

the expulsion of Socialist forces from the German Democratic Republic: in other words, the liquidation of Socialism in the German Democratic Republic and the creation of a single capitalist Germany which
would, no doubt, be a member of NATO. As for our own position on
this issue, we wanted simply to sign a peace treaty that would recognize the existence of two German states and would guarantee that
each state be allowed to develop as its own people saw fit.[13]

Over the next several years both sides returned to the German
question in the context of security arrangements for central Europe.
Because, however, those arrangements were about the status of Germany, changing them meant contemplating change in Germany's
status. By now the Federal Republic had become a player, with
stakes of its own; and while it was not quite realized at the time, so
had East Germany. The stakes of those two states intruded into the
political deliberations in Washington and Moscow.

On paper the two sides were not all that far apart. Yet since the
real question was Germany, the distance was greater than it seemed.
Rather than might-have-beens, the proposals were more has-beens;
their interest now that the Cold War order has passed away lies in
how statesmen then thought the solidifying of that order might have
been prevented.

The Eden plan in Berlin had been about German elections, not
European security, but in the next year and a half the three western
powers developed the security aspects of the Eden plan, calling for
a security agreement between all four powers and a reunited Germany under which all five would aid any victim of attack; the four
would also agree to limits on their forces in and around Germany.
Later versions proposed an inspection system in which joint teams
would operate by mutual consent within a specified area on both
sides of the East-West divide in Europe, and, at Bonn's urging, they
tightened the link between German unity and European security.

At the Geneva summit in July 1955 the Soviet Union elaborated
a proposal for a fifty-year security pact it had presented at Berlin.
The new pact would be accomplished in two phases. In the first,

two to three years long, existing obligations in NATO, the Warsaw Pact, and the WEU would remain in force, and the parties would agree only to renounce armed force and settle disputes amicably. In the second phase, existing alliances would lapse, to be replaced by a pan-Europe collective security system; until it became operational, NATO and the Warsaw Pact would conclude a provisional non-aggression pact.[14]

The echoes in Soviet proposals thirty-five years later are unmistakable; dusted off, the 1955 proposal would have served as a talking paper for Gorbachev and Eduard Shevardnadze in the spring of 1990. The difference is that later the proposals were driven by the imminent unification of Germany, while earlier it was unification that foredoomed them. Then, Moscow insisted that reunification could be considered only after, not as, the security system was in place. And so the argument returned to Germany and elections.

On that score, Moscow hardened and softened in apparent response to events. Since 1950 it and East Germany had proposed various forms of an all-German council, one that would equally represent East and West Germany, and that would among other duties organize all-German elections. In 1951, in an action by the East German People's Assembly (*Volkskammer*), the requirement of parity between East and West was dropped, at least provisionally, and the preparation of elections became the proposed council's paramount task, not just one among many—both nods toward the position of the Federal Republic and its allies.

This change prefigured the Soviet March 1952 note. After the Bonn treaties the Soviet view hardened, and did so again during the Berlin conference. Molotov spoke of preparing elections as a task for Germans themselves, not the occupying powers. Moscow's view softened after France defeated the EDC, and it declared its readiness to consider the Eden plan as a basis for discussion.

At the Geneva summit, the four powers agreed on "free elections," but it was doubtful that they agreed on what they had agreed. When the four foreign ministers met a few weeks later to follow up that agreement, Molotov returned to East German ideas for a council, arguing that after the Paris treaties, reunification could only be achieved through rapprochement between the two German states. A Soviet note to Bonn the next year put the point sharply, concluding that "talks about German reunification by all-German elections no longer have any real foundation. At the present moment, the conditions requisite to holding such elections do not exist in Germany."[15]

FROM GERMANY TO ARMS CONTROL

The deployments, actual and impending, of nuclear weapons in central Europe added urgency to the cottage industry of security proposals. However, with the division of Germany a fact, along with the links of the two to their superpower patrons and alliances, proposals that ran to the German question were more and more impractical while those that did not run so far were more and more beside the point. Proposals of both sorts were alike in seeking to solve the political problem in central Europe with military measures. In that they began a line of policy, later called "arms control," that ran down to the fall of the Berlin Wall.

For instance, in 1956 Erich Mende, then a Bundestag deputy from the Free Democratic Party (FDP) and later foreign minister in SPD-FDP governments, argued that the first step to unification was four-power agreement on the military status of Germany.[16] He proposed mutual pullbacks of western and Soviet forces from their respective zones, with a constrained German armed force defending Germany. Germany would then either join the four in a five-power pact or become part of a broader pan-European security arrangement.

In either case, the two Germanys would leave their respective alliances. Mende made clear, however, that an American military presence in Europe would remain a prerequisite for German security. Other than reshuffling its forces after the departure of American troops from Germany, for Mende, NATO was not immediately in question; its future would depend on the effectiveness of the European security system.

Hugh Gaitskill, the British Labour Party leader, speaking to an audience at the Free University of Berlin in March 1957, added Poland, Czechoslovakia, and Hungary to the Germanys as countries to be stripped of foreign troops and released from their respective alliances; a control system would monitor national forces permitted in those states.[17] Germany would be unified in free elections. The security of the neutral zone would be guaranteed by a mutual European security arrangement, with special commitments by the four powers.

Gaitskill's theme was echoed by others, by the German SPD in its May 1957 Ollenhauer plan, and by George Kennan the next autumn in his Reith lectures for the BBC, who named it "disengagement":

> If there could be a general withdrawal of American, British and Russian armed power from the heart of the Continent, there would be at least a chance that Europe's fortunes might be worked out, and the competition between two political philosophies carried forward, in a manner disastrous neither to the respective peoples themselves nor the cause of world peace.[18]

Kennan, who consistently argued that the threat of a Soviet invasion had been overestimated, nonetheless believed that the political benefits of a Soviet military withdrawal had been sharply undervalued. On the core issue, Germany, though, he was vague, seeming to suggest four-power imposition of a limited, armed neutrality—something akin to the Austrian solution.

That same autumn, Poland's foreign minister, Adam Rapacki, outlined to the United Nations the first of a series of Warsaw Pact proposals for special zones of disarmament in Europe.[19] His version was focused and spare, its targets nuclear weapons and Germany. His rhetoric was the threat posed to Poland and its neighbors by a nuclear-armed Federal Republic in the NATO alliance. He proposed that nuclear weapons be neither produced nor stockpiled in either Germany, and he indicated that Poland was prepared to join the prohibition.

The Rapacki plan probably was tactical in its intention, the latest in a series of attempts to frustrate West Germany's arming and its integration into NATO, with nuclear weapons the target this time, an emotive one. So it was then interpreted by the western countries. It was unacceptable to NATO, which deemed nuclear weapons necessary to offset Soviet advantages in conventional forces; thus a no-nukes-for-no-nukes trade, symmetrical on its face, was not in fact.

West Germany was to be defended all the way to its border, so-called forward defense. For Bonn that was imperative, then and later. Moreover, a special zone in central Europe meant singling out the Federal Republic; "singularization," a Soviet *droit de regard* over its military decisions, was also unacceptable both then and later.

The Rapacki plan, though, also demonstrated how far European statecraft had drifted from the central issue of Germany. Put the other way around, Germany was a settled issue; there would be two. Whatever might have been, the superpowers and their allies had fumbled toward a status quo that was perfect for neither side but acceptable to both. It would take something dramatic to change that calculation. Certainly no tinkering with disengagement, mere arms control, would do the trick.

CRISIS OVER BERLIN

Seen in this context, the second Berlin crisis, in 1958–61, the tensest moments of the Cold War until the Cuban missile crisis, with Soviet and American tanks facing off at Berlin's Checkpoint Charlie, did not change all that much. It began a decade-long process of tidying up the status quo toward which the superpowers had stuttered. If Moscow was willing to run risks in Berlin, the point of those risks, at least in hindsight, seems less a strategic adventure and more a persistent problem—the stability of its client, East Germany, the German Democratic Republic.

The stakes of the East German regime, visible through the backings and fillings of the Soviet position, seem evident enough in retrospect to have been calculated by western leaders at the time, especially since by this time those leaders were plainly aware of how much *their* policy was affected by *their* German ally. Then, however, the image of the Soviet bloc was overpowering, for officials in Paris and London little less than for those in Washington. If anything, that image became even more dominating during the crises over Berlin: in western eyes, when Moscow said "jump," East Berlin said "how high?"

To be sure, the East German regime was much more the creation of the Soviet Union than the West German one was of its three western founders. Disagreements among the three opened space for the new government, and all three were prepared to let West German politics run, albeit within limits. By 1958–61 the Bonn government, in form still not a participant in three-power decisionmaking, in fact had acquired what amounted to a veto over American policy.

By contrast, East Berlin was the creature, not just the creation of the Soviet Union; it was brought into existence by the formation of the Federal Republic, much as the Warsaw Pact mimicked NATO. Moreover, the numbers of German communists who sought wartime refuge in the Soviet Union only to be slaughtered by Stalin ensured that when created, the East German regime could be recruited from a select group of German communists, to put the point gently. The East German leader, Walter Ulbricht, probably had more standing, if not stature, in Moscow than he did among his own compatriots.

Yet, however much the East German regime was Moscow's creature, once created, it was an actor. In that regard, the spate of revelations after the fall of communism in East Germany was as much misleading as instructive. It was stunning to see just how pervasive the East German security service, the Stasi, was and how intertwined it was with the KGB. Yet institutional connections across bureaucracies do not automatically make for acquiescence at the top of government. As a rough analogy, think of U.S. military and intelligence relations with Israel.

Since in the 1950s no one, east or west, doubted that free elections would mean the East German regime's elimination, its interest in how those elections would be carried out was correspondingly powerful. The tugging of these East German stakes must have compounded Moscow's own hesitation to hazard fresh proposals over Germany. Soviet leaders presumably were prepared to sacrifice the specific East German regime if they could have their first-best. But once reunification came to seem like a gamble they could lose as well as win, the concrete stake in East Germany, now pressed on them by East German leaders, must have reinforced their disinclination to gamble over Germany as it increased their inclination to gamble on behalf of East Germany.

The second Berlin crisis began with a November 10, 1958, speech by Khrushchev, by then the clear winner in Moscow's latest power struggle. His immediate theme was "the atomic arming of the Bundeswehr"; his rhetoric was fierce; his argument was that the time had come to "renounce the remnants of the occupation regime in Berlin and therefore make it possible to create a normal situation in the capital of the German Democratic Republic"; and his threat was that "the Soviet Union . . . would hand over to the sovereign German Democratic Republic the functions in Berlin that are still exercised by Soviet agencies."[20]

In a Soviet note of November 27, the rhetoric was no less tough and the message was more explicit: the status of Berlin is an anachronism and must be ended, thus "the Soviet Union regards as null and void" the 1944 agreements on occupation. With regard to timing, the note was both vague and explicit. Moscow would enter into negotiations with East Germany "at an appropriate time" to transfer Soviet functions to the government in East Berlin. However, Moscow also proposed, in what it argued was a compromise, turning West Berlin into "a free city, without any state, including both existing German states, interfering in its life." On that score the timing was more threatening: the Soviet Union would make no change "in the present procedure for military traffic" of the western powers to West Berlin "for half a year," but at the end of that time would feel free to "carry out the planned measures through an agreement with the GDR."

Khrushchev's turning up of the international temperature over Berlin is usually interpreted in broad strategic terms, as the reflection of Khrushchev's harder line, a probe of western firmness, or an attempt to forestall the deployment of American nuclear weapons in Europe, especially Germany, or, with hindsight, as in part a response to the emerging Sino-Soviet rivalry. Dulles, for instance, characterized the Khrushchev speech as another in a series of probing operations designed "to find out whether they are up against firmness and strength and unity."[21] All these surely played a role, nuclear weapons in particular, against the backdrop of Kremlin politics.

What is striking, however, is the plain acceptance of two states reflected in the Soviet language. Indeed, Moscow demanded specifically that the western powers accept the legitimacy of the East German state. The Soviet language described West Germany harshly but did not characterize it as illegitimate: "two states came into being in Germany," in the language of the November 27 note. Hence the crisis was about either more or less than the status of Germany—more if it was interpreted, as did most of official Washington, as a strategic probe, less if it was seen in the context of East Germany's struggle for legitimacy. The 1953 uprising in Berlin had demonstrated just how precarious the East German position was; in 1958 Berlin continued to be an open sore.

In a memorandum to the president on November 13, Christian Herter, the acting secretary of state during Dulles's illness, listed first among Soviet motivations the "long-standing desire to force the Western Powers into *de facto* recognition of an East German regime through the creation of situations on allied access routes to Berlin calculated to compel the Western Powers to deal with East German officials." The next day state's intelligence bureau put the Soviet purpose in similar language, adding that it seemed "unlikely that the USSR plans at the present time to use force against the Western position or to blockade the city."[22]

Soviet and East German interests converged. Moscow could hardly be expected to stand by and watch West Germany acquire access to nuclear weapons. That was all the less acceptable because, for their alliance purposes, American officials had to blur the issue of exactly how much access Germans would have: different audiences made for different messages. While Eisenhower, like Kennedy after him, seems never to have seriously entertained the prospect of giving Germans (or anyone else) real control over the firing of nuclear weapons, the public pronouncements by him and his associates were not so clear on that point.

For instance, Secretary of Defense Neil McElroy announced at a meeting of NATO's parliamentarians in November 1957 that the United States wanted to base intermediate-range missiles in Europe and would consider giving the allies control not just of the launching vehicles but of the nuclear warheads as well. Dulles tried several days later to soften the menacing spin, by saying only that the United States wanted "a very considerable measure of allied participation."[23] Still, the language was hardly reassuring in Soviet ears, all the less given the presence as West German defense minister of Franz-Joseph Strauss, a man who minced no words about German equality, including in matters nuclear.

For an East Germany whose legitimacy was doubtful, West Berlin was an embarrassment at best, a running sore at worst. Ulbricht, who had served Khrushchev well during the latest turns in Moscow's power struggle, had been dropping hints about West Berlin since 1956. He laid claim to the city in a public speech on October 27.[24] Eleanor Dulles, the secretary's sister and a senior Germanist at the state department, suggested Ulbricht had pressed Khrushchev to act during a visit to Moscow in 1958.[25]

ALLIED REACTIONS

John Foster Dulles's public reaction to the Khrushchev speech was firm but flexible, emphasizing negotiation not confrontation, and seeking to narrow the issue, not broaden it. In these respects he set the line of American approach that continued across the Eisenhower and Kennedy administrations. The narrowing of the focus was particularly evident after the failure of the Geneva meeting of the big-four foreign ministers in May 1959; President Kennedy mobilized troops in Berlin, but he too sought secure access to Berlin and feared a repeat of the 1948 blockade.

At a press conference on November 26, Dulles called normal access to Berlin for the western allies "an obligation, an explicit obligation, on the part of the Soviet Union." Yet while the United States would "not accept any substitute responsibility," it would not rule out dealing with "minor functionaries of the so-called GDR" so long as they were agents of the Soviet Union, not substitute authorities.[26]

Dulles's words prompted "shock and dismay" in Willy Brandt, then mayor of West Berlin and later chancellor. When Dulles went still further and suggested, in January 1959, that free elections were not the "only method by which reunification could be accomplished," he provoked the same reaction from Adenauer and his foreign minister, Heinrich von Brentano.[27] For the social democrat Brandt the Berlin crisis was first and foremost about West Berlin, its status as a western island in an East German sea.

Eisenhower himself had always thought the West's agreement to creating that island was a terrible mistake, and he was willing to entertain the possibility of making Berlin a "free city," perhaps with a special connection to West Germany and access guaranteed by the United Nations. After all, the West could hardly, in the line attributed to NATO secretary general Paul-Henri Spaak, risk nuclear war to force the Russians to stay in Berlin! Meeting with Khrushchev at Camp David in September 1959, Eisenhower's tone on Berlin was conciliatory, noting that Berlin's situation was unusual, perhaps a mistake, one that could be rectified "with great patience" and not in the "long distant future."[28]

He was stayed from trying, however, by the knowledge that Adenauer's great fear was precisely that the United States would abandon him by doing a deal over his head. As Eisenhower's aide recorded him musing in October 1959: "he thought he could strike a bargain on his own with Khrushchev if he were to try to do so, but he knew our allies would not accept his acting unilaterally."[29] Adenauer's Rhineland heart was not in Berlin—when Dulles suggested to him that if war broke out over Berlin, nuclear weapons might have to be used, Adenauer replied, "For God's sake, not for Berlin!"

Rather, for Adenauer, Berlin was about *his* policy, *Westpolitik*, the alignment with the West and the attempt to isolate East Germany. On that score no American reassurance could be reassuring enough. Dulles's January language was the opposite of reassuring and called forth a blast from the chancellor to the American ambassador in Bonn: the repercussions of Dulles's words "in Germany would be momentous," undermining his position that "reunification could only be achieved through free elections" and encouraging his opponents, "those naive people" who thought it possible to talk to East Berlin. Such talk "was for him inadmissible" and the idea of "confederation in any form" to which talks might lead "totally unacceptable."[30]

By separate paths and with different implications, both Britain and France had confided to themselves what the United States government had not quite yet—that Germany would remain divided. For France, "would" was also "should" and the policy implication was tactical support for the Adenauer view: better not to risk a slippery slope to confederation, let alone unification. Accordingly, France tugged at the United States for a harder line on Berlin.

Britain's logic went exactly the other way: Germany was divided but the western position in Berlin was vulnerable. The British prescription—a forthcoming posture that had run through its sponsorship of the Eden plans—fit Tory Britain's broader interest in *detente* with the Soviet Union. British leaders continued to mouth support for unification through free elections but in fact, as a state department intelligence report of April 9, 1959, put it, they were "losing interest in identifying a *detente* in Europe with reunification by free elections"—a view that got them branded "soft" by Washington throughout the crises.

If the Soviet security proposals of 1955 provided a script for Gorbachev and Shevardnadze thirty-five years later, by the 1959 meeting of the big-four foreign ministers in Geneva, the United States and its allies had come remarkably close to what in 1990 they proposed—and succeeded in persuading Moscow to accept. The government of a unified Germany would have "full freedom in regard to internal and external affairs," thus could stay in NATO if it chose. No country could station forces in that Germany without its consent.

Perhaps most intriguingly, in talking of broader European security arrangements, the allies prefigured the 1990 Hans-Dietrich

139

Genscher proposal for not stationing NATO forces in the territory of the former East Germany: "should the all-German Government decide to adhere to any security pact"—for which, read NATO— "there might be special measures relating to the disposition of military forces and installations in the area which lies closest to the frontiers between a reunited Germany and countries which are members of another security pact."[31]

The proposal is more tantalizing in retrospect than it was at the time, for then it was almost anachronistic as one last try at linking unification to broader European security arrangements. Khrushchev made painfully clear just how anachronistic in June 1959 to a visiting Averill Harriman, the former ambassador and Marshall Plan administrator. Khrushchev began, in passion, with a crude joke that spoke reams about his peasant bluster: seen naked and from behind, Chancellor Adenauer demonstrated why Germany was divided; seen from the front, he showed why that Germany could not stand.

> We will not agree to your taking over western Germany. We will not agree to a united Germany that is not socialist. In fact, no one wants a united Germany. De Gaulle told us so; the British have told us so; and Adenauer himself when he was here said he was not interested in unification. Why, then do you insist on talking about it?[32]

Bluster aside, Khrushchev seems to have drifted from his second-best toward his third. At most, perhaps he could head off or limit the nuclearization of West Germany; more likely, he could shore up the position of his East German ally. In retrospect, he seems to have had little stomach for a military confrontation and thus no objectives of commensurate sweep. His deadlines twice came and went; moreover, advertising advance warning would seem a strange way to enter a confrontation. Rather, the pattern suggests an interest in negotiating. He said as much, bluster again aside, for instance to Senator Hubert Humphrey in December 1958. If negotiation were the intent, Berlin and East Germany were the logical subjects.

In October 1962 Berlin ceded place to another crisis, missiles in Cuba. In the meantime, though, Khrushchev's Berlin problem had been solved another way—the building of the Wall in August 1961. The Kennedy administration's initial military buildup, announced by the president at the end of July, provoked Khrushchev speeches in return, ones taken as toughness at the time but that, read now, seem to indicate a fear that things were spinning out of control. On August 7 he said "let us not create a war psychosis," and on Berlin specifically ruled out "any barring of access to West Berlin, any blockade of West Berlin is entirely out of the question."[33]

The Wall was an eyesore, tangible evidence of communism's failure, but it was still better than the sore of open access to West Berlin. It was the price of sustaining the German status quo, for East Germany was losing 2,000 able refugees a day to the West—the same number, suggestively, as in 1990 after the Wall came down but before economic union between East and West Germany. As Llewellyn Thompson, the American ambassador in Moscow, had cabled Washington in March 1961: "If we expect [the] Soviets to leave [the] Berlin problem as is, then we must expect [the] East Germans to seal off [the] sector boundary in order to stop what they must consider [an] intolerable continuation of refugee flow through Berlin."[34]

OSTPOLITIK AND THE MOSCOW TREATY

What next reconfigured Moscow's German problem was not its own actions but rather those of the West and ultimately of the Federal Republic. In the sequence begun haltingly with President Kennedy's "strategy for peace" in the early 1960s and confirmed more explicitly in President Johnson's "bridge building" speech of 1966 (not to mention French president Charles de Gaulle's visit to Moscow the same year), the Federal Republic's allies had decided that the way to mitigate the effects of Europe's division lay in negotiating with the East, not trying to isolate it—*Ostpolitik* in its German version.

The seeds of the new policy ran back into the early postwar years. Adenauer himself had not been above harboring heretical thoughts about Germany's postwar status. He told McCloy in 1950 that it was better to "renounce for a time the thought of a reunited Germany" than to break the Federal Republic's western ties by negotiating with Moscow.[35] He seems to have acknowledged, to himself if not to his political associates, that Germany's eastern territories were lost forever at the same time as he talked publicly about their recovery.

He put his private office to work on alternatives in preparation for his negotiation of diplomatic relations with Moscow in 1955, work perhaps reflected several years later in the chancellor's suggestion to the Soviet ambassador in Bonn that the Soviet Union consider an "Austrian status" for East Germany. In secret discussions with Moscow as early as 1962, Adenauer had also foreshadowed *Ostpolitik*'s willingness to put the German question in abeyance, instead focusing on living conditions in East Germany.

The pieces of the new approach had been visible between the lines of the most recent Berlin crises. If holding western policy hostage to reunification was making less and less sense to Bonn, that was even more the case with other western capitals. Paris had come first to the conclusion that reunification was not going to happen soon anyway, in France's case the wish perhaps siring the thought. Britain had been ahead of France during the 1950s in concluding that the way around reunification lay in negotiations with Moscow—a conclusion evident in the Eden plans and in London's approach to Berlin. By 1959 Herter recorded what was becoming conventional wisdom in Washington as well: "the Germans themselves will have to find the answer to their own reunification."[36]

Among German social democrats, yearnings for a third force in Europe had lingered on; along with the party's dogmatic commitment to socialism, this allowed the CDU to tar it with the epithet "unfit to govern." It took the SPD a decade, until 1959–60, to reverse course in both economics and foreign policy, accepting the political and military arrangements of the Atlantic alliance. In 1966 it was rewarded with admission to the "grand coalition" with the Christian Democrats. The coalition's chancellor, Christian Democrat Kurt-Georg Kiesinger, spelled out the dilemma of the new approach in a 1967 speech:

we ought not to duck the question of how . . . [to] combine our policy of detente as a precondition for overcoming the division of our people, with our Western allegiance and with our efforts to[ward a] united Europe. Does the one not cancel out the other? Is this not where the tragic contradiction lies in the way we think and feel about our entire policy? Germany, a reunified Germany, would be of critically large size. It is too big not to have an effect on the balance of power, and too small to be able itself to hold the balance with the powers round about it. It is there[fore] in fact very hard to imagine that the whole of Germany could without further adjustment belong to one or other side, if the current political structure in Europe continues. For this very reason, one can see the separate halves of Germany growing together only if this is firmly anchored in the process of overcoming the East-West conflict in Europe.[37]

Once the social democrats were the senior partner in government after 1969, for the first time in the Federal Republic's history, in coalition with the Free Democrats, Willy Brandt and Walther Scheel hurried their country to the front of the logic of reconciliation lest their allies, and especially their superpower patron, deal with the Soviet Union over their heads. They accepted the inevitable—that reunification was a hope, not an operative goal, and that the path to it lay through dealing with their eastern neighbors, including the Soviet Union and, in particular, trying to improve the living conditions of those neighbors, especially the German Democratic Republic.

Moscow's brutal crushing of the Prague spring of reform in 1968 had, somewhat paradoxically, underscored the logic of a new approach for both West Germany and the Soviet Union. The invasion forced West Germany to deal with Moscow, for the road to Prague, not to mention Warsaw or East Berlin, ran through Moscow. But Moscow also realized the limits to utilizing France as a mediator, for Germany held the keys to detente.

Ostpolitik culminated in West German treaties with the Soviet Union and Poland in 1970, the four-power agreement on Berlin in

1971, and parallel agreements between West and East Germany.[38] Together, they completed the tidying up of the postwar order. The Federal Republic and its allies did what Khrushchev had sought in 1958: they recognized East Germany, with the two Germanys establishing representation to each other. In return, the Soviet Union recognized the links between West Berlin and West Germany and agreed to improve access to the city; travel between the two Germanys became much easier, especially from west to east.

The solution to Khrushchev's problem—consolidating East Germany by recognizing its borders in international law—freed Moscow to seek improved relations with Germany's other half, the Federal Republic. Doing so, though, required the removal of East German leader Ulbricht, the last surviving of Lenin's immediate colleagues. Just two weeks before his departure, Ulbricht spoke to the 24th Soviet Party Congress:

> He [Brezhnev] underlined the importance of the international recognition of the GDR by many states and the immutability of existing frontiers. He made it clear beyond any doubt that the ratification and, hence, the implementation of the Moscow and Warsaw treaties with the FRG must be regarded as an important task in the interest of European security.[39]

Ulbricht's colleagues suggested that there could be no "special relations" between East and West Germany while the latter remained an imperialist state and NATO member.[40] But Ulbricht went and the point for the Soviet Union was precisely to establish limited "special relations" with West Germany. In the ten years after 1971 Soviet imports from the West more than quadrupled, and the Federal Republic was Moscow's principal western trading partner. West German leaders met their Soviet counterparts at the summit more often than those of any other western nation.

This was the state of affairs Mikhail Gorbachev inherited. East Germany was a loyal and fellow socialist state, on German territory moreover; to all appearances it was prosperous and stable, if not by comparison to the West Germany whose television all its citizens watched, then surely by comparison to Gorbachev's own country.

For communist ideologues, it was as much of a success as they could point to. For the military, it was the cornerstone of their forward deployment in Europe; without it, Soviet troops would have had to retreat to the Soviet border. It was also the best duty in the Soviet army, even if its troops remained buttoned-up in garrison much of the time to avoid too much contact with East Germans. It had become common practice for Soviet military wives in East Germany not to follow their Soviet doctors' prescriptions for their children until they had a second German opinion.

Perhaps most of all the Soviet position in eastern Europe was the tangible fruit of victory in the Great Patriotic War, and East Germany as a symbol of the main enemy conquered and divided was the sweetest morsel of that fruit. As has been so often observed, World War II, relegated to cinematic nostalgia in most of the West, is on the tongues as well as the memories of many Soviets. If Gorbachev was young enough so that the repetition of war stories could perhaps be tiresome, as Americans of his age might have tired of tales of Depression hardships, he was still part of that historical legacy. To tamper with East Germany was to run not just ideological risks or institutional ones, but fundamental political ones. As Gorbachev told French president François Mitterrand in late 1989: "the same day the reunification of Germany is announced, a general will be sitting in my chair."[41]

THE DOMESTIC IMPERATIVE

Why should Gorbachev have taken the risk of changing the happy state of affairs in relations between Moscow and East Berlin? His predecessors had first flirted with a neutralized, demilitarized Germany then, perhaps more fleetingly, with some kind of special relationship to the Federal Republic. Those flirtations had ceased by the mid-1950s; Moscow had come to regard Germany's division as tantamount to a permanent state of affairs, while hoping for some military limitations on the western part and seeking recognition for its East German ally.

By about 1970 Soviet leaders seem to have settled on a combination of a tight hold on East Germany and limited detente with the Federal Republic. That approach meant they could pursue the course of seeking to loosen the Federal Republic's ties to the West without having to face the question of whether they would like actually to succeed at that task. Khrushchev is reported to have said to the Frenchman, Guy Mollet, in 1956 that he preferred 17 million Germans on his side to 70 million in a neutral and reunited Germany.

Yet as Gorbachev confronted *his* problems, he was persuaded, and persuasive to his Politburo colleagues, to take unprecedented risks.[42] American actions affected these Soviet calculations only indirectly, mostly through their effects on West German policy. Dramatic change in Soviet policy toward Germany resulted from internal factors, as earlier foreign policy shifts had ensued from Soviet domestic politics: witness Soviet acceptance of Romania's limited independence and of the Austrian State Treaty, both of which owed something to intraparty maneuvering in the wake of Stalin's death. The second Berlin crisis did not mark a significant change in Soviet foreign policy, but it too may have been in part a refraction of the power struggle from which Khrushchev emerged.

Part of the reason for risk-taking was German but most was domestic. Gorbachev and his colleagues evidently came to believe that the Soviet economy required a massive military withdrawal from eastern Europe; or that domestic reform required different responses from—even different regimes in—eastern Europe. Once again events, domestic needs in particular, reconfigured Moscow's German problem.

Surely, history suggests that East Germany was as central to Gorbachev's European policy as West Germany was to America's.[43] It accounted for a tenth of Soviet trade and was the major supplier of industrial goods, all the more because technology seeped easily through inter-German trade. After the deployment of American missiles in western Europe in 1983, the Soviet Union watched warily as the two Germanys sought to insulate their relations from superpower tension and succeeded in achieving a measure of such insulation. And who would have thought two decades ago that pan-

German sentiments would have been more alive by the 1980s in the east than in the west, complete with a bizarre celebration of Martin Luther's birthday?

The state of affairs in East Germany was not as happy as it seemed. After all, for East Berlin, celebrating Luther, a German Christian, was to clutch at legitimacy wherever it could find it. If Gorbachev's party colleagues might have been expected to argue the brief of their German fellows, his KGB would have had grounds for suspecting that neither East Germany's economic success nor the domestic political acquiescence that so bedazzled western students of East Germany were what they seemed. So the West German government suspected.[44] The same KGB under Gorbachev's mentor, Yuri Andropov, in possession of information about just how bad the Soviet Union's own economy was, had begun to sponsor reformist thinking at home.

How the military came down, and how hard, will be intriguing to learn. On one hand, the Group of Soviet Forces in Germany (GSFG) was not just pleasant duty, it was the army's elite. On the other, the Soviet army, like its counterparts elsewhere, would have had little stomach for continuing military missions once it sensed the political basis for them was eroding. The vision of East Germans demonstrating around Soviet casernes would have been a particular nightmare. Moreover, the Soviet army, like others when faced with declining budgets, no doubt would have opted for a smaller, more professional, and better equipped force rather than one that was larger and less soldierly. That might have argued for preserving something like the GSFG at home if need be, rather than as the forward edge of a huge military establishment abroad.

In the 1980s Gorbachev must have calculated that his chances of reform at home would be diminished if the status quo in eastern Europe remained, or at least that he had little choice but to let the eastern Europeans go.[45] The fellow socialist regimes were either dinosaurs or drains. Either they had to be pushed to reform, or let go. In the early 1970s Moscow had finally had to engineer the replacement of East German leader Ulbricht, a man with friends and stature in Moscow. Erich Honecker, the faithful apparatchik, was hardly of *that* stature, certainly not for Gorbachev, a generation younger. To try to sustain him and his kin in eastern Europe against the kind of internal pressure Gorbachev was promoting at home would have been to unite Gorbachev's domestic enemies and his erstwhile socialist allies.

In this he underestimated the risks. His foreign minister, Eduard Shevardnadze, hinted as much at the 1990 party congress: Did he know what would happen in eastern Europe? Yes,

> We felt that if serious changes did not take place, then tragic results would ensue. In principle, we sensed this, we knew this. But we could not, proceeding from and guided by the principles of new political thinking interfere in the affairs of others, the affairs of other states.[46]

Need at home had made second-order business of eastern Europe, even Germany, the focal points of Soviet foreign policy. When Gorbachev's former colleague, then rival, Boris Yeltsin, visited the United States in the winter of 1989–90, he barely mentioned eastern Europe. Thinking hopefully, Gorbachev must have anticipated a string of little Gorbachevs in eastern Europe. None of his sources, not even the KGB, would have been better than western observers at predicting how thin the façade of communist rule was after forty years, and most of those sources would have been much worse. At any rate it is hard to believe Gorbachev would have started as easily down the path of pushing on those eastern European dinosaurs had he known the alternative to them was not little Gorbachevs but Mazowieckis, Havels, and, worst of all, Helmut Kohls—nothing little about him!

And so Gorbachev pushed the German question forward, probably without meaning to. He did so, in general, by raising the prospect of unfreezing the status quo in Europe, and, more specifically, by undermining, again unwittingly, the legitimacy of the remaining Stalinists in eastern Europe, in the German Democratic Republic above all. Those conservative eastern Europeans found themselves sandwiched between the blandishments of the West and the reformers in Moscow.

By the logic of events set in motion by Moscow, reform was the order of the day and opening the East-West border a means. What place was there in such a logic for a neo-Stalinist rump Germany, justified by ideology, the division of Germany, and Soviet troops? And, more to the point, what more logical course for that rump than some form of association with the rest of Germany?

REUNITING GERMANY

In retrospect, the turning point came in relations with Poland, not East Germany. On August 22, 1989, Gorbachev called the Polish communist leader, Mieczyslaw Rakowski. The message was plain: the party's over. He encouraged the Polish communists to participate in a noncommunist government led by Tadeusz Mazowiecki.[47] If noncommunists were to be permitted to share power in Poland, how could Hungary settle for less? And so the timid steps toward reform became a rush; what had been negotiations with existing rulers over how to share power became talks on how those rulers would surrender it.

In the crunch, during the visit to commemorate East Germany's fortieth anniversary, Gorbachev made clear he would not back the use of force; no Tiananmens. The message was discernible even between the lines of his public speech. His words were a sharp contrast to Honecker's insistence on the division of Europe and Germany. Gorbachev stressed that "issues concerning the GDR are decided not in Moscow but in Berlin." That said,

> it is the recognition of postwar realities that has ensured peace on the continent . . . the Helsinki process . . . promises to lead to further positive changes in the entire European situation, to the building of a common European home.
>
> In short, existing realities on the continent, including such a key component of these realities as the borders of sovereign states, do not block the path to progress in international relations.[48]

As unification became inevitable, Gorbachev's Moscow, not surprisingly, found it hard to come to grips with the fact. In January 1988, Shevardnadze had said in Bonn about the division of Europe that "everything can and should stay as it is." And Gorbachev said that reunifying would be dangerous, although he was less adamant in private.[49] Until April 1990 Moscow publicly sought a neutral Germany. It opposed the fast track of unification—that through Article 23 of the West German constitution, which meant that East Germany would simply be absorbed into the Federal Republic.[50]

Then, it moved from outright opposition to a unified Germany remaining in NATO to various proposals for a vague transition, suggesting, for instance, that Germany might remain in both alliances for a transition period of perhaps five to seven years leading to a new pan-European security order. Shevardnadze all but admitted that the pace of events was baffling.[51]

Yet it took just seven months to do the deal. At the critical moments, the doers were Kohl and Gorbachev. Under the "two-plus-four" formula worked out in Ottawa in February 1990, the two Germanys were to negotiate their union, and the four wartime powers—the United States, Britain, France, and the Soviet Union—would then ratify the results. The "two" were essentially one from the beginning, a state of affairs that was confirmed with the stunning victory by Kohl's recently organized Christian Democratic allies in the March 1990 East German elections—a result that was more surprising at the time than in retrospect it perhaps should have been.

Throughout the spring, the Federal Republic and its allies sought to make it easier for the Soviet Union to accept a unified Germany remaining in NATO. Foreign Minister Hans-Dietrich Genscher proposed the 1990 version of the western allies' 1959 plan—that a unified Germany be a member of NATO but with the former East Germany not a military part of the alliance during some transition period. Official Washington first judged the idea a little *too* clever—or forthcoming—but came to see merit in it as a face-saver for Mikhail Gorbachev.

NATO promised to reduce its forces and change its political profile at its London summit in July 1990; Gorbachev was invited to meet with NATO leaders at the next summit.[52] Behind the scenes, Kohl's NATO colleagues agreed to let the chancellor commit a unified Germany to a ceiling on its future armed forces, thus removing the last obstacle.

Moscow finally accepted that a unified Germany would remain in NATO later in July, in private talks between Kohl and Gorbachev, the Soviet leader taking the chancellor to his home town. Kohl pledged to cap the forces of a united Germany at 370,000, a hundred thousand fewer than the Federal Republic's forces alone. That pledge, along with others to respect existing German borders and to abide by West Germany's nonnuclear commitment, were embodied in the final two-plus-four treaty, signed in September and put in a broader European framework, that of the Helsinki Final Act, the Conference on Security and Cooperation in Europe (CSCE), when it met in November in Paris. Soviet forces were to be withdrawn by the end of 1994. Separately, Bonn promised upwards of $10 billion in aid to Moscow; it agreed to continue paying for the Soviet troops as long as they stayed in Germany and to help fund new living quarters for them once they returned to the Soviet Union.

Plainly, whatever Gorbachev's private calculations of Soviet national interest, presiding over the transition of a unified Germany into NATO was a stunning political defeat. It amounted to relinquishing the last fruit of the Great Patriotic War, the division of the main enemy, Germany. The unthinkable—what Gorbachev as late as March 1990 had described as "totally out of the question"—had happened.[53] Paradoxically but not surprisingly in politics, the extent of the crisis at home probably lessened the pain of defeat abroad. By 1990 everything, even Germany, was secondary to the crisis in the Soviet Union.

Gorbachev accepted defeat with characteristic grace. He did not play the last several cards in his weak hand, perhaps calculating that they would fail and, to boot, poison relations with his main hope for money and advanced technology, Germany. Bonn was not above demonstrating the point. When the chancellor met Gorbachev in February 1990, he brought with him $150 million worth of aid in foodstuffs.[54]

Gorbachev came to the unification of Germany in a way, perhaps, not too different from how Stalin arrived at division—by stages. He first decided he could not have reform at home without sponsoring it abroad. Once reform in eastern Europe ran ahead of his assumptions, there was no way short of bloodshed to save his position in East Germany. Once he decided against bloodshed, probably because of its effects on reform at home, he became hostage to events in East Germany. And from then on the logic of unification was inexorable.

Shevardnadze's speech to the 28th party congress in July 1990 was moving and revealing. He applied the economic diagnosis directly to military spending: "it is obvious that if we continue as we did before . . . to spend a quarter . . . of our budget on military spending—we have ruined the country—then we simply won't need defense, just as we won't need an army for a ruined country and poor people."[55] Was a divided Germany comfortable and the prospect of unity discomforting? The answer was "yes," with passion. Yet "can there be such a reliable guarantee which is based on the artificial and unnatural division of a great nation? And how long can this last?" After outlining the shape of a possible agreement, he argued that "it is not in our interests to drag out the resolution of the external aspects of German unity within the framework on a general settlement."

The postwar order was over. Moscow had given up on it.

CHAPTER SIX

Europe's Past, Europe's Future

W ITH THE Cold War over, we know best what Europe's future will not resemble, and that is the last forty years. In neither security nor economics will the future have the clarity of sharp division, with the armies of opposing alliances poised along the German-German border and with western Europe's continental economic system, the Common Market, ending at the boundaries of the security order, excluding all Europe east of West Germany. So, too, the glacial stability of the old order, however unappealing it could be, is gone. That Humpty-Dumpty cannot be reassembled, not to mention the Wall, and it provides few pointers to Europe's future.

The old order had its virtues, ones driven home after 1990 by the process of disintegration in eastern Europe and the Soviet Union and by the unpredictability of what would replace the nations that were the Cold War's artifices. The status quo served Europe well by dividing German power, and so solving the problem with which the continent had grappled unsuccessfully for over a hundred years. Because it also justified a permanent American military presence, what the order accomplished for western Europe was summarized in the pithy line by Lord Ismay, an early NATO secretary general: NATO is intended to keep the Russians out, the Americans in, and the Germans down.[1]

If dependence on the United States was grating to European elites and occasionally terrifying to people in the streets, the American connection in combination with the Soviet threat provided both insurance and incentive to integrate—conditions for unprecedented prosperity. The nations of western Europe were spared some of the burdens of self-defense, both cost and the historical millstone of competing military establishments. The order suppressed traditional antagonisms among large European powers as they integrated and muted the concerns of small European states, which preferred a distant preeminent power to dominant states nearby—two sets of concerns that ran through the constructions of the early postwar period.

The status quo served the Soviet Union's communist leaders even better. By dividing German power, it diminished the threat; by dividing the continent as well as Germany, it conferred the Soviet Union leverage over the Federal Republic, justified a large Soviet military presence in eastern Europe, and provided some legitimacy for regimes in eastern Europe that would otherwise have been unacceptable. Indeed, the Cold War order justified not just the external Soviet empire but the internal one as well, the Soviet Union itself, as the pace of disintegration after the fall of the Wall testified.

From an American perspective, that status quo was a good second-best: the division of Europe, and of Germany, justified a permanent American presence there; while western Europe's partial integration provided a shape to trans-Atlantic relations without creating a real competitor to the United States. The latter language is loose economics but seems apt politics, for notice the comparison to Japan. Currently, the EC is a much larger economic unit than Japan, but no individual state approaches Japan's size and so serves as a comparable target of American frustrations. Unified Germany represented, initially, less than two-thirds of Japan's economic power.

Now, only one thing seems clear. What happens in the Soviet Union or Russia will matter to Russians and their neighbors, and conceivably, in the presence of nuclear weapons, to world peace. But if it is barely conceivable that Europe might again be divided east to west, with Russia dominating the east, Germany will not be redivided short of a war. And yet Germany's own role in west and east Europe, and America's, and that of Europe east of Germany's border, plus the definition of Europe itself: all these are in question.

In thinking about what will follow the Cold War order, "choose your analogy" can be a useful game to play. Certainly no new order in Europe will resemble any past one in all particulars. Yet because the Cold War order was so fixed and so comprehensive, earlier analogies can kindle the imagination, particularly for those of us whose personal experience reaches no further back than the Cold War.

Analogies—to the nineteenth-century Concert of Europe, or to Europe after the first German unification in 1871, or to the interwar period initiated by the peace of Versailles in 1919—can be suggestive of what has changed and what has not. And they can help us calibrate the impact of what does seem truly distinct from older history in this era of Europe's construction—in particular, nuclear weapons and the kind of institutional interdependence, to use the fashionable term, embodied in the European Community.

THE NUCLEAR QUESTION

Nuclear weapons, no part of any older European system, were at the center of the Cold War order. The advent of nuclear weapons muted, though it did not end, the arguments of the early 1950s over how many divisions NATO needed and who would provide them. Europe, with America, opted for deterrence on the cheap through nuclear weapons.

The price for America, once the Soviet Union had a survivable nuclear arsenal, was vulnerability: as the line had it, would a U.S. president trade Chicago for Hamburg? The price for western Europe was increased dependence, sharpening the anomaly of nations that had reacquired all the attributes of sovereignty save the most important—responsibility for their own defense.

The Federal Republic was twice exposed: as the most important state on the front line, it was the most vulnerable; as the largest non-nuclear state in NATO, deprived by treaty of nuclear weapons, it was the most dependent. Now, the retreat of Soviet power from the center of Europe makes it less exposed, but it is still dependent, and so for all the stunning political transformation there is some continuity in the strategic realm. The Soviet Union is less of a threat, but unless Russia disintegrates entirely, it will remain Europe's largest military power, and its largest nuclear power. That will be so if Russia is reduced to the Duchy of Muscovy.

In strategic terms, the biggest change is German unification itself: if Germany now is less subject to fear of the Soviet Union, it is also less subject to influence by Russia, for the hand of Moscow is lifted from eastern Germany. Reasons for special deference toward Russia will be less, for Moscow will have less and less access to levers about which (west) Germans care, either in eastern Germany or eastern Europe. In August 1991 Helmut Kohl's government, by then weakened because of its domestic circumstances, nevertheless condemned the coup attempt in Moscow more forthrightly than would have been imaginable two years earlier; it did so notwithstanding the 275,000 Soviet soldiers still remaining on (east) German soil.

Alliance arrangements in the early postwar period reflected European fears both of and about Germany. If Germany was to be rearmed, better to embed those armaments in alliance. And even if Germany was to be rearmed, it still had to remain nonnuclear. Germany accepted those limitations, even sought them, as a reasonable price to pay for rejoining the West and rebuilding its economy. So long as Germany was consigned to a nonnuclear status in the western alliance, it literally had no alternative to dependence on the United States—a fact which is much of the reason why that anomaly of dependence was prolonged.

Over the last three decades, fears *of* Germany on the part of its neighbors became less in evidence, but they were and are still present beneath the surface. And concerns *about* Germany continued to be at play even before unification was a near-term prospect—for instance in France as the German social democrats seemed to be wandering off the NATO reservation in the early 1980s. German sensitivity to both sets of concerns also continued, another reason why the anomaly was prolonged.

Unified Germany is still dependent because it is nonnuclear. Dependence will be less grating if happy politics in Europe permit American and other nuclear weapons to retire, perhaps taking their soldiers with them, and if the need for spending money and taking unpleasant decisions over nuclear weapons recedes. But it will endure.

During the Cold War there were in strategic logic two broad alternatives to the dependence of trans-Atlantic alliance for the Federal Republic—nothing or nuclear weapons. With some variations, they were the alternatives for western Europe as a whole. They are now the alternatives for unified Germany. Pursuing either would diminish the need, and perhaps preclude the possibility, of an alliance with the United States, certainly in anything like its current form.

Deterrence based only on conventional weapons, conventional deterrence, so called, is not one of these alternatives and never was. The conditions under which it might become a real alternative are hard to imagine. Not only does the European distaste for and distrust of conventional deterrence seem likely to persist—after all, Europeans have seen it fail horribly in two wars this century—Europe would still confront a nuclear Russia and would need somehow to neutralize the threats or leverage that might derive from those weapons.

The first of the alternatives to dependence—doing "nothing"—would be to decide that the Soviet Union or Russia no longer was a strategic threat worth paying much attention to. Forces and alliances would then become matters of less account, and western European states might settle for promises of nonaggression from their Soviet neighbor. This strategic hope animates interest in pan-European systems of collective security, like one based on the Helsinki Final Act, the Conference on Security and Cooperation in Europe (CSCE), a view that regards modern Europe as altered beyond relevance for the analogies of Versailles or the Concert.

By this hope, perceptions of threat will diminish as arms are reduced. That will be especially true in the nuclear arena, where nuclear weapons will be more and more stigmatized, less and less usable even as symbols of power. In these circumstances, a broad—and thus necessarily thin—collective security order eventually will be enough. What centers of power remain will be seen as benign enough not to require counterbalancing or deterring.

Such a hopeful vision cannot be ruled out but neither can it be counted upon. It surely is true that the retreat of the Soviet Union from eastern Europe all but nullifies the Soviet conventional threat to western Europe, Germany included, at least in the form against which NATO insured for forty years. However, the Soviet Union or Russia will not cease being a military superpower, a fact Europe will confront no matter what its judgment about Soviet intentions. Its nuclear weapons will remain. And so, in strategic logic, a collective security system is not likely to be enough for Germany in the long run.

Europe may be more likely to arrive at something like this hopeful vision by the opposite route, not through collective security east and west but through disintegration in the east. If the Soviet Union fell into chaos and practically ceased being a major power, something like its situation following the Crimean War, Germany and western Europe could settle for almost any security arrangements except for one crucial particular: Russia would continue to be a nuclear power.

The other alternative is a nuclear Germany, perhaps as the senior partner in a nuclear western Europe. General de Gaulle's strategic logic was impeccable, though he was careful not to carry it to its logical extension: if Europe—and Germany—fear that America will not push the button, then they need buttons of their own with nuclear weapons to match. For Germany, half-way measures—say, loose association with British or French nuclear systems—would not do. Strategically, they would not do because those British and French forces are small and for the most part designed as last-ditch retaliators.

"Tearing off a Soviet arm," as the British put it, may be credible enough to deter an attack on one's homeland even if the tearing is tantamount to suicide. Such deterrence cannot be credibly extended to one's neighbor, however; that is true even though France and, to a lesser extent, Britain, would not be decoupled from Germany by geography. Put differently, if strategic logic makes it unconvincing for the United States to threaten the use of nuclear weapons in Germany's defense, it is still less convincing for Britain and France to do so.

To be credible, a European nuclear force would have to have a Europe to defend, requiring decisionmaking and command and control arrangements to match. It would also require a Europe in which France could not be separated from Germany, so no salami-slicing could be tempting. The Common Market works in that di-

158

rection, with its movements of people and corporations. But a Europe-as-strategic-unit would also require, if not a single armed force, then considerable mixing and cross-stationing of national forces under a combined staff at the top. Germany would have to have not just a finger on the nuclear trigger, but a finger to match its size in Europe.

Otherwise, strategic logic points to a nuclear Germany.[2] The idea strains the imagination. No Germans are flirting with the idea now, while some were three decades ago.[3] Yet a nuclear Germany is the *strategic* track Europe is on. To be sure, that is strategic logic, not political. What the former indicates, the latter seems to rule out.

Yet, strategically, a future German government might find nuclear weapons a means of minimal deterrence on the cheap, all the better if the bulk of those weapons were strategic and thus based at sea, not on land. Stretching the speculation still further, the nuclear option would, it seems to me, be more appealing to a German government of the left than of the right, one that would be nationalist but primarily interested in social spending, hence unwilling to build a serious conventional defense even if the weather to its east turned dark.[4] To be sure, such a government would first have to control the nuclear allergy that has been so much in evidence in recent years.

What is the case for Germany is also true, strategically, for other states in Europe. Europe's bipolar landscape of the last forty years had plenty of ugly terrain, but it did level any temptations to nuclear proliferation, in the west by making nuclear weapons unnecessary and in the east by making them impossible. Europe's most authentic armed neutral, Sweden, did contemplate nuclear weapons as the logical extension of its strategy. It concluded that it could deter potential aggressors without nuclear weapons, in part because it was remote enough to go around, and in part, no doubt, because it was backstopped by NATO.

Now, however, eastern Europe is spawning new neutrals not quite sure what they are neutral about but living in a dangerous neighborhood. By strategic logic, nuclear weapons would provide them with relatively cheap insurance. A Polish nuclear force might solve Poland's historic problem, the inescapability of its geography, providing it with a measure of deterrence against its two neighbors. A nuclear Ukraine, which inherited Soviet nuclear weapons, could make a more credible claim to independence from Moscow. Hungary could plausibly threaten nuclear retaliation if bizarre politics in Romania led to risks of armed attack. And so on.

There are many reasons why this strategic logic may not determine Europe's future, or Germany's. Some have to do with the nature of the nuclear decision itself: the sanction against going nuclear is strong, so breaking it would set off alarm bells well beyond the domestic politics of the would-be nuclear power. Nuclear transitions are also dangerous, for the state that seeks nuclear weapons for deterrence invites preemption lest it steal a nuclear march on its rival(s).

More important, perhaps, there are positive political reasons to believe Europe's future will not be that of a nuclear Germany and other nuclear powers beyond today's few. In the future as in the past, the shape of Europe will be determined by the hurly-burly of its various politics, national and across nations, not by the rational calculations of states conceived as unitary actors.

Yet the abstracted analyses of strategic logic frame the terms within which those politics operate, and that logic also serves as a baseline for assessing those politics, a goad to ask "why not?" questions if outcomes seem to diverge from strategic logic. The changes in Europe's politics may make building nuclear weapons seem not only too risky to contemplate but unnecessary.

THE INTERDEPENDENCE PRESUMPTION

For Germany, part of the answer to "why not go nuclear?" is interdependence given form in the European Community. What distinguishes interdependence now from earlier periods in Europe's history, other than simple scale, is institutions—the Common Market and its workings, which, if they do not command much loyalty, are widely recognized as necessary. By this view, economic interdependence given form in the EC has changed the nature of the state system in (western) Europe, and, as the traditional security concerns evoked by the Soviet Union wane, by extension the EC can serve as the organizing structure for all of Europe.

There are a number of ways to evaluate this clutch of presumptions, but none of them can be conclusive. Simple scale surely matters, as does the structure of interdependence. For instance, the percentage of production for export—the nation's dependence on exports—doubled for the Federal Republic from 15 percent in 1950 to 28 percent in 1985; of those exports in 1985 half went to EC partners, compared to 35 percent in 1958.[5] However, pre–World War I Germany was also highly dependent on exports, its dependence not surpassed by the Federal Republic until the 1970s. And it went to war.

So, too, while Germany's economic straits after World War I were such as to render it a smaller trader—from 13 percent of world trade in 1913 to 9 percent in 1928—the pattern of its trade changed remarkably little. Three-quarters of its imports were food, raw materials, and half-finished goods, while a similar portion of its exports was finished goods. After as before the war, its largest trading partners were its once and future enemies—Britain for exports and the United States for imports.[6]

The pattern did change dramatically by the outbreak of World War II—trade as a proportion of domestic product was reduced to six percent (today the figure is thirty percent), and the share of Germany's imports provided by Britain, the Soviet Union, and the United States all dropped by at least half. The change might be seen as evidence for interdependence's presumption that states that trade more, war less; it was, though, a result of Hitler's conscious determination to prepare for war by reducing Germany's vulnerability, especially with regard to possible enemies.

Pre–World War I Germany, as well as its Weimar successor, had mostly imported agricultural products and raw materials. This form of interdependence underlay John Maynard Keynes's forebodings about the Versailles treaty of 1919:

political considerations cut disastrously across economic. In a regime of Free Trade and free economic intercourse it would be of little consequence that iron lay on one side of a political frontier, and labor, coal, and blast furnaces on the other. But as it is, men have devised ways to impoverish themselves and one another; and prefer collective animosities to individual happiness.[7]

By the 1980s, primary products accounted for less than three-tenths of West German imports, imports of finished goods having gone up sixfold since 1950. Importing more refrigerators and less wheat hardly precludes conflict, but it does mean less reason to argue—or war—over which state has coal mines and which does not. Economic value attaches less to territory and resources and more to production processes, and more visibly to the order that permits those processes to be transferred.

By the logic of interdependence, states recognize that all are made better off by sustaining a liberal economic order within which their firms can compete fiercely. A certain amount of political cooperation is necessary to create and sustain that structure, and, moreover, once the system is in place, each state realizes its well-being is hostage to the others, in a way not so different logically from the mutual hostage relationship between the superpowers in the nuclear realm.[8] Thus, the recognition of shared fates makes conflict less likely, and political cooperation makes it still less so.

Investment abroad and foreign ownership at home is blurring what is a "British" or a "German" company. That, logically, ought to make it harder for nations to protect "their" national champions in industry. Indeed, it may join nations in shared frustration at their declining ability to control economic activity within their borders—vulnerability of another sort.

Yet is it self-evident that mutual vulnerability makes for less conflictual political relations? Even if the particular form of interdependence reflected in the liberal international order makes all participating states better off and thus provides all with incentive to manage the politics of their condition, still, those politics will not be easy to manage.

162

Vulnerability is uncomfortable and so breeds temptation to circumvent it. Nuclear vulnerability may be too emotive to serve convincingly as an analogy, but, logically, both the United States and the Soviet Union were beneficiaries of the stability their mutual vulnerability produced. Neither had an interest in upsetting the status quo; nuclear defenses by either were the enemy of both. But neither found the vulnerability comforting, and both were tempted to escape it through erecting defenses against the other's nuclear missiles.

Moreover, if interdependence produces gains for all nations, this is not the case for all sectors of all those states. When domestic politics elevates those concerns, the states will simply have more about which to squabble. Whether the squabbles will be harder or easier to manage in the future than in the past is a matter of judgment. The incentive to manage them is greater, the more all recognize their stakes in the existing order. Moreover, forty years of economic growth in Europe, along with a dampening of social and economic inequalities, make "losers" very relative: Europe's farmers, like America's, demand and receive government help, but few of them are poor; their protection owes less to absolute need than to hard political calculation overlain with softer sentiment about rural tradition.

This question of absolute versus relative position raises another critique of interdependence. The logic of interdependence assumes states care primarily about their absolute economic well-being. If they do, then so long as interdependence provides an expanding pie from which all benefit, all will have an incentive to sustain the framework of interdependence. If, however, states also care about their *relative* position, their incentive to cooperate will be weaker. They will ask not just whether they will gain, but whether they will gain more or less than other states.[9]

If states care only about their relative positions—in economics or security—then cooperation is impossible. The more they care about relative position, the more difficult is their cooperation. Again, nuclear deterrence is a vivid example. The United States and the Soviet Union cared about the absolute value of not obliterating themselves,

and so shared an interest in sustaining the stability of shared vulnerability. At the same time, however, they also cared about their relative nuclear positions in an uncertain world; to some extent, they
may have allowed themselves such concerns precisely because their
nuclear relations were so stable. And so both were tempted to gain
an advantage, in particular through building defenses.

It is hard to believe that in the nineteenth century the fact that
Germany had overtaken Britain as an industrial power did not de-
stabilize the European order. By the same token, after World War I,
Germany, which had barely grown economically until 1929, grew
rapidly between 1929 and 1938 (nearly 5 percent annually), while
France's economy was actually declining and the British growth rate
was only a quarter of Germany's—a fact that sharpened French worries if it did not actually sap French confidence. And so by the outbreak of World War II Germany's economy was Europe's largest,
slightly larger than that of the Soviet Union, a quarter larger than
Britain's, and nearly twice the size of the French economy.[10]

Plainly, relative gains matter less the more nations regard themselves as a community, which might be defined as putting a positive
value on other's gains as well as one's own. Logically, the force of
relative gains thinking is also diminished as numbers of states go
up.[11] The risk that a would-be cooperator will steal a march by re-
neging on cooperation is more and more overwhelmed by the gains
any two states can make through cooperating. Put differently, the
risk of being left out of cooperative ventures grows.

What happens in groups of states like Europe after the Cold War,
when the number is larger than two but less than many and where
the states are of unequal weight, is logically indeterminate. To the
extent they care about relative gains, the larger states will measure
themselves in comparison to each other, disregarding the small
states, making cooperation among the large states difficult. After
German unification, for instance, France seemed visibly to alternate
between its two logical concerns—on the one hand, the unpredictable, that Germany might forsake its European vocation and, on the
other, the predictable, that if Germany did not, it would be too big,
shattering the "balance of imbalances" among western Europe's

larger states and, in particular, threatening France's privileged position in the European Community.

The small states might reckon themselves in relation both to the larger ones and to their fellow small states. To the extent they are wary of the larger states, those larger states will have to entice them into cooperation. On the other hand, if there are traditional rivalries among second-rank states, those states will incline toward larger states as protectors.

THE FORCE OF SHARED INSTITUTIONS

In modern western Europe's case, political structures have been erected to make possible the shared gains of interdependence. Those will act to reduce future conflict. It is not just that states have incentives to avoid conflict, they also have mechanisms for containing disputes—an executive in the form of the council of ministers and commission, a parliament, and a European court. When interdependence, predictably, produces losers, EC as well as domestic political structures are available to compensate them and adjudicate their grievances.

Moreover, once created, the institutions themselves bind Europe's states and provide warning lights if participants seek to escape the bonds. For an individual EC member to cut a separate deal on trade with a nonmember is both difficult in fact and a visible symbol of noncooperation. In the summer of 1990 West Germany simply told its EC partners it was establishing a currency union with East Germany. If, however, the EC's monetary union had been as far along as its trade, Bonn would not have had that luxury; its partners would have had a say, although the outcome hardly would have been different.

The process of EC integration establishes benchmarks for the behavior of its members. In the run-up to unification, West Germany was under pressure to demonstrate that its preoccupation with its eastern half would not deflect it from its EC vocation; at the time it acceded to the pressure eagerly, as a reassurance to its partners. In the future its behavior, especially, will be judged against the benchmarks of integration: is it stalling on monetary unification, or going it alone in eastern Europe? If Germany or another member sought to reverse the process of integration, the warning signal would flash bright red.

Another part of the EC presumption is that democracies, while not less likely to make war than autocracies, are less likely to make war on other democracies.[12] Democratic ideology provides no justification for making war on other democracies, no argument for a democratic empire run from the center. And democratic leaders can make war on other democracies only with the assent of their own citizens, a demanding condition. Europe is not yet the United States, but if American states are a century past thinking of fighting each other, (western) European states are several generations past such imaginings.

In other respects, the differences between Europe and the United States are apparent. For all the growth of the EC, the power to tax remains preeminently with the states, not the federation. But notice that the burdens of taxation have been shifting back toward the states in America as well. Nor is it self-evident that the United States is the "right" or most stable balance of powers among federal, local, and intermediate levels, or that there might not be some advantages in an intermediate level—nations in Europe—with a stronger claim on public loyalties than American states command.

More strikingly, Europe's states retain armies, while America's retain only vestigial militias. If they are beyond imagining conflict, they are not beyond accomplishing it. The context of national armies is changing, but they are not about to go away. They will become more "interdependent" in that their sources of armaments will be less and less national companies, more and more transnational conglomerates. The EC will edge into security matters, but the process will remain slow.

The last forty years of western European history make the strongest case for interdependence as a muter of conflict. After 1871, Europe's states traded with each other considerably, and both their elites and the royal families were interconnected through ties of kinship. They were "interdependent." Their systems of government were not the same but their range was not all that much greater than in Europe today, for all the reform in eastern Europe. Interdependence did produce a long period of peace. But it ended in war, evidence that the fashionability of the term "interdependence" can mislead. In contrast, the achievements of the period after World War II by states that were destroying each other a half century ago are impressive testimony to the power of shared stakes and shared institutions.

INCORPORATING EUROPE'S EAST

It takes no crystal ball to foresee a bumpy road ahead for politics in Europe's east. Nor is it undue pessimism to imagine that those politics might be both parent and child to various sorts of internal and interstate violence.[13] The prewar histories of those countries, Czechoslovakia excepted, are not reassuring about their democratic vocations. Nor is the presence of irredentist and ethnic tensions reassuring about their pacific future; Woodrow Wilson's post–World War I handiwork is not as bad as is often supposed, but neither could it completely situate ethnic groups in their own states—as the conflict in Yugoslavia or between Hungary and Romania over ethnic Hungarians in Transylvania has made vivid.

With what turned out, in hindsight, to be no more than a totalitarian façade now ripped off, the political conflict among groups with stakes will be stark. In many cases, there will be only weak agreement on rules of the game and only limited acceptance of institutions as mediators of conflict. The experience of power monopolized by a single party, the communists, provides no model of pluralist parties and considerable distaste for the whole notion of "parties."

If the totalitarian police apparatus was not ultimately effective, it was pervasive, tarnishing and thus eliminating most claimants to political leadership. The more diffuse interests of less organized citizens may lack political expression, and so national policy may be captured by narrow interests, perhaps in coalitions with each other, with appeals to nationalism drawing acquiescence from unorganized citizenry.[14] Communism leveled societies, literally and figuratively, a kind of universal pauperization. Now, however, inequalities will at least be more evident, perhaps greater in fact, hence there to provide grievance, the fodder for nationalist or other demagogic appeals.

These political patterns are more than echoes of pre–World War I Germany. Industrialization had come late to Germany, before the rise of a bourgeoisie had displaced the feudal order. Prussian Junker landowners formed uneasy coalitions with rising industrialists—the "iron and rye" connection—and both reached out to civil servants and the armed forces. The Reichstag (parliament) had the power to tax and spend but not to unseat ministers; forming cabinets thus meant jockeying for favor around the emperor.

This sketch is stylized, but the politics that are emerging in Europe's east bear resemblance to it: restricted democratic institutions with limited legitimacy; entrenched bureaucratic and other interests; new losers and new winners seeking redress or accommodation; incomplete agreement on rules of the game. The transition, moreover, is just beginning. These patterns, should they persist, need not necessarily be a recipe for violence across borders, whatever their internal consequences. The two notorious disturbers of the peace this century, Germany and Japan, had politics that resembled the pattern, but there are other explanations for their aggression. And in many other such states, conflict turned inward. So it will for the most part in Europe's east.

Still, politics plus ethnic and irredentist tensions and the prospect of economic straits is at least cause for concern about conflict spilling across borders. In any event, a Europe with aspirations to be a "common house" cannot be indifferent to conflict even if that conflict is confined to single rooms in what used to be the servants' wing. So the question arises: might interdependence as embodied in the EC help contain that conflict?

The answer is "yes" in several ways, none of them, however, decisive. If not much else about western Europe's experience of the

Marshall Plan seems applicable to eastern Europe's current reconstruction, the joint learning process it entailed does. In most other
respects the two cases differ sharply, sadly so: eastern Europe needs
to build market economies, not rebuild them, so relevant expertise
cannot be assumed to be at hand; forty years of communism have
silenced anticapitalist ideologues in eastern Europe comparable to
those in Atlee's Labour Party or Schumacher's SPD, but essential features of free markets—profit, middlemen, and inequality—are still
misunderstood, objects of suspicion.

Eastern Europe's problem is thus not so straightforward as postwar western Europe's: widening the bottleneck of hard currency
alone would not suffice, even if there were an "America" on which
eastern Europe could count for generosity. But eastern European
states do resemble postwar western Europe's in their ignorance of
each other's economies and their competition with each other, in
this case for links westward. Cooperating with each other seems to
risk being consigned to an eastern ghetto. Something like the
Marshall Plan's process, perhaps in association with the EC, would
at least break down their isolation from each other and might lay the
basis for converting their regional trade from a ghetto into a benefit.

More important, the eastern Europeans are desperate for any association with the "Europe" of which they feel themselves a part but
from which they have been excluded, and the EC is the ultimate
symbol of that club, quite independent of economics. They know
that if their politics take an authoritarian turn, or their foreign policies an aggressive one, they will be excluded, just like the Greek
colonels or the Turkish generals. This awareness will not prevent
erratic politics or hostile policies but will serve to deter them.

To the extent that western economic help, in and around the EC,
can cushion the pain of economic transition and temper the consequences of internal inequalities, it mitigates internal politics as well,
although plainly the relationship between economics and happy,
democratic politics is not always straightforward. Moreover, help
will be accompanied by conditions on policy, some of which will
sharpen, not relax internal conflict (shrinking government spending, for example). And some of what would help eastern Europe

169

most—opening markets in western Europe above all—runs into the bargains implicit in the existing European Community.

As eastern European countries become candidates for EC regional assistance, that money can forestall national policies that might otherwise cause conflict with neighbors—tariffs on agricultural imports, for instance. Those EC policies may then, to be sure, raise objections from outsiders, like the United States, who see their own interests as hurt; when Spain joined the EC it became eligible for regional assistance but also became enclosed in the EC's common external trade walls, which thus became higher for American agricultural exports to Spain.

These partially affirmative answers to the question of whether the EC can reduce conflict in eastern Europe rest more on institutions than vague notions of interdependence. Europe's interdependence today is different in some respects from that before World War I— the cross-national patterns of corporations, for instance—but what is most different is the institutional framework around it. The EC provides visible incentive to sustain cooperation (notice British prime minister Thatcher's grudging conversion at each stage of the process), mechanisms for resolving (economic) disputes, and tripwires for would-be departers from cooperation (notice how much German chancellor Kohl had his feet held to the fire to prove he was a loyal European in the process of German unification).

OPEN QUESTIONS

The historical analogies suggest how much "Europe" in modern times has been *western* Europe. On that score, Cold War language, often unusual, was not misleading in conflating Europe into western Europe. The core of Europe has been there, in the Rhine valley and its tributaries, with Russia becoming a European power almost by act of will and England remaining aloof, an external balancer. The small lands between the core and Russia have defined themselves in relations to that core.

Americans see those in-between lands through Wilsonian lenses adjusted by American ethnic politics as gallant little states struggling for freedom and democracy. By contrast, for Europe and especially for Germany, now on a new front line, the perspective is more like America's with regard to *its* southern neighbors—unstable, faintly inferior lands that can cause trouble or provoke immigration. The lands to the east are western Europe's Latin America.[15]

To be fair, the Stalinist ice age glazed over very different countries, and so distinctions between east central Europe and west central Europe are again coming to be heard. In Milan Kundera's phrase, "*Mitteleuropa* is a piece of the Latin West which has fallen under Russian domination . . . which lies geographically in the center, culturally in the West and politically in the East."[16] The communist ice age shifted what we used, too easily, to call eastern Europe further west. Central Europe became eastern Europe. Now, those countries will seek their relation with western Europe. The shape of those connections will vary, but the point of reference will be the same.

Yet how this Europe will be defined is an open question. *Mitteleuropa* in German, for instance, is not the same as English "central Europe," for the former term connotes a sphere of German influence that the latter does not. And how can Russia be included, for it is too big, too poor, and too Asian: on that score, Adenauer's language was anachronistic but on the mark.

During the Cold War, a loose, confederal *Europe des états* seemed attractive for reasons that appealed to de Gaulle as much as for reasons that tugged on Britain—and as much to hold open the long-run possibility of reintegrating Europe's east as because of the pain involved in yielding sovereignty to a supranational Europe. Such a Europe foreclosed neither independent national action nor real union with the East. Now, the arguments for a *Europe des états* are not so different—limiting the transfer of sovereignty while making easier the integration of eastern Europe and even, if Europe were thin enough, somehow incorporating states on the territory of the existing Soviet Union, Russia included.

Another open question is the future role of the United States. Europe's steps toward federation, especially its early ones, came under the shadow of the Soviet threat, as vivid in 1950 for Britons or Germans as for Americans, and under the wing of the American engagement. The presence of a shared threat muted both the rivalries among the larger European states and the wariness of the smaller ones. Indeed, the smaller states, like Belgium, keenly remembered their vulnerability, and so took the lead in assembling European arrangements. The need to balance Soviet power made the first steps toward political cooperation more necessitous, hence easier to accomplish.

At points early on the United States literally pushed the European states together. Throughout, it served not only as the ultimate guarantee against the Soviet Union, but also as insurance to the larger European states against their gravest fears of each other and to the smaller states against their misgivings about the larger states. In particular, the American presence in Germany forestalled worry about the worst German futures. If American dominance occasionally was grating to European elites, that irritation, too, was probably more unifying than divisive for Europeans.

Looking to Europe's future, the reversal of German and Soviet roles from 1945–55 is stunning: now it is the Soviet Union, not Germany, that seems less an actor than an object, something to be brooded over because of its weakness, not hedged against because of its strength, while Germany is now the driving force. But what about the American role? Is that role relevant still, or is it only an artifact of the Cold War, now only a piece of distant history? Germany's place in the future Europe is the subject of the next chapter, while a concluding word turns to the prospects for America's European engagement.

A European Germany or
a German Europe?

T HE ANXIETIES provoked among other Europeans by Germany's unification, visible enough beneath the surface, centered not on the Soviet Union's weakness but on Germany's strength. The fact that those anxieties were more prominent in older rather than younger Europeans suggests they may be simply anachronisms. But a Europe with a dominant Germany had not always been a stable or happy Europe. Isn't Germany simply too big, eastern Europe too unstable, and Russia too weak? If not, why not? What has changed to make what has been unhappy before not so this time?

THE LEGACY OF HISTORY

When the history of the postwar order in Europe is written, the position of Germany seems likely to look exceptional. Not so much the division of the country per se, for German history is that of several German political units, states, within the broader German nation. The precedent of Germany before its first unification, the nineteenth-century confederation, or *Bund*, briefly tempted scholars as a model in 1989 before it became evident that there was no need and no will to sustain a separate state in eastern Germany. Still, Germans have always been able to be nationalists without necessarily being unifiers.[1]

Rather, what will look unusual is the extent of the western tug on the biggest part of that postwar Germany, the Federal Republic. In that sense, federal Germany was the most "western" it had been since the Holy Roman Empire. The forced loss of East Germany left the Federal Republic more Catholic and dominated by the part that had historically been closest to the West, especially France. For Konrad Adenauer, in particular, the heart had always led him westward. It is said that as mayor of Cologne from 1917 to 1920 and then as president of the Prussian state council, he had always felt some hesitation in crossing the Elbe eastward.[2]

He had little affection either for Prussia or for Bismarck's Prussian-centered Reich. It was plain enough during the crises over Berlin in 1958–61 that he did what his country's position and its alliance commitments required but that he felt little affection for the city thus safeguarded. Virtually unknown abroad before World War II, he was above all a Rhineland Catholic. He had been confronted in 1919 with the prospect that his Rhineland would be dominated, annexed perhaps, by France. The prospect led him away from the *Schaukelpolitik*—or see-saw policy between East and West—and toward reconciliation with France and western Europe.

Seeking to square the incompatible, a Prussian-centered Germany and French anti-Prussianism, he imagined a Rhineland that was still part of the German federation but with close economic ties to France. The idea was ahead of its time in 1919, but the Nazi defeat gave Adenauer the opportunity to pursue it virtually unchanged a generation later, this time a western Germany built around the Rhineland and tightly bound westward, to France in particular.

In the trauma of Nazi defeat, the Federal Republic made a sharp break with history by identifying firmly with the West. Germany, an integral part of the West during the medieval period, had become less so thereafter. The romanticism that influenced European culture in the first half of the nineteenth century became for Germany, in the historian Gordon Craig's words, "that peculiarly German sense of inwardness, or remoteness from reality, of intimate community between self and the mysterious forces of nature and God."[3]

Both German nationalism, under an autocratic regime with a dominant military, and economic growth occurred in the second half of the nineteenth century within an emphasis on "a combination of inward-looking faith and outward obedience." Germany became the land of *Zwischenkultur*—the culture of the "middle." No less a cosmopolitan than Max Weber spoke, on the eve of World War I, of the special mission of German culture "between Anglo-Saxon materialism and Russian barbarism."[4]

Before the Nazi defeat, Germany had been *Mitteleuropa* in policy as well as geography. The *Schaukelpolitik*—or see-saw policy—attempting to balance the western nations against Russia, came naturally to Bismarck and his successors under the Wilhelmine empire. It seemed to them what Germany's position indicated and its interests required. It came less naturally to the politicians of post–World War I Weimar Germany, but they, too, attempted a balance, despite, or perhaps because of, their anticommunism and their interest in reconciliation with the western victors of World War I.

Like Bismarck, Weimar Germany's statesmen did what they felt their state's interests required—the European, and especially German, tradition of statecraft as a reflection of the state's intere ts, not passions or ideologies. The famous quote from Bismarck captures the essence of what later came to be called *Realpolitik*:

> Sympathies and antipathies with respect to foreign Powers and persons I cannot justify to my sense of duty to the foreign service of my country. . . . Therein lies the embryo of disloyalty toward one's master or the land one serves. . . . In my view, not even the King has the right to subordinate the interests of the fatherland to personal feelings of love and hate toward the foreigner.[5]

In this spirit, the German diplomats, conservative anticommunists, who crafted the 1922 Rapallo agreement with the Soviet Union—and thus created "Rapallo" as the West's catchword for German unreliability—did so for fear of an Anglo-French-Russian deal because they felt their state's interests required it.

For Americans, *Realpolitik* became during the Cold War a four-letter word connoting amorality in foreign affairs. For West Germans then and for all Germans now, however, the observation that they share the continent with Russia was and is more than a simple commentary on geography. After all, Moscow occupied half of Germany until 1990, divided its capital, and gave away German territory to its eastern neighbors. For Germans, the strand of crusading moralism in American foreign policy is dumbfounding and sometimes frightening, whether the crusade is Wilsonian internationalism or Reaganite anticommunism.

Realpolitik was linked to another historical tradition, also common to Europe but also, perhaps, strongest in Germany—the relative isolation of foreign policy from domestic politics. Before 1919 the United States was a democracy and Germany was not; while Bismarck engaged in logrolling with parliament to secure military appropriations, he was nearly as much constrained by the preeminent role of the military as by domestic politics in any wider sense. Both the role of the military and the discretion for the government continued into the Weimar period and, needless to say, during the Third Reich. Weimar Germany's chaotic domestic politics left the foreign ministry free to pursue Rapallo, not to mention letting the general staff sustain military cooperation with the Soviet Union, first in secret and then openly, if discreetly.

Whether the balancing act actually served German interests is a grand historical puzzle that hangs over Europe's future. When Bismarck's diplomatic mastery was not matched by his successors, and when both ends of the see-saw, France and Russia, joined in Bismarck's nightmare alliance, the eventual result was World War I.

Yet what bears remembering is that a balance between East and West has been traditional German policy, and so the postwar ties westward were correspondingly unusual. It would not be surprising if the approach of unified Germany, its capital moved from Germany's western edge to its eastern, reverted more to historical form. Indeed, it would be surprising if it did not.

THE IMPACT OF *OSTPOLITIK*

In fact, the Federal Republic's two decades of absorption in *Westpolitik*, its exclusive western connection, ended well before the high drama of the Berlin Wall's fall, unification, and the capital's move to

Berlin. The change was visible in the late 1960s. *Ostpolitik*, the policy of reconciliation with the Federal Republic's eastern neighbors, one that began more with Germany's allies than with itself, was practical mediation between East and West in new circumstances.

Ostpolitik as public policy marked a break with previous efforts to isolate East Germany and limit relations with the Soviet Union. As such, the new line was initially opposed by the Christian Democratic Union (CDU) and its Bavarian sister party, Franz-Josef Strauss's Christian Social Union (CSU). During the long years of SPD governments under Brandt and Helmut Schmidt from 1969 to 1982, however, the two conservative parties came to accept it, for much the same reasons of state interest as had impelled conservative German statesmen in the 1920s. In the process, *Ostpolitik* came to seem part of the landscape of West German politics.

In the early 1980s a chancellor characterized the Federal Republic's relations with the East:

> Because of our geographic situation and because of our history, we Germans are obligated to maintain good relations with West and East. For us Germans there are many historical ties to the East. We share a deep understanding of the cultural unity of Europe, in all its variety and with all its differences.[6]

The chancellor was Helmut Kohl long before the fall of the Wall, but the words might have been Helmut Schmidt's. Schmidt's own conversion—from a politician whose ties were all with the West to a chancellor who spoke often and passionately about the Federal Republic's links eastward—was surprising enough.

Even more surprising, though, was how quickly and completely the CDU/CSU government made the SPD's policies, and accompanying language, its own once in government, just as it had adopted *Ostpolitik* and the eastern treaties after opposing them a decade earlier. In 1983 the conservatives made a fresh loan of over a billion Deutschmarks to East Germany, a loan, moreover, negotiated for the government by Strauss, CSU leader and fervent anticommunist.

Ostpolitik foreshadowed the Helsinki Final Act, also known as the

Conference on Security and Cooperation in Europe (CSCE), in its ambivalence: on the one hand, it could be seen in the short run as ratifying Germany's division by recognizing East Germany, and on such grounds it was mightily criticized by German anticommunists. On the other, its long-run effect, one not quite recognized by its architects, was subversive of communist control. East-West relaxation meant more contacts, more television seen by more East Germans, more chances to raise questions of internal governance. Trying to isolate the East had also insulated it; seeking contact infected it with western ideas and western standards.

Similarly, hard-minded western conservatives feared at the Helsinki Final Act in 1975 that CSCE's human rights commitments were no more than a lofty façade covering the ratification of communism's hold in eastern Europe. They turned out to be wrong, for surely when historians write the story of 1989 they will be impressed by how, little by little, the internal arrangements of Europe's states came onto the international agenda. The oppressors found it harder and harder to hide their acts—from the world or their own people. In the future, too, CSCE's human rights provisions will continue to underline the connection between internal governance and external behavior.

The tug of domestic politics on foreign policy in the Federal Republic has become more apparent. Adenauer talked about recovering German territories lost in the east even while privately accepting that the loss was permanent in part because the organizations of Germans expelled from those territories were vocal parts of the chancellor's constituency. And it took Brandt and his like-minded SPD leaders a decade to turn their party around.

European foreign policies, German included, are becoming more "American" in the degree to which they are influenced by domestic politics, and American foreign policy is less "American" in this dimension than Europeans often suggest: the pullings and haulings of American politics masked considerable continuity in postwar policy toward Europe and the Soviet Union. Still, it is small wonder that Germans often saw American foreign policy through the lens of their own tradition as inconsistent, hostage to the passing passions of domestic politics. What conclusions they will draw about the policy of a united Germany as their own politics incorporates new forces and strains is an intriguing question about the future.

OLD SOLUTIONS AND STREET POLITICS

Behind the rhetoric of support for a unified Germany, most of us, Germans included, assumed that unification would never occur; the rhetoric was "purposeful hypocrisy," easy because, at base, we assumed that Moscow would prevent unification. And almost all of us, including many Germans, rather preferred that state of affairs; as reflected in the remark attributed to François Mauriac, we liked Germany so much, we were happy there were two—three if Austria were included. If unification ever happened, it would come only at the end of a long period of change in Europe. This fall-back assumption, charmingly naive in retrospect, amounted to expecting Germans to wait patiently in line while Europe's divisions ended before raising their own concern—their German question.

When the fall of the Berlin Wall cast those convenient assumptions into doubt in the autumn of 1989, they were replaced by another, that political union between the two Germanys would be slow, the two states staying in their respective alliances while gradually working out the terms of their association. That was yesterday's school solution, and most of the world, Europeans, Russians, and Americans, including many Germans, would have liked it that way. It underlay the ten-point plan for a confederal Germany that Chancellor Helmut Kohl offered—without consulting anyone outside his own politics—in November 1989.

However, street politics in East Germany interacted with electoral politics in both Germanys to deny the luxury of a gradual transition. Gorbachev's reform had set loose the possibility of reform in eastern Europe, and once loose it came to Germany first, not last. Once reform was afoot, the logic of unification became inescapable; notions of a third way between communism and capitalism disappeared once East Germans learned that West Germany's social welfare net

179

was better than their own. With East Germany visibly disintegrating, why endure the pain of trying to create what already existed on the other side of the Wall that was no more?

Unification became only a matter of time, and West Germany was in the driver's seat. Kohl's achievement was crowned by his party's triumph in the first all-German election in December 1990. The chancellor, often underestimated as a windy, shambling local politician, had seen the chance to make history earlier than almost anyone, and he had pursued it single-mindedly. Second thoughts about the cost of unification were already in evidence, and even in victory the CDU came nowhere near achieving an absolute majority in the Bundestag.

But the voters rewarded the governing coalition, especially Genscher's junior partners, the Free Democrats, and punished those who had not grasped the moment of unification. The Greens, explicitly antiunification, all but disappeared from the parliament. The SPD suffered badly from its evident ambivalence over unification as well as the taint of its earlier party-to-party contacts with the ruling East German communist party, contacts accompanied by occasional flights of rhetoric about "convergence" between the two systems.

American policy publicly embraced unification from beginning to end: unification was in train, American leaders had said for forty years the United States was for it, and so it made no sense to hesitate when past rhetoric was becoming current fact. Despite Gorbachev's interest in recruiting Washington to a "slow unification" banner at the 1989 Malta summit and after, it did not happen. Indeed, at points Washington was perhaps a little too supportive of the Kohl government; a little stern lecturing in private to Mr. Kohl during the winter of 1989–90 about his muddle over whether Germany was committed to its existing eastern border with Poland would not have been amiss, provided the strong public support for unification had continued.

British policy, however, fell into the error of appearing antiunification and thus anti-German; when Nicholas Ridley, Prime Minister Margaret Thatcher's confidant and minister of trade and industry, implied in an interview that the next steps in EC integration were "a

German racket designed to take over the whole of Europe," with France acting as Germany's "poodles," his comments were instructive mostly because they strengthened the impression that he had said what she believed.[7] French president Mitterrand was all over the lot about unification, first acting out the instinctive French fear of Germany by seeming to oppose unification while seeking aid and comfort from Moscow. French and British foot-dragging made it seem to Washington and Bonn all the more important that West Germany have one unquestioning friend. To its credit, Washington was that friend.

The Bush administration also deserves high marks for holding firm to its objective of a unified Germany in NATO. In December 1989 a prudent bettor would not have laid money on that outcome: Moscow still had cards to play. It never, for instance, probed the limits of West German public opinion with careful proposals for unification coupled with withdrawal from NATO, or simultaneous pullbacks of Soviet and American troops. In retrospect, the Genscher compromise—Germany in NATO but no NATO troops in former East Germany—seemed almost unnecessary, and the chancellor pulled some of it back by agreeing to the non-NATO status for eastern Germany only until the last Soviet troops were withdrawn.

It is interesting that no one, including in Moscow, ever doubted that East Germany would become part of the European Community when it joined West Germany; it would not have been so two decades earlier when Moscow still railed against the EC as a capitalist plot. In economic terms, a Germany of 77 million instead of 60 million is not too much to handle, and to argue so is to make the worst mercantilist mistake. Its economy represents more than 20 percent of the western European economy, breaking any pretense of equality with France or Britain, but it is still less than two-thirds the size of Japan's and only a fourth that of the United States. Indeed, a dynamic Germany, even if given to bouts of tactlessness, will be a plus for its neighbors, not a minus; Oregon and Nevada are advantaged, not disadvantaged, by the proximity of California (though they do not always feel so!).

However, the timing is awkward because unification caught the

EC in the middle of its 1992 program and before the next steps in European integration, labeled European monetary union and European political union (EMU and EPU), were in train. The EC had wanted to deepen cooperation among its existing members; instead it widened to include East Germany immediately and came under pressure to stretch into Europe's east before it was ready.

The old question of widening versus deepening the EC arose in a new form. So did questions about Germany's role suggested by older analogies. In the run-up to unification, with Bonn under pressure to demonstrate that it would not renege on its EC commitments, Kohl uttered reassurance in his speech opening the Conference on Security and Cooperation in Europe (CSCE) meeting in March 1990: "We start from the assumption that the united Germany will be a member of the Community. . . . This will not hamper or delay European integration. On the contrary, it remains our objective to speed up the process of European integration wherever possible."[8]

In the event, for Germany, once united, the 1992 program suited perfectly: it got a bigger market and a freer flow of goods and services, plus loose monetary coordination around the Bundesbank without sharing any real power over German fiscal policy. Moving toward a monetary union, however, will mean sharing real power with less inflation-phobic Europeans, like Italy, a prospect all the less appealing as the cost of integrating eastern Germany puts upward pressure on German inflation and interest rates.

Almost certainly, Europe will become what the EC has sought to avoid: a Europe of several speeds or tiers, in and around the EC. Austria and Sweden easily qualify for full EC membership on economic grounds, as do Norway, Finland, and Switzerland. Not all of these, though, will necessarily want to be full participants in EC political cooperation. Conversely, economies in Europe's east will not soon be ready for full EC membership, but states there hanker for tighter political association. One answer might be a confederated Europe around the EC, as suggested by French president Mitterrand; another would be variegated national associations with the EC itself.

Germany, with Britain, has been the strongest proponent of widening. In Britain's case the stance reflected Britain's familiar preference for a wider, thinner Europe, especially so before domestic politics took Margaret Thatcher from the scene. In the case of Germany, the desire for widening inevitably was seen in light of older history and so fed questioning about just what Germany intended in *Mitteleuropa* and beyond. After all, if the sea change of 1989–90 had been set in motion less by governments than by the politics of the street, especially in eastern Europe, it was also the case that insofar as any government drove the process, that government was neither superpower. Rather, it was Germany, which had its way precisely because the Soviet Union was weak.

INSTITUTIONS AND PURPOSES

With the unification of Germany the postwar security order in Europe ended. That order was stable, glacially so, but it had been constructed on the backs of the eastern Europeans. What lies ahead is happier but less predictable: the Soviet Union, instead of menacing the West with an attack across the north German plain—the contingency around which both NATO and the American government organized their defenses for forty years—now threatens to implode, yet it remains the largest military power on the continent, with tens of thousands of nuclear weapons; eastern Europe, instead of existing only as a marginal accretion to Soviet military power, now faces the challenge of building free economies and societies.

The collapse of the old order catches western Europe prosperous but in the middle of its next steps in building the European Community. At the same time, traditional security concerns have not gone away, and "new old" ones arise out of ethnic conflict and internal turmoil in Europe's east. The time may come when the EC can be Europe's confederation, but that time is not yet at hand. Meanwhile, there remains a need for some elements of a security order.

That new order will be a patchwork of institutions: the EC plus the Conference on Security and Cooperation in Europe (CSCE) as the embryo of a pan-European collective security structure, with NATO serving as residual insurance. The order presumes not the absence of conflict but the absence of a determined upsetter of the system; it presumes that Europe's weather bodes tolerably fair. There are grounds for concern about that optimism, but they are mostly for the long term. Now, the political task is to bet on hopes while allowing for time to respond if the benign assumptions prove wrong.

The place to start thinking about a new security order in Europe is with purposes, not institutions. A new order should be judged against seven requirements:

Make central and western Europeans, and especially a nonnuclear but united Germany, be safe and *feel* safe from coercion by Moscow, no matter what happens in Moscow.

Do the same for eastern Europeans.

Make western Europeans feel comfortable in the company of united Germany.

Do the same for Poles, Czechs, and Hungarians, which may have rather different implications than doing so for western Europeans.

Make Germans feel they are both sovereign and equal, not the objects of continued occupation or political imposition.

Avoid an American role that domestic politics will not sustain.

Be tolerable to Moscow.

If a new order could meet two further requirements, it would be so much the better:

Make central and eastern Europeans feel safe from each other.

Make both any new states that emerge from Soviet territory and the remaining Soviet Union or Russia feel tolerably comfortable with the process of secession.

These last two requirements are especially challenging. NATO, a formal alliance organized around a palpable threat, played some role in containing but never came close to settling the dispute between two of its members, Greece and Turkey—a conflict that is suggestive of some of those that lie ahead in eastern Europe. And decolonization has rarely been easy; the secession of near or contiguous territories often has been particularly bitter (Ulster, Bangladesh, Biafra, Eritrea).

The continued membership of unified Germany in NATO reassures central and western Europe about the Soviet Union and assures everyone about Germany. But it leaves the eastern Europeans hanging, perhaps with reason to fear hostile emanations from former Soviet territory if no longer the Soviet Union itself. And Germany in NATO is unappealing to Moscow, still more so with the Warsaw Pact having vanished.

For its part, the European Community provides everyone with some reassurance about Germany. Yet while the states of the existing European Community are almost as much past fighting with each other as are American states, the EC will have problems enough in the aftermath of German unification, let alone extending its community of peace eastward. Because states in Europe's east desperately want to be admitted to Europe's "club" and know that erratic politics or conflict with their neighbors will earn them blackballs, the EC provides some deterrent to conflict simply by existing—for governments if not for street politics. And in any event actual membership in the EC is a long way off for most; nor does the EC provide any reassurance about Russia or the Soviet Union.

A pan-European collective security structure—of which the Conference on Security and Cooperation in Europe (CSCE) is one—has the benefit for the Soviet Union of including it, hence certifying it as "European" and giving it a role in reshaping Europe's security order to match. CSCE also provides a forum for the eastern European states departing the Warsaw Pact and for what used to be called Europe's neutral and nonaligned states.

In principle, there are advantages to pan-European arrangements like CSCE. Unlike alliances, which accomplish deterrence through balancing military power, they seek collective security through commitments undertaken by all; they depend as much on shared norms as military power. NATO was formed against an explicit potential

185

enemy; CSCE would, by contrast, presume the absence of such a threat and so would depend on participating states holding compatible views of the desirable future order in Europe.

Balancing power magnifies the significance of every imbalance; NATO's nuclear history is one of worrying over this or that category of weapons Moscow had and NATO did not. By contrast, successful collective security arrangements could deemphasize military measures, thus save all states money, encourage transparency, and so make wars by accident less likely. They could diminish the political effect of minor perturbations in the military balance to the extent that all participants were tolerably confident the others shared a long-run stake in sustaining the system.

The worry is that collective security systems may work best when they are not needed. So long as all states share the presumptions of the system—which amounts to saying that as long as there is no real security threat—they do fine. When they are needed, they do not. They depend on the weather remaining fine. In particular, they are hard-pressed to cope with a major power pushing the limits of the system. They call to mind one of Bertrand Russell's critiques of metaphysicists who "like savages, are apt to imagine a magical connection between words and things."9

A FAIR-WEATHER SCENARIO

Not surprisingly, then, a hopeful vision for Europe's security is an institutional patchwork dealing with a future in which traditional security concerns wane, and interdependence in the form of an expanding EC becomes the principal framework of European order. NATO would provide insurance against disastrous reversals in the Soviet Union, but, with fair weather, would in the long run cede place to CSCE or another pan-European organization as the guarantor of what residual security problems Europe confronted.

At present, the defects of CSCE as the embryo of a pan-European arrangement are all too evident. It is *too* inclusive, nearly forty nations, the ills of inclusiveness compounded by its operating principle of unanimity, which means tiny nations can hold it hostage (and they do, as anyone who has dealt with Malta over CSCE matters can testify). And before 1990 CSCE hardly existed; it was a convener, not an institution. It will for a long time be the umbrella body for smaller "groupings of the willing"—an extension of CSCE's past practice in arms control negotiations. Smaller groups can report their results to the full CSCE but with nonparticipating nations not able to veto them.

The CSCE nations recognized some of the organization's defects in their Charter of Paris, signed in November 1990. In the charter, CSCE foreign ministers undertook to meet as a council at least once a year. The charter established a small secretariat in Prague, a conflict prevention center in Vienna, and an office for free elections in Warsaw, as well as stipulating that follow-up meetings would as a rule be held every two years and calling for a CSCE parliamentary assembly.[10]

Making the CSCE into a binding treaty would give its confidence-building and other transparency measures more weight. It would mean, however, confronting the principle of unanimity, risking either a fight with the small countries to break the principle or having it engraved in a treaty. *Who* got to sign would raise again and again the question of how permanent are Europe's boundaries. Whether disintegrating states in Europe's east would permit secessionist states to join is in question, to put the matter gently.

A CSCE inner core or security council—comprising, say, the "two-plus-four" powers, the United States, Germany, France, Britain, and the Soviet Union or Russia, plus Poland and several other rotating members—makes sense but probably cannot be established formally. The Europe of the 1990s is not that of the Concert in 1815. Still, it would be natural for the two-plus-four powers to meet informally but frequently, not a new Concert of Europe exercising tutelage over smaller states but a core taking special responsibility.

Interestingly, though, in post–Cold War Europe's first test of conflict in eastern Europe, in Yugoslavia in 1991, it was the EC that was, if not the grouping of the willing, then the grouping of the resigned. With members adjacent to the conflict and others with interests, it simply did not feel it could remain aloof. The EC has the political infrastructure the CSCE lacks, for the cabinet ministers of its members meet almost constantly. The CSCE quickly demonstrated it could not act—Yugoslavia would not permit it, although the EC secured a CSCE mandate.

What the EC lacks is any military backstop, a want it quickly discovered once it sent unarmed observers to Yugoslavia. While it will be a long time before the EC has military forces of its own, if it ever does, it will be pushed toward some military arrangements. Events will exert that pressure despite the qualms of American administrations, especially that of George Bush, which have worried that any EC role in military or security issues will undercut NATO. There might be a new role for the Western European Union (WEU)—the vehicle in Eden's brainchild for rearming West Germany in 1954, which is revived periodically when someone thinks of a new purpose for it.

The WEU nations could undertake peacekeeping or other military tasks on behalf of the EC (or the CSCE), or on their own, much as they have several times used the WEU to coordinate their naval forces in the Persian Gulf. The WEU is acceptable to France because it is not NATO, and its forces might be more acceptable in Europe's east because they are European, excluding the remaining superpower, the United States. Forces deputed to WEU would be ones that might otherwise be assigned to NATO, but since the two organizations have been intertwined since 1954, some coordination should be easy enough.

A WEU rapid reaction force might be deployed outside Europe as well as inside it, and so diminish the chances of a replay of the Gulf conflict of 1990–91, when Europe's political cooperation was effective but coordination among its military powers was ragged. Such a force would also provide a home for German soldiers as and if German politics permit. And in the process France might even sneak closer to NATO through the back gate.

These European groupings of the willing may be preferable to, or complement, the United Nations. Faintly racist feelings of European superiority aside, consensus among the major powers might be

188

easier to come by in a European body, much as it was easier to associate the Soviet Union than China with UN sanctions against Iraq. Some parties to European disputes might prefer the UN, but others might prefer a body in which their say was greater. And there seems little reason to believe that the weight of a European action would be less than one by the UN, and some reason to think it might count for more with European states eager to join the European "club."

The CSCE "common house of Europe" might even come to make the break-up of European states easier than it now seems—for the secessionists, the residual states, and for the safety of the rest of Europe. All the parties to, say, Yugoslavia's internal strains seemed initially to prefer a European body to a global one. Hard cases make bad law, but if the Soviet Union were prepared to seek the assistance of *any* organization with its breakup, it too, might prefer a European one. At least CSCE might be a forum for communication and, eventually, a face-saving way to accept, for instance, redeployments of forces out of separating republics.

The operations of such groupings of the willing would hardly be tidy but over time could begin to add some shape to European security. The track is clearer with regard to arms control. There, groupings of the willing could negotiate additional measures of both what is now regarded as "arms control" and what are seen as "confidence-building measures." The latter was primarily the province of the full CSCE, the former of one such grouping, the CFE (conventional forces in Europe) negotiations between NATO and the erstwhile Warsaw Pact.

But the Warsaw Pact is gone, and the distinction between how *many* forces states have and how they are *used* was always arbitrary, so bringing the two approaches together is overdue. Indeed, foot-dragging by the Soviet military in completing the first CFE agreement during 1991 was taken by other participants as a warning signal; failure to follow through on arms control itself affected confidence.

CSCE might have one set of confidence-building measures agreed upon by all members (and, ideally, ratified in treaty form), but then smaller groups might negotiate further measures as part of additional arms control agreements. The broadest and loosest set of confidence-building measures might be agreed upon, as in the past, by all CSCE states. Groups of states that deploy forces in particular subregions could then negotiate additional constraints for those subregions, a process that will be especially important as the eastern European states reshape their military relations with the Soviet Union absent the Warsaw Pact.

The agreements might range from specific constraints on forces deployed along single borders, like those between Hungary and Romania or Poland and Germany, to something as broad as limits on the total forces of all participating states. Nations would participate individually in any such negotiation, but NATO could constitute a kind of informal caucus, much as it does already.

All of this depends, however, on the necessary condition for collective security: a relatively benign future course of events in Europe. Two assumptions, both more implicit than explicit, are worth exploring:

1. Europe's security problems will be minor ones, if not necessarily so for the peoples concerned. They will arise from ethnic and cross-national tensions in Europe's east. Some European grouping may or may not deal with them; in either case, however, the danger for Europe as a whole will be minor.

2. If storm clouds appear, Europe will scurry under its remaining cover; NATO's draw-down of forces, for instance, could be halted. The movement away from existing structures will not be irreversible, and so the transition to a new order could be fairly rapid if fair weather holds, or much slower if it does not.

IMAGINING THREATS TO EUROPE'S SECURITY

Certainly, the fair-weather projection of Europe's future is improbably smooth in light of the upheavals of 1989–90. Events may turn out that way, but it would be foolhardy to count on it. The bumps in the road for eastern Europe and the Soviet Union are easy to foresee if impossible to make out in detail. Predicting whether or when

Soviet and Russian leaders will fall, or be pushed toward or away from reform is madness. Yet that there will be bumps is certain, as the attempted Moscow coup of August 1991 testified. A smooth transition to liberal polities and open economies in eastern Europe, let alone the Soviet Union, simply is not in the cards.

One fair-weather assumption does seem on the mark: turmoil in eastern Europe probably will not threaten Europe's security. Current fashion overstates the sources of conflict in that region and enthuses too much about Europe's indivisibility.[11] The fashion is also a little too Marxist in assuming that frustrated economic reform automatically will undermine democracy. No doubt the eastern Europeans will be disappointed both by their own internal progress and by the helping hand they receive (or do not receive) from the EC, but they will continue to seek admission to the club in any event.

If, the incentive of the club notwithstanding, eastern European states fall into turmoil, even armed, that will be a blow to democracy, not to mention to visions of a Europe "whole and free," in George Bush's phrase.[12] It should goad Europe's institutions, the EC and CSCE in particular, to do better. But existing armed forces should be enough to contain any possible spillovers of violence.

For all the talk of ethnic conflict within and across existing borders in eastern Europe, the region is not seething with irredentist minorities. Woodrow Wilson's post–World War I handiwork (as adjusted by Stalin) is not that good, but neither is it that bad. When in breaking up, Yugoslavia fell near civil war, that was, not to be too cold-hearted, bad for it and for Europe. Nevertheless, the situation was a far cry from the Cold War, when Yugoslavia's disintegration risked Soviet meddling and, with it, a dangerous East-West confrontation. Indeed, in 1990 and 1991, the United States felt it could remain aloof from Yugoslavia's turmoil.

Economic failure east of the Oder-Neisse will produce waves of refugees moving westward, not columns of tanks. As labor shortages in western Europe take hold, its nations will face the choice of more immigrants or slower growth. On current projections, western Europe confronts a demographic time bomb. Now, the combined population of western and eastern Europe is about 500 million; by contrast, the Islamic periphery of North Africa and the Middle East totals only slightly more than half that. However, if current birthrates continue, that Islamic periphery would catch western Europe in population by the turn of the millennium, and all of Europe west of the Soviet Union by 2015.

The process of accommodation will not be easy for European societies, homogeneous and with traditions as exporters of people, not importers. It will be at least as straining for Germany as for its neighbors. It will take time, and meanwhile the threat of immigration will call forth a messy combination of aid designed to forestall emigration and barriers to would-be emigrants. Italy's handling of economic refugees from Albania has provided a foretaste of both. But the challenge is political and economic, not one to which security arrangements are immediately relevant.

That leaves the question of what might happen in the territory of the Soviet Union. Its transformation will be slow, moving by fits and starts, steps forward and back, and some of the backward steps will be long ones—and violent ones. What kind of tolerably stable arrangement might emerge is as much an imponderable as when one might ensue. Yet even a Prussian-style federation around Russia would have more buffers between it and Europe's core than did the Soviet Union. It might be ugly for its immediate neighbors but would pose less threat of unleashing a great war.

For as far as the eye can see, which is not very far, the Soviet Union, or an independent Russia, will be the largest military power in Europe, and its thousands of nuclear weapons will not go away. Their existence leaves no alternative to deterrence, for both the United States and western Europe; the Soviet or Russian weapons will remain long-range even if it is easier to imagine them being used in civil war than in transcontinental conflict.

Paradoxically, the risk of a nuclear weapon being used, irrationally, in desperation during a Soviet civil war is probably greater than that of the purposive Soviet nuclear strikes NATO belabored to deter during the Cold War. Soviet nuclear weapons plants are spread around the various republics much more than Soviet nuclear weapons (and the weapons are based in at least Kazakhstan and the

Ukraine, as well as Russia). Irrational threats are, however, by definition hard to deter, and the requirements of deterring purposive threats will be even less demanding than they have been heretofore. Indeed, the specter of chaos on Soviet territory provides a stronger argument for U.S.-Soviet negotiations to sharply lower numbers of weapons than any of the nuclear theology or fears of nuclear winter during the Cold War.

Nuclear weapons will continue, in Pierre Hassner's words, to "exert to some degree their double effect—potential destruction and actual restraint."[13] For the United States and its allies, precise deployments will matter less than they have. For instance, modernization of NATO's short-range nuclear forces (SNF) was not going to happen even before the Berlin Wall crumbled. Now, SNF have no purpose and no place to be deployed, a fact Mr. Bush recognized in September 1991 when he proposed eliminating NATO's land-based SNF—and called on Moscow to reciprocate.

The argument, sometimes still heard, that American soldiers should not remain in Europe without nuclear weapons to protect them is curious, for NATO always had trouble figuring out exactly how the use of SNF could help its defense more than the inevitable retaliatory strikes hurt it. Curious arguments sometimes make good politics, but this one seems likely to fade along with the imminence of the Soviet threat in Europe.

At some point, NATO may think of modernizing its nuclear forces in Europe—with a new standoff air-delivered missile, for instance—but that task is not urgent. NATO defended Berlin with nuclear danger, in McGeorge Bundy's words, not nuclear warheads in the city. It could defend Germany in the same way, all the more so if the threat of a conventional blitzkrieg is reduced through unilateral Soviet reductions and through conventional arms control. In the end, a nuclear-free Germany might be comforting all around—and might offer the American administration an excuse for a few B-2s, suitably armed.

The massive Soviet military threat *through* eastern Europe *to* western Europe that was the defining feature of the Cold War has disappeared for the near term and seems all but incredible in the long run. But the future is unpredictable enough that simple prudence indicates sustaining some hedge against the worst, if very unlikely and rather distant, Soviet contingencies. For this purpose, NATO has, like CSCE for its purpose, the virtue of existing, and the two would complement each other. If a reconstituted federation threatened to attack an eastern European state, CSCE would provide a forum for ostracizing the aggressor while NATO had warning time to reconstitute its own forces.[14]

If NATO is viewed in this way, as a hedge and a skeleton structure to be fleshed out if need be, its specific configuration can vary. How big it is, whether national armies are exclusively committed to it, whether the supreme commander is American or European: all these matter less than simply whether there is *some* command structure to reconstitute.

So, too, the precise American contribution is not a matter of great moment. The smallest force that can be defended on military grounds as an integral unit would be in the range of 100,000. While "instability" is not a threat against which military commanders can plan, for the near future the basic mission would be serving as the leading edge of reinforcement should a threat again appear in the east. Military commanders will be clever enough to work out the details.

NATO would be useful reassurance, though perhaps not necessitous, in a thousand chaotic futures that can be imagined: suppose Moscow used force ostensibly to protect ethnic Russians but actually to keep some part of the old empire in some federation; or that civil war broke out in the Ukraine; or ethnic kinsmen crossed the border to aid Moldavian or Estonian separatists. In all there would be some chance of conflict spilling across borders into eastern Europe, if not western. It plainly is too much to expect any CSCE to limit these conflicts, though not too much to expect it to try, so sustaining some structure of military power in NATO as a residual deterrent makes sense.

If the nations of Europe's east become more democratic and more connected to western Europe's economy, Soviet (or Russian) leaders will be both deterred and self-deterred from attacking in any case. Certainly a Soviet decision to use military force on Polish territory, for whatever purpose, is already very different than it was before 1989, quite independent of whether Poland is somehow associated with NATO or not. Yet suppose a turn to repression sent Moscow's troops into Lithuania. Suppose, in those circumstances, a democratizing Poland said fine words were not enough; it wanted tangible support, soldiers or planes. The West's choice would be dangerous, and sending NATO forces might be deemed too dangerous. But NATO would be a welcome option, and a deterrent.

THE SHAPE OF A NEW GERMANY

The other possible upsetter of the system is Germany, though it will not be such in military terms over any reasonable future. If history suggests that a unified, more self-confident Germany will be given to bouts of tactlessness and may not always be the best judge of its own longer-run self interest, the same might be said of the United States. Germany will be preoccupied with its eastern half and then may be drawn further into eastern Europe than its interests warrant. It may drag a more ragged EC with it.

It is uncertain how long the integration of the two Germanys will take, how expensive the process will be, and thus how much political backlash it may generate. But there is little doubt about the economic end point of German unification. It will be a stronger Germany. Unification will break any sense of parity among Europe's major economies. Before unification, the West German economy was less than a third larger than France's; once East Germany's economy begins to converge with that of West Germany, the combined German economy could be nearly twice France's—thus confirming the French nightmare of 1950.

A short drive in 1990 through the cobblestone highways and blackened valleys of eastern Germany, through towns whose architecture seemed untouched for seventy-five years, not just forty, made it hard to believe NATO intelligence agencies could have calculated East Germany's economy as nearly equal per capita to West Germany's just a few short years before.

The realization of just how backward eastern Germany is provoked disillusionment on both sides of the erstwhile Wall. To the east, the "Ossis" anticipated the German life they had seen on television and resented being told they had to keep their wages low lest their economy be uncompetitive. They felt colonized by suddenly ungenerous "Wessis." Protest marches appeared. For their part, the Wessis behaved as though they had expected unification not to disturb their comfortable life, and took their disaffection out on Chancellor Kohl when he raised their taxes despite his campaign promise not to do so.

Yet taxes on Wessis spent on infrastructure for Ossis are Keynesian pump-priming for the German economy. West German growth rates rose sharply in 1990 as Ossis satisfied some of their pent-up demands for consumer goods. It bears remembering that after the currency reform in the western sectors of Germany in 1948, industrial production rose at an annual rate of 50 percent in the first five months, and GNP grew in real terms by 20 percent annually in 1949–51. The analogy is imperfect, in particular because the military occupiers then could rely on market economics to an extent German politicians cannot now. But there will soon begin to be success stories in former East Germany. If success in the form of equality between Germany's two halves is a long way off and will be more expensive than most Germans expected, there is no doubt that Germany has the resources to make it happen. In the process, Germany will become the "expert" in reconstructing communist economies.

Rebuilding eastern Germany was rapidly turning around Germany's balance-of-payments surplus even before the Gulf war and its aftermath added additional claims on German money. That turnaround will be welcome as increasing German demand for imports erases Germany's trade surpluses with its EC partners and the United States but unwelcome for the United States if the disappearance of the surplus makes it harder to find foreign financing of the huge American deficit and for European states east of Germany if they had counted on German money.

However, this richer Germany will also have fewer Germans. In the nineteenth century, European birthrates were Third World–scale, so Germany grew from 40 million in 1870 to 50 million in the early 1890s to 68 million by the outbreak of World War I. Then, Austria-Hungary had a population of 50 million, giving the two German-speaking empires a population greater than that of the United States.

Not so today, for Germany, like the rest of western Europe, has falling birthrates; nor has erstwhile communist East Germany been any more fecund. Thus, unified Germany will, on current projections, fall to the population of West Germany today by 2025. There do not remain large numbers of ethnic Germans elsewhere in Europe to repatriate; the biggest group is in the Soviet Union, perhaps as many as four million but perhaps only half that. In 1989 some 750,000 ethnic Germans from other than East Germany, Poland for the most part, emigrated to the Federal Republic (340,000 emigrated from East Germany). Those Poles have become more and more dubious in their German ethnicity; they are drawn to Germany more by economics than the tug of kinship, and while the process for becoming certified as "German" is thorough, falsified papers are easy to come by and hard to dismiss.

Unification will add new streams and new strains to German politics. As is now commonplace to observe, however hard the Federal Republic has found it to come to grips with its past, East Germany never began; socialist Germany was absolved of any blame for fascist war. In the short run, politics in a unified Germany seem likely to become less predictable, and the surprisingly tidy results of the first all-German elections in December 1990 not a good predictor.

East German Protestants were seen in light of prewar patterns as natural social democrats, but many of them have so far turned out to want that which least resembles what they have had, and so have voted conservative. The rightist Republicans were eclipsed in the national feeling of unification, but immigration will give them or their kin fresh issues, and their uglier side will find resonance in former East Germany.

Surely a unified Germany will be different from the West Germany Europe has known: less western, less reticent, perhaps less predictable. The politics of that adjustment will not be easy. The EC may well lose some of its claim on German attentions, even money.

In the military area, Germany will be less introverted than it has been, but the process will be gradual. For instance, what seemed a modest change—altering the German constitution's interpretation to permit military deployments outside Europe, at least for UN peacekeeping, with German forces reconfigured accordingly—proved controversial even after the Gulf war of 1991. No strand in German politics agitates for a larger German military, and almost all favor a smaller one.

Indeed, public opinion polls in the wake of unification yielded a picture of a green and introverted Germany. Three-quarters of respondents thought the country should remain aloof from international conflict; and among a dozen possible areas in which the nation might spend more money, defense came last, behind sport, culture, and art. The highest priority was the environment, chosen by 71 percent of the respondents (here the east-west difference was marked, 59 percent of westerners and 74 percent of easterners, no surprise given the ecological disaster of former East Germany).

Only 6 percent of those polled selected the United States as a model, while 40 percent chose Switzerland and 29 percent Sweden. When asked with which countries respondents wished good relations, the Soviet Union led with 59 percent—perhaps little surprise given that the departure of Soviet troops was only beginning—followed by the United States and France with 44 and 36 percent respectively. Somewhat ominously, Israel led the list of candidates for more distant relations, cited by 32 percent overall and 52 percent of the easterners.[15]

As with the elections, public opinion polls taken in the midst of unification are not good predictors. A commitment to neutrality is not part of the German tradition; Germany has always been too big to be neutral—Europe's problem. Neutrality-for-reunification was, for the SPD in the 1950s, more a hope than a policy, and it was rejected in 1960 when the party got serious about governing.

Unified Germany enters the post–Cold War era with a relatively high degree of consensus on foreign policy. The consensus will not always make for easy relations with Germany's partners, especially the United States, but it is notable. Its emergence was visible in the preunification Federal Republic in the 1980s; writing in 1987, I characterized its main features:

> The primacy of German stakes in a stable Europe. Hence:
>
> Trade and humanitarian contacts across the East-West divide in Europe are a good thing in any season. Economic sanctions, for any purpose, are correspondingly bad. And:
>
> Arms control is similarly good almost irrespective of agreements. More is better.
>
> Given the minimal threat of Soviet adventure in Europe, nuclear deterrence is a fact and would be with many fewer nuclear weapons based in Germany.
>
> In the interest of stability in Europe, the Federal Republic should decouple itself from the United States in areas beyond Europe.[16]

In the 1990s the consensus might be described as "the same only more so." It reflects the inheriting of the SPD's clothes by the CDU, the seeping into mainstream politics of the antinuclear allergy, and self-preoccupation, all redoubled by the fall of the Wall. The old reasons for German deference to Moscow are gone, but there are new reasons for contacts across the former East-West divide.

Against this consensus, Saddam Hussein's invasion of Kuwait in August 1990 caught Germany by surprise. Germans first tended to think that Germany would take care of eastern Europe and the Soviet Union while America tended the Gulf. Kohl and Genscher, neither an instinctive America-watcher, took little heed of months of evidence that Mr. Bush had bet his presidency on the Gulf.

Zwang nach Osten

If the Soviet Union or Russia remains weak, it is worrisome to recognize that no guarantees of the Polish-German border, no matter how firm, can be final. With the political map of Europe changing, why should this one particular piece of Stalin's legacy be regarded as sacrosanct? The expulsion of twelve million ethnic Germans from what is now Polish, Soviet, and Czech territory is a human rights violation that pales only by comparison to Hitler.

There, too, though, the sources of tension will be economic and political, not military. Eastern Europe seems destined to return to its prewar pattern, its economies organized around Germany's; prewar Germany had at least a quarter of eastern Europe's trade. Territories adjacent to Germany, especially the former German ones, will wind up bearing the same relation to Germany as northern Mexico does to the United States—independent in sovereignty but in practice of a piece with the German economy.

Germany will be pulled into eastern Europe whatever its inclinations. The process may be more *Zwang nach Osten* than *Drang nach Osten*, more the pull of perceived obligation than the push of imagined destiny: eastern Europeans will feel they have little alternative to seeking trade and aid from Germany. Germany's presence will be heaviest in those areas where history gives it a basis—for instance Czechoslovakia, whose regions of Bohemia and Moravia have long, if not always happy, ties to Germany, or Croatia and Slovenia and the Baltics. That may be uncomfortable for those areas in political terms and also, in another way, for other parts of eastern Europe, like Poland and Hungary, whose economic benefits from Germany will be less than they hope.[17]

The history of Germany's relations with Poland makes adjusting to a world in which their relations are not artificially frozen by Cold War structures difficult for both.[18] Poland's ambivalence over unification was reflected in the internal debates of Poland's revolutionary government, visibly divided over whether a unified Germany was good or bad for it and whether in the circumstances Soviet forces should stay or go from Poland.

And Germans' disdain for Poles was not far beneath the surface, reflected in one way in the reluctance of their businesses to move in and, in another, by reactions in Berlin to the flood of Poles that arrived after the Wall came down to trade goods for hard currency. Absorbing new waves and new kinds of immigrants will strain western Europe's societies, Germany perhaps most of all. Germans will worry about the implications of instability, however defined, for them; the prospect of new waves of Polish immigrants, for instance, will be unattractive politically even after it has been necessary economically.

Yet there is also a romantic edge to the German attraction; when Germans talk of their responsibility, or even their mission, in eastern Europe, they are sincere despite the odd ring to their statements in light of not-so-distant European history. The image of Luftwaffe planes flying relief supplies into Romania in 1989 was unusual because it was Germany. Because Germany starts from such a base of introversion, as it becomes less so the world will be constantly surprised.

Eastern Europe, having moved westward in the Stalin ice age, will now move eastward. The Baltics, then Byelorussia and the Ukraine, will seek escape from or more elbow room with regard to the remaining federation. In most of them, the elites will be pro- not anti-German; the last forty years of history have made them more so, and the process of moving away from the federation's Russian or pan-Slavic core will make them more so still. Already, Germany's democratic institutions are coming to be seen as a model—a far cry from the worries of the late 1940s.

In these respects, the Europe emerging will resemble that of pre–World War I. The differences, though, are instructive, and most are hopeful. It is a different Germany in a different Europe. It will be a smaller Germany, one more entangled with its western European partners and intertwined with Europe's east through people flows if not institutional arrangements.

The less hopeful difference between then and now is the structure of power. Eastern Europe is at least as much of a power vacuum now as then, and the uncertainties as great, and Russia is weaker; in that sense, the closer analogy may be Russia after World War I, not before, after its wartime reverses and revolution.

Unless Russia collapses entirely, the remaining core, nuclear armed, will watch its disintegration with alarm—or regard its new neighbors with suspicion. Germany will be like the rest of western Europe only more so, caught between its desires for more self-determination in an eastern Europe that extends further east and its fear that the process will get out of hand. It and the rump Russia will in any event share a stake in what happens between them. That Russia, moreover, is likely to have its own exaggerated hopes for what Germany can do for it.

In any event Germany will be Russia's sponsor for membership in the European "club," if not soon the EC itself. That sponsorship was obvious, and obviously self-interested, in the immediate process of securing Soviet assent to German unification. Beyond immediate self-interest, Germany will be tempted to return to the old balancing policy in a new form. If the military threat from the East dwindles to the vanishing point, so will the value of military currency and Germany's need for military alliance with the West.

Particularly if Germany were disappointed by its western partners, if the EC proved too weak and if the United States retreated from the scene, then Germany might again turn eastward toward Russia for reasons as much romantic as economic. It would then be tempted to convert its economic power into leverage in both directions. Shifting the analogy to the post–World War I era, special relations eastward would confer influence in the other direction, and vice versa. Germany could return to the land of the middle, committing to neither East nor West but playing both off against each other.[19]

The presence of nuclear weapons in Europe complicates these calculations, raising the question of whether at some point a unified Germany might not feel compelled to have them as well. Since nuclear weapons are not easy to share, nor nuclear deterrence to extend—as NATO has found for forty years—German nuclear weapons as an inexpensive deterrent would make strategic logic. Continued weakness in the Soviet Union coupled with the continuing delegitimization of nuclear weapons in global politics, however, might make Germany reckon that the benefits of not having them outweighed the costs.

Or further progress toward European integration might make some sleight-of-hand pooling of existing British and French nuclear weapons both acceptable to Germany and unprovocative to Russia. But neither path seems one on which to bet. And so hedging against nuclear proliferation in Europe by beginning to construct elements of some new security order seems all the more important.

BETTING ON HOPES

Behind thoughts of new architecture is the looming question of whether the nature of the European state system has changed fundamentally. In power terms, that question amounts to asking whether a Europe in which Germany is as powerful as it has been for a century, while Russia is as weak and eastern Europe as unstable, can be a peaceful Europe. In another form, the question is whether what has seemed unstable before—a Europe dominated by a powerful Germany at its center—still is. Or has economic and cultural blending so changed interstate relations as to render rivalry harmless amidst gains for all? In yet another form, can Europe be left to the Europeans, as the Soviet Union ceases to be an immediate threat and the United States becomes a lesser actor?

The echoes of the Soviet 1955 proposal for European security in the trial balloons floated by Gorbachev and Shevardnadze in the spring of 1990 are arresting. Yet in power terms it is easier to see why in 1955 Moscow should have favored a pan-European system than in 1990. Thirty-five years ago a unified Germany would have been relatively weak and perhaps susceptible to Soviet meddling, as the West feared. In 1990, a broad, thin security system, like the CSCE, seemed ideal for Germany, which got plenty of room for maneuver, but less so for the Soviet Union, which got little influence over German actions—unless Moscow could have a special German connection as leverage.

There are grounds for both optimism and skepticism about the European order. An optimist would point to the peaceful nature of the revolutions in eastern Europe, the consolidation of West German democracy, the formidable gains of the Common Market, and, not least, the fact that, with luck, this period of European construction will begin not with an aggrieved Germany but with the opposite, a Germany that feels its future is fulfilling.

By contrast, a skeptic hears echoes of earlier periods. The ethnic conflicts and the possibility of erratic politics in eastern Europe recall the interwar period. So, too, does the prospect that the preeminent actor in that region will be Germany. By almost any reading, the economic interconnection of the European economies is vastly different from the period before the war, notably in the institutional framework of the EC. But Britain and Germany then too were prime trading partners—testimony to the dubiousness of any too straightforward reasoning from economic benefit to political comity.

The optimism would be greater if the western European foundation were stronger. Britain's position in 1989–90 was unhappily reminiscent of its role in 1950 at the beginning of European economic construction; under Ernest Bevin, it had been the godfather of NATO but then parted ways with the continent as economic integration began. This time the political map of Europe changed at a stroke, but Britain was carping from the sidelines, not leading the next steps of European construction.

France, too, stopped short of a new version of its historic gamble of 1950, the Schuman plan, when it decided that if it could not beat Germany it would join it, and so began shaping what became the EC. In 1990, the waning of Soviet power seemed to make serious thought about defense unnecessary, while the shock of German unification, though real, was less than that of prospective German rearmament in 1950; it was not enough to call forth a new vision. Instead, France clung to Gaullist orthodoxy, trying to sustain the same policies when circumstances no longer permitted.

The logic of integration would indicate real efforts to build *western* European defense arrangements even if that risked seeming to move closer to NATO through the back door. It would mean proposals for more than symbolic mixing of French and German units and for the stationing of German, if not American, forces on French soil. It might even mean consideration of sharing nuclear weapons with Germany in a European army—a return to France's other proposal of 1950, the Pleven plan for the European Defense Community (EDC). It would mean real thought about European security roles beyond Europe, a need underscored by the late and frayed European cooperation during 1990–91 in the Persian Gulf, cooperation cobbled together under the Western European Union (WEU).

Despite these qualms, the basis for optimism is strong. The emerging European order will be messy by comparison to the tidiness of the Cold War division. It will be an institutional patchwork quilt, pieces of overlapping institutions. Some will work, others not. At this point, as with nuclear matters, too much reliance on abstract, and fundamentally apolitical, mental exercises in architecture can only get in the way of good outcomes. Not every bad possibility can be hedged against, and to try—for instance, by pushing too hard for American troops to remain in Germany against that country's political inclination—will produce just those setbacks that American policy should be seeking to avoid.

In the end, no formal arrangements can protect all concerned against nightmarish scenarios. Yet unlike nightmares, political disasters seldom happen overnight. The political task is thus to construct practical arrangements that are reasonably safe and sensibly hedged, in particular by building in enough warning time. With time, all parties can react to persistent movement in dangerous directions.

A Final Word

THERE IS A PLACE in the future Europe for the United States, but it is a far less prominent one than in the first decade after World War II. Europe still needs America but not with the same desperateness it did then, and American attentions are not nearly so concentrated on Europe as they were then. The time may come again when Europe will need America desperately, and the need may call forth comparable American attention. That time might come if real danger again appeared in Europe's east, from Russia, if Europe's core around Germany disintegrated, or if both occurred in some combination.

For now, though, there is no need and no basis for reconstructing the intensity of American engagement that was called forth by first rebuilding, then defending western Europe. So much has changed, and so much clamors for attention at home. It will suit everyone, Europeans east and west, and Americans, to have the United States remain engaged in Europe, including with its military forces. But those forces and the NATO structure that surrounds them will not be the centerpiece of American foreign policy that we became accustomed to in the nearly half century before 1989.

A stripped-down American military presence in NATO will remain useful insurance, for NATO has the great virtue of existing. Clay's 1947 threat of a "war that may come with dramatic suddenness" is gone; America and its western European partners would have years of warning before it returned. But Europe's east, including the lands of the former Soviet Union, will be tempestuous, and so a residual military structure, including the visible presence of the remaining superpower, will be reassuring for Europe's core. It can be so too for Poles or Lithuanians or Ukrainians.

That structure also spares western Europe the divisiveness of too much arguing over military matters. Those western Europeans will move, haltingly, toward greater military cooperation among themselves, impelled by the need to cope with conflict to their east. However, Europe is a long way from the kind of federation in which military matters would not be contentious among member states. Who commands and who produces what and how many are not yet inconsequential questions. Until they are, the American presence and the insurance of NATO can mute the force of those questions while Europeans grope toward the serious military arrangements among themselves whose lack was so evident after the fall of the Wall.

And, for all the change in Germany and in Europe, the American presence will remain reassuring *about* Germany as well as *for* it. Whether the combination of Germany's preoccupation with its unification and the EC's need to somehow reach out to eastern Europe would have strained cohesion within the existing Community, between France and Germany in particular, is now moot, for the disintegration of the Soviet Union adds new tasks and new claimants for attention. Now, the prospect that Europe's center will be strained by contending with Europe's east seems undeniable. The strain was evident in the disagreements over how to deal with a disintegrating Yugoslavia during 1991 and is bound to be reflected in suspicions over national intentions, not least Germany's, in the lands of the former Soviet empire.

In those circumstances, the presence of American forces can be a tangible sign of reassurance. If the troops are to stay in Europe in anything like numbers of 100,000, they will have to be in Germany, for there is nowhere else. Hence, for Germany to move toward expelling American forces in the absence of visible agreement by its neighbors and alliance partners would be to set off warning signals about its intentions.

Yet Europe's need for insurance and reassurance is a far cry from the dark days after World War II. Western Europe, prostrate and disheartened then, is now as rich as the United States. The European Community exists. Germany, a divided shambles then, is rich and unified now; it is fulfilled, not aggrieved. Europe's preoccupation now is itself, and the focus of American attentions is much less exclusively Europe than was the case in the decade after World War II.

Predicting short-term economic trends is fool's play, but the long-term *relative* decline of the United States, apparent for all to see, does not seem likely to be reversed, and surely not soon. It is true but not very comforting to say that so far much of the decline can be seen as redressing the effect of World War II, America's emergence from the war unscathed and so temporarily huge by comparison to war-torn Europe. It is also true but no longer very relevant to say that the change reflected the success of American policies.

And it is also true that the United States has attributes of soft power—the appeal of its culture, for instance, or the spread of multinational corporations that are less and less national but still probably "American" in a pinch. It is not, however, very reassuring to notice these have been discovered or rediscovered now that measures of harder power are less in America's favor.[1]

Since most people live within their national economy, they do not have immediate bases for comparing their standard of living with that of other nations, and so the force of relative change is mitigated. They simply notice, or after a time take for granted, that more and more of what they used to make is now made elsewhere. Americans thus may emulate those British who managed to condescend toward the French long after France had become richer than Britain.

However, if relative decline does not at some point resemble absolute decline, its effects may not be much different. "Japan-bashing" in the United States stems at heart from frustration over relative decline, notwithstanding the kernel of truth in American feelings that Japan still does not play by the rules of international commerce. The sense of decline was also a perceptible undertone during America's triumphal moment, the Gulf war of 1990–91. Americans' desire to continue acting in the world as before was mingled, crabbily, with the feeling that their country could not quite afford it anymore. It could if other nations' arms could be twisted to pay part of the bill, and so in the aftermath of Iraq's invasion of Kuwait the United States was tempted to try to get others to share the burden without much say in deciding what the burden would be.

The Gulf war also underscored another contrast between the years ahead and those after World War II. In retrospect it is arresting how focused official Washington was then on Europe—Dulles and Eisenhower only a little less so than Truman, Acheson, and Marshall. It was not that nothing else was happening. Trouble in the Middle East was predictable enough; and the Truman administration probably made it more firmly America's trouble, for understandable reasons, by hastily recognizing Israel in 1948. And civil war raged in China.

But the United States acted from the premise, not always articulated and later contradicted by rhetoric about communism's global threat, that Europe was the highest stakes game. It had been the wartime theater of first priority, and it was the premier theater of the Cold War. During Eisenhower's six-month stint as acting chairman of the joint chiefs of staff in 1949, he articulated for his colleagues the stark proposition that the paramount American objective, after preserving its homeland, was preventing the Soviet Union from taking over western Europe.[2]

His proposition did not go uncontested. Herbert Hoover and his kin who would have drawn the American defense perimeter more narrowly were paralleled by those inside officialdom who sought more flexibility in countering the Soviet threat. By the lights of both, Eisenhower's proposition risked creating a modern-day Maginot Line. The negotiation, then ratification of the North Atlantic Treaty brought the argument to a head and began to bring the dissenters around. By July 1949 an interagency memorandum circulated as guidance for testimony before Congress said:

> The United States cannot, without dealing a mortal blow to the civilized world, and risk of vastly increased U.S. and Allied casualties and cost, abandon Western Europe to enemy occupation with the later promise of liberation. Military strategy, in the long view, must, in the event of war, envisage the containment and thereafter the defeat of any aggressor.[3]

Official Washington paid a price for conceding priority to Europe, most evidently in the "fall of China" that hung over America's Asian policy like a right-wing ghost of Banquo for two decades, but agonizingly if slowly in the Middle East as well. Yet in these early years the United States held to its strategic priority. Other regions would be second-order; they would be less ends in themselves than means for achieving first-order goals.

Not so now. The American administration, fixed on Europe during Germany's unification, quickly turned its eyes to the Gulf after August 1990. American and German officialdom, so close during the process of unification, drifted quickly apart, and so did their respective politics. Even in more normal times now, absent war, the Middle East is a continuing preoccupation for American leaders. So, to put it mildly, is Japan. Lands to America's south, perennial losers in the Cold War competition for U.S. attention save when "communists" threatened to take them over, may do better, Mexico in particular, now that the coin of the competition is economics.

And so on. The list could be extended. No American administration would find it easy to keep its attention focused on Europe, or anywhere else, even if it had the strategic wit to try. And there is less urgency about trying, for the international environment of the next decade or so will be *relatively* benign for the United States. America will confront no shortage of international problems but no mortal threats of the sort that animated it for the last forty years.

The Soviet Union or Russia, its threat to the United States overstated in the past, may be underestimated now. But the threat, for the next decade or more, is more one of implosion than expansion; it is dangerous, especially for Europe, but does not pose a direct threat to territorial integrity, sovereignty, or political institutions, not for western Europe and surely not for the United States.

Notwithstanding the Gulf war, the same seems to be the case for threats from the south, what used to be called the Third World when there still existed a communist second. Terrorists will outrage Americans, understandably, well beyond the extent of their damage to the United States. An occasional Saddam Hussein or Qadafy will pose a more genuine threat, and some of those will require military force. But those contingencies seem more likely to resemble Libya or Grenada than the Gulf war—quick, sharp dispatches of small forces, not prolonged engagements of large ones.

If the international realm is less threatening than it was over the last forty years, domestic affairs seem more urgent. America's pressing business now lies at home, not abroad; the tails of those problems stretch across borders, but their roots are at home. For instance, no amount of beating on Japan to open its markets, however appropriate, will help American industry as much as competing better with Japanese products in the United States.

If America's urgent business is at home, the same is perhaps the case for Europe and for Japan as well. Europe's business is constructing itself, moving through the 1992 project and beyond while opening to Europe's east. That is plenty to do. Like America's business, the international tails of it are long, but its roots are in Europe; for example, nothing the United States might do for eastern Europe would help as much as more open access to western Europe's markets.

There is no obvious requirement to reconstruct a basis for an American engagement comparable to the Marshall Plan and NATO. Nor is such a basis near at hand. On its face, rebuilding Europe's east seems like it provides one; moreover, as a project after the Cold War it is temptingly analogous to the Marshall Plan after World War II. For forty years America spent national treasury to keep the Soviet Union out of western Europe and prise it out of eastern Europe, so it would seem a shame to stop now. When communism fell in Poland and Hungary, the United States responded with half a B-2 bomber's worth of aid, a symbol of the shame.

Yet, perhaps inevitably, eastern Europe will be Europe's responsibility. On its own terms, eastern Europe as a project is unpromising by comparison to the western Europe of the Marshall Plan for all the reasons that have run through previous chapters. Further east, even the names of the units to be reconstructed are in doubt. More to the point, though, the lack of American money reflects a lack of will. Eastern Europe makes for good rhetoric and for specific claims from specific groups of ethnic Americans. But it does not seem likely to call forth an American project anywhere near comparable to the Marshall Plan. There is neither the Soviet threat in the background to concentrate the mind of the American body politic nor economic self-interest to reinforce principle, as there was for western Europe at the time of the Marshall Plan.

Another possibility, a new trans-Atlantic bargain for dealing with security issues beyond Europe—out of area, so-called—also seems unpromising as a project on which to stake a renewed American engagement in Europe. In principle, trans-Atlantic imaginings might run to agreement by western Europe on what it has been edging toward for a decade or more—that NATO has a global role as a forum for consultation and concerted action. For its part the United States would agree to consultations that were substantive, not merely over how to divide the cost of policies made in Washington, and would accept that the Europeans might wish to consult each other first, in the Western European Union (WEU) or, eventually, the EC.

Yet having first spurned giving NATO a role beyond Europe, the United States has found it hard to turn around its own arguments. Moreover, critical out-of-area issues will, with luck, be few and each case different; there is no place called "out of area." They will, to boot, be divisive, as they have in the past, an incentive to find a framework for managing disagreement but hardly the makings of a successful trans-Atlantic project. Nor is the NATO structure at hand exactly right, for it stretches existing military configurations into politics, and so leaves out Japan and leaves Germany hanging in a kind of limbo, involved but pressed to contribute where it least can—structural shortcomings that were more than evident during the Gulf war.

The grandest of possible projects would be joint management of the global economy. Yet it would be necessarily trilateral, including Japan, and therefore awkward as the basis for a European engagement. And it also seems a project whose time is not yet.

The need seems plain, for on the surface what passes for cooperation at present is mostly shapeless arguing, driven by domestic considerations on both sides of the Atlantic, over who will be the "locomotive" for global economic growth. It is probably a mistake, though, to assume that the lack of visible institutions for managing the global economy means no managing is going on. And so to make trilateral management explicit would court the objections of those excluded, like the Asian "tigers" or Brazil.

Trilateral management is problematic for another reason: there is yet no "Europe" for this purpose. The EC's mandate in trade is not yet paralleled for international money or fiscal policy. When EMU comes, it will bring in train a Europe for fiscal policy. On that score, Monnet's and Schuman's logic of successive steps holds with a vengeance, for there can be no European central bank, no Eurofed, without a common European fiscal policy. With a common currency, Britain and France would be no more able to run separate economic policies than are California and Texas. But there is not yet a common currency.

Recognizing that there may be neither need nor basis for a reconstructed American engagement in Europe akin to that of the last forty years is not disengagement, let alone isolationism in whatever "neo" incarnation. Economic connections across the Atlantic would still be important; so would tourism and cultural connections. So, I hope, would American troops in some numbers. Thinking about a rough new bargain over issues beyond Europe could still be on the agenda, and a way to better manage the trilateral global economy would remain a goal.

Explicitly disengaging, for instance by announcing America's departure from NATO, would be unwise at home, never mind its effects abroad. After a half century, the politics of domestic and foreign policy cannot be so easily disentangled. I doubt that the United States could be creative and generous at home if it were crabby and narrow-minded abroad. And the obverse is also telling: if America's domestic travails were left untended, the basis for a constructive policy abroad would eventually unravel.

Postwar containment of the Soviet Union, however one assesses it in retrospect, did come to serve as the organizing core of American foreign policy. The people who shaped postwar American foreign policy did not locate that polestar quickly. They acted one stage at a time, impelled by the immediate circumstances; they hoped, whatever their fears, that each action would be enough—first aid to reconstruction, then security guarantees, then formal alliance. The Marshall Plan itself was improvised. One of the officials working on international economic matters confided to a colleague abroad in a July 1947 cable: "The 'Marshall Plan' has been compared to a flying saucer—nobody knows what it looks like, how big it is, in what direction it is moving, or whether it really exists."[4]

It took most of a decade for containment to evolve as a relatively coherent approach, and so it would be foolhardy to imagine the United States will find a new polestar more quickly this time. There is no Stalin to concentrate minds and politics. Nor is there much evidence of the kind of consensus that is so striking in Marshall's invitation to his would-be successor, Dulles, to join him at Moscow in 1947, even granting that Marshall's action, still statesmanlike, was that of a desperate administration expecting to be turned out of office the next time around.

That leaves a final challenge for the United States, one for which Europe provides a pivotal instance. Can the United States participate constructively in international arrangements it does not dominate? Clayton's answer in 1947 about the Marshall Plan was "no." The United States had to run that show, he thought. George Bush's conduct of the war with Iraq was masterful international coordination. But it was clear who ran the show. By the same token, part of Americans' attachment to NATO surely derives from the fact that we have run it.

Yet America's days of running the show in Europe are over. They were good days, so nostalgia for them is understandable. But they are over, at least for the future immediately ahead. And we have essential business at home to tend to in reconstructing the basis for an American role in the world as forthcoming and productive as that of those good days.

Notes

INTRODUCTION

1. Quoted in Robert D. Kaplan, "Germany: The Character Issue," *The Atlantic*, May 1990, p. 34.

CHAPTER ONE
DIVIDING GERMANY

1. These debates are discussed in more detail in John H. Backer, *The Decision to Divide Germany: American Foreign Policy in Transition* (Durham, N.C.: Duke University Press, 1978); and John Lewis Gaddis, *The United States and the Origins of the Cold War, 1941–1947* (New York: Columbia University Press, 1972), pp. 95–132.

2. On the treaty and its effects, see, among many others, Winston S. Churchill, *The World Crisis*, vol. 2, *The Aftermath* (New York: Charles Scribner's Sons, 1923–29); Pierre Renouvain, *War and Aftermath, 1914–1929* (New York: Harper and Row, 1968); Howard Elcock, *Portrait of a Decision: The Council of Four and the Treaty of Versailles* (London: Willmer Brothers, 1972); and Charles L. Mee, Jr., *The End of Order: Versailles 1919* (New York: E. P. Dutton, 1980).

3. Recommendation by the State Department Interdivisional Country Committee on Germany, September 23, 1943, quoted in Gaddis, *The United States*, p. 98.

4. Quoted in John Morton Blum, *Roosevelt and Morgenthau* (Boston: Houghton Mifflin, 1970), pp. 581, 583.

5. Directive to SCAEF Regarding the Military Government of Germany in the Period Immediately Following the Cessation of Organized Resistance (Post Defeat), September 22, 1944, in *Foreign Relations of the United States, 1945*, vol. Yalta, pp. 143–54. Hereafter cited as *FRUS* followed by the year and volume.

6. Policy minutes 42 (National Archives, SDF, Record Group 59, Notter Files), cited in Backer, *The Decision*, p. 19. See also "H-24 Germany: Partition," in ibid, pp. 20ff.

7. For the British and Soviet proposals, see *FRUS*, 1944, 1:150–53, 177–78.

8. See the map in *FRUS*, 1944, 1:facing 196.

9. The JCS minutes of their meeting with the president are in *FRUS*, 1943, vol. Teheran, pp. 253–56, 261.

10. Roosevelt to Churchill, February 29, 1944, *FRUS*, 1944, 1:189.

11. Winston S. Churchill, *Triumph and Tragedy* (Boston: Houghton Mifflin, 1953), p. 443.

12. *FRUS*, Conference of Berlin, 1945, 2:1504.

13. Truman to Stimson, July 29, 1945, in ibid., p. 822.

14. *FRUS*, 1945, 2:1029.

15. It is printed in *FRUS*, 1948, 2:449–55.

16. Lucius D. Clay, *Decision in Germany* (Garden City, N.Y.: Doubleday, 1950), pp. 73–78.

17. Quoted in John Gimbel, *The Origins of the Marshall Plan* (Stanford, Calif.: Stanford University Press, 1976), p. 107.

18. Printed in Department of State, *Bulletin*, September 15, 1946, pp. 498–99.

19. Ibid., p. 499.

20. *FRUS*, British Commonwealth, 1946, 5:516–20.

21. His January 17 speech is reprinted in "Europe Must Federate or Perish," *Vital Speeches of the Day*, February 1, 1947, pp. 234–36.

22. Eugene V. Rostow, "The Partition of Germany and the Unity of Europe," *Virginia Quarterly Review* 23, no. 1 (Winter 1947): 24.

23. Dulles, "Europe Must Federate," p. 236.

24. Rostow, "The Partition," pp. 20, 27.

25. *FRUS*, 1947, 2:201–34.

26. Backer, *The Decision*, p. 174.

27. See *FRUS*, 1947, 5:32–37.

28. Dean Acheson, *Present at the Creation: My Years in the State Department* (New York: Norton, 1969), p. 220.

29. *FRUS*, 1947, 2:191.

30. John Foster Dulles, *War or Peace* (New York: Macmillan, 1950), pp. 102–3.

31. V. M. Molotov, *Speeches and Statements Made at the Moscow Session of the Council of Foreign Ministers, March 10–April 24, 1947* (London: Soviet News, 1947), p. 34.

32. Council of Foreign Ministers, Minutes of the Twelfth Meeting, March 22, 1947, cited in Backer, *The Decision*, p. 166.

33. Council of Foreign Ministers, Fourth Session, Moscow, "Summary of Discussion on Report of Allied Control Council," cited in ibid., p. 168.

34. *FRUS*, 1947, 2:274.

35. Clay, *Decision in Germany*, p. 174; and Edward S. Mason, "Reflections on the Moscow Conference," *International Organization* 1, no. 3, (September 1947): 475–87.

36. See Backer, *The Decision*, p. 177ff.

37. March 22, 1947, quoted in Molotov, *Speeches*, pp. 41–42.

38. George Kennan, *Memoirs, 1925–1950* (Boston: Little, Brown, 1967), p. 178.

39. For the Acheson quote, see Daniel Yergin, *Shattered Peace: The Origins of the Cold War and the National Security State* (Boston: Houghton Mifflin, 1977), pp. 275, 296; for Kennan, *FRUS*, 1946, 6:699.

40. Walter Lippmann, "A Defective Policy," reprinted in Thomas G. Paterson, ed., *Containment and the Cold War: American Foreign Policy since 1945* (Reading, Mass.: Addison-Wesley, 1973), p. 51.

CHAPTER TWO
CREATING DEPENDENCE

1. Quoted in Walter Millis, ed., *The Forrestal Diaries* (New York: Viking Press, 1951), p. 387.

2. Paul-Henri Spaak, *The Continuing Battle: Memoirs of a European, 1936–1966*, trans. Henry Fox (Boston: Little, Brown, 1971), p. 141.

3. Quoted in Don Cook, *Forging the Alliance: NATO, 1945–50* (New York: Arbor House/William Morrow, 1988), p. 88.

4. Reported in *FO 371*, 67673, Z 8579/251/17/G, Memorandum, September 26, 1947, cited in John Baylis, "Britain, the Brussels Pact and the Continental Commitment," *International Affairs* 4 (1984): 619.

5. *FO 371*, 67674, Z 11010/25/17/G, Anglo-French conversation, December 17, 1947, cited in Baylis, "Britain," p. 619.

6. Sir Nicholas Henderson, *The Birth of NATO* (Boulder, Colo.: Westview, 1983), p. 2. This is the official British history, written in 1949 by Henderson, who had taken part as a young diplomat in the events recorded, but not declassified for thirty years.

7. Escott Reid, *Time of Fear and Hope: The Making of the North Atlantic Treaty 1947–49* (Toronto: McClelland and Stewart, 1977), p. 37.

8. *FRUS*, 1948, 3:5.

9. Quoted in Reid, *Time of Fear*, p. 36.

10. Quoted in Cook, *Forging the Alliance*, p. 118.

11. Quoted in Theodore H. White, *Fire in the Ashes: Europe in Mid-Century* (New York: William Sloane Associates, 1953), p. 295.

12. For instance, "British Policy towards Western Europe," *Cab 80/44*, Secret COS (44)113, June 3, 1944; and "Security in Western Europe and the North Atlantic," a fascinating preview prepared by the interdepartmental Post-Hostilities Planning Staff, *Cab 81*, PHP (44)27(Q), Final, November 9, 1944, both cited in Baylis, "Britain," pp. 616–17.

13. Quoted in Henderson, *Birth of NATO*, p. 7.

14. The conversation and Lovett's subsequent note are reprinted in *FRUS*, 1948, 3:12–20.

15. *FRUS*, 1948, 3:7.

16. Memorandum of Conversation, January 21, 1948, *FRUS*, 1948, 3:11.

17. *FRUS*, 1948, 3:7–8.

18. George Kennan, *Memoirs 1925–1950* (Boston: Little Brown, 1967), pp. 402–3, 408.

19. *FRUS*, 1948, 3:285.

20. *FRUS*, 1948, 3:287.

21. *FRUS*, 1948, 3:287.

22. See, for instance, the cable from the American chargé d'affaires in Brussels to the state department, March 14, 1948, in *FRUS*, 3:52.

23. For the text, see *American Foreign Policy, 1950–55, Basic Documents*, 1:968–71.

24. The full speech is reprinted in Department of State, *Bulletin*, March 28, 1948, pp. 418–20.

25. Joint message to the Secretary of State, March 17, 1948, *FRUS*, 1948, 3:55–56.

26. Henderson, *Birth of NATO*, p. 15.

27. The minutes of the meetings and related material are printed in *FRUS*, 1948, 3:59–80.

28. Quoted in Henderson, *Birth of NATO*, p. 18.

29. *FRUS*, 1948, 3:66.

30. See Article 31 of "Reciprocal Assistance (Rio Treaty)," in Charles I. Bevans, ed., *Treaties and Other International Agreements of the United States of America, 1776–1949*, vol. 4, *Multilateral 1946–49* (Washington: Department of State, 1949), pp. 560–61.

31. *FRUS*, 1948, 3:72–75.

32. *FRUS*, 1948, 3:213.

33. See *The Vandenberg Resolution and the North Atlantic Treaty*, Hearings Held in Executive Session before the Senate Committee on Foreign Rela-

tions, 80th Cong., 2d sess. on S. Res. 239, and 81st Cong., 1st sess. on Executive L, the North Atlantic Treaty, Historical Series, (Washington: 1973), p. 87 for Acheson, p. 159 for Vandenberg.

34. Ibid., p. 99.

35. See *North Atlantic Treaty, Part I: Administration Witnesses*, Hearings before the Senate Committee on Foreign Relations, 81st Cong., 1st sess. (April 27–29, May 2–3, 1949), p. 47.

36. Ernest May and I spell out this point in more detail in our "Defence Relationships: American Perspectives," in Hedley Bull and W. Roger Louis, eds., *The "Special Relationship": Anglo-American Relations since 1945* (Oxford: Oxford University Press, 1986).

37. William T. R. Fox, *The Superpowers: The United States, Britain and the Soviet Union—Their Responsibility for Peace* (New York: Harcourt, Brace, 1944).

38. Bernard L. Montgomery, *Memoirs of Field-Marshall Montgomery* (Cleveland: World Publishing Company, 1958), pp. 448–49.

39. Montgomery, *Memoirs*, p. 450. On the later decision, see *Cab 131*, 8 DO (50), 5th mtg., cited in Baylis, "Britain," p. 623.

40. *FO 371*, 73045, Z 814/273/72/G, cited in Baylis, "Britain," p. 624.

41. Ibid.

42. *FRUS*, 1947, 3:230–31.

43. *FRUS*, 1947, 3:232.

44. Ernst von Schenk, quoted in Wilfried Loth, "German Conceptions of Europe during the Escalation of the East-West Conflict, 1945–49," in Josef Becker and Franz Knipping, eds., *Power in Europe?* (West Berlin: Walter de Gruyter and Co., 1986), p. 522.

45. See Loth, "German Conceptions of Europe," pp. 517–36.

46. Konrad Adenauer, *Erinnerungen, 1945–1953* (Stuttgart: Deutsche-Verlags-Anstalt, 1965), p. 39.

47. Hans Peter Mensing, ed., *Adenauer, Briefe 1945–47* (West Berlin: Siedler Verlag, 1983), p. 191.

CHAPTER THREE
INTEGRATING GERMANY, ENGAGING AMERICA

1. Quoted in Phil Williams, *The Senate and US Troops in Europe* (New York: St. Martin's Press, 1985), pp. 37–38.

2. *FRUS*, 1950, 1:261, 275.

3. *FRUS*, 1950, 4:634.

4. Quoted in C. G. D. Onslow, "West German Rearmament," *World Politics* (July 1951): 455.

5. U.S. Department of State, *Documents on Germany, 1944–1985* (Washington: 1985), p. 311.

6. *FRUS*, 1950, 4:687, 688.

7. Quoted in Geoffrey Warner, "The British Labour Government and the Atlantic Alliance, 1949–51," in Olav Riste, ed., *Western Security: The Formative Years: European and Atlantic Defence, 1947–1953* (New York: Columbia University Press, 1985), p. 251.

8. Konrad Adenauer, *Erinnerungen, 1945–1953* (Stuttgart: Deutsche-Verlag-Anstalt, 1965), p. 345.

9. Dean Acheson, *Present at the Creation: My Years in the State Department* (New York: Norton, 1969), p. 437.

10. Harry S. Truman, *Memoirs*, vol. 2, *Years of Trial and Hope* (Garden City, N.Y.: Doubleday, 1956), p. 253.

11. *FRUS*, 1950, 4:691, 693.

12. *FRUS*, 1950, 4:692.

13. *FRUS*, 1950, 4:702.

14. *FRUS*, 1950, 3:138.

15. *FRUS*, 1950, 3:180–81.

16. Both Churchill and the Council resolution are reprinted in Onslow, "West German Rearmament," p. 456.

17. The quotes are from the August 17 memorandum, reprinted in *FRUS*, 1950, 3:221–222.

18. *FRUS*, 1950, 3:223–224.

19. See Acheson's memorandum of conversation with the president, July 31, 1950, in *FRUS*, 1950, 3:167–68.

20. Acheson, *Present at the Creation*, p. 438.

21. For McCloy and Bruce, see *FRUS*, 1950, 3:206, 194–95; see also Laurence W. Martin, "The American Decision to Rearm Germany," in *American Civil-Military Decisions: A Book of Case Studies* (Birmingham: University of Alabama Press, 1963), p. 654.

22. *FRUS*, 1950, 3:250.

23. *FRUS*, 1950, 3:273–75.

24. *FRUS*, 1950, 3:264–66.

25. See Jean Monnet, *Memoirs* (Garden City, N.Y.: Doubleday, 1978), p. 341–42; the Acheson and Schuman quotes are from p. 342. See also *FRUS*, 1950, 3:1191–97, 1201. Acheson's own memoirs do not men-

tion the ten division figure. See Acheson, *Present at the Creation*, pp. 441–45.

26. *FRUS*, 1950, 3:294, 299, 1230.

27. *FRUS*, 1950, 3:299.

28. *FRUS*, 1950, 3:1296–99.

29. Acheson, *Present at the Creation*, p. 441.

30. *FRUS*, 1950, 3:340.

31. *FRUS*, 1950, 3:1392, 344.

32. *FRUS*, 1950, 3:344.

33. Jules Moch, *Histoire du réarmement allemand depuis 1950* (Paris: Robert Laffont, 1965), p. 78.

34. *FRUS*, 1950, 3:350–52.

35. The speech is reprinted in Norman A. Graebner, ed., *Ideas and Diplomacy* (Oxford: Oxford University Press, 1964), pp. 742–45.

36. This and the following quote are from *Congressional Record—Senate*, January 5, 1951, pp. 59–61.

37. *Congressional Record—Senate*, January 16, 1951, p. 322.

38. See, for instance, their comments in *Congressional Record—Senate*: for Douglas, January 5, 1951, p. 62; for Morse, January 5, 1951, pp. 65–66; and for Connally, January 11, 1951, pp. 144–46.

39. This and the next quote are from *Congressional Record—Senate*, January 11, 1951, pp. 154, 147.

40. For a nice table of the changing resolution, see Williams, *The Senate*, pp. 87–91; see also the quotes from pp. 86, 95.

41. *Assignment of Ground Forces of the United States to Duty in the European Area*, Hearings before the Senate Committees on Foreign Relations and Armed Services, 82d Cong., 1st sess. (February 1–28, 1951), pp. 19, 74.

42. *Congressional Record—Senate*, February 8, 1951, p. 1123.

43. April 14, 1954, quoted in Sir Bernard Burrows, "European Defence," in Bernard Burrows, Geoffrey Denton, and Geoffrey Edwards, eds., *Federal Solutions to European Issues* (New York: St. Martin's Press, 1977), p. 187.

44. Anthony Eden, *Full Circle* (Boston: Houghton Mifflin, 1960), p. 168.

45. This and the following two quotes are from "The London Conference: Final Act, U.S., United Kingdom and Canadian Assurances," in Council on Foreign Relations, *Documents on American Foreign Relations, 1954* (New York: Council on Foreign Relations, 1955), pp. 113, 117.

46. This is nicely put in Josef Joffe, "Europe's American Pacifier," *Foreign Policy* 54 (Spring 1984): 71ff.

47. This language of protector and pacifier is Uwe Nerlich's. See his "Western Europe's Relations with the United States," *Daedalus* 108, no. 1 (Winter 1979): 88.

CHAPTER FOUR
ECONOMICS AND SECURITY

1. The speech is reprinted in *FRUS*, 1947, 3:237–39.

2. For a polemical view along these lines, see Tyler Cowen, "The Marshall Plan: Myths and Realities," in Doug Bandow, ed., *U.S. Aid to the Developing World: A Free Market Agenda* (Washington: Heritage Foundation, 1985).

3. Two of the best of the recent studies are Alan S. Milward, *The Reconstruction of Western Europe, 1945–51* (Berkeley: University of California Press, 1984), and Michael J. Hogan, *The Marshall Plan: America, Britain, and the Reconstruction of Western Europe, 1947–52* (New York: Cambridge University Press, 1987). See also William Diebold's insightful review of these two and other recent works in *Journal of International Affairs* 41, no. 2 (Summer 1988).

4. For a semiofficial summary of how the Marshall Plan worked, see Harry Bayard Price, *The Marshall Plan and Its Meaning* (Ithaca: Cornell University Press, 1955). I have also benefited from Thomas Schelling's reflections on his experience with the plan in Paris, and from William Diebold's comments.

5. Gaddis Smith, "The Marshall Plan," in Alexander DeConde, ed., *Encyclopedia of American Foreign Policy* (New York: Charles Scribner's Sons, 1978), p. 544.

6. *FRUS*, 1947, 3:224–25.

7. Price, *Marshall Plan*, p. 162.

8. See Ludwig Erhard, *Prosperity through Competition* (New York: Frederick A. Praeger, 1958), pp. 13ff.

9. Speech to the OEEC, Paris, October 31, 1949, ECA pamphlet on microfilm.

10. Robert Schuman, *French Policy towards Germany since the War* (Oxford: Oxford University Press, 1954), p. 21.

11. *FRUS*, 1950, 3:692–93.

12. Quoted in Derek C. Bok, *The First Three Years of the Schuman Plan* (Princeton: Department of Economics and Sociology, 1955), pp. 3–4.

13. Konrad Adenauer, *Memoirs, 1945–53* (Chicago: Henry Regnery, 1966), p. 196.

14. For Adenauer's reflections, see his *Memoirs, 1945–53*, pp. 256–66, 329–43, 383. The Schumacher line is from *Die Zeit*, May 18, 1950.

15. *FRUS*, 1950, 3:719.

16. The French text is excerpted in William Diebold, Jr., *The Schuman Plan: A Study in Economic Cooperation, 1950–1959* (New York: Frederick A. Praeger, 1959), p. 49.

17. *FRUS*, 1950, 3:711–12.

18. *FRUS*, 1950, 3:712–14.

19. Quoted in Diebold, *Schuman Plan*, p. 58.

20. *FRUS*, 1950, 3:752.

21. This episode is well described in John Gillingham, *Coal, Steel and the Rebirth of Europe, 1945–1955* (Cambridge: Cambridge University Press, 1991), pp. 270ff.

22. Dean Acheson, *Present at the Creation: My Years in the State Department* (New York: Norton, 1969), p. 395.

23. See *FRUS*, 1950, 3:701.

24. See, for instance, Richard N. Coudenhove–Kalergi, *Pan-Europe* (New York: Knopf, 1926).

25. *The Private Papers of Senator Vandenberg* (Boston: Houghton Mifflin, 1951), pp. 488–91.

26. *FRUS*, 1950, 3:723.

27. *FRUS*, 1950, 3:696–97.

28. On Skybolt, the classic source is Richard E. Neustadt, *Alliance Politics* (New York: Columbia University Press, 1970); see also John Newhouse, *De Gaulle and the Anglo-Saxons* (New York: Viking Press, 1970).

29. I spell out this conclusion in chapter 5 of my *Making the Alliance Work: The United States and Western Europe* (Ithaca: Cornell University Press, 1985).

CHAPTER FIVE
MOSCOW'S GERMAN PROBLEM

1. Charles de Gaulle, *Discours et Messages* (Paris: Plon, 1970), pp. 339–41.

2. The note was reprinted in *Current Digest of the Soviet Press* 4, no. 7 (1952): 7–8. It and the following note of April 9, along with the western replies, are printed in Council on Foreign Relations, *Documents on American Foreign Relations, 1952* (New York: Council on Foreign Relations, 1953), pp. 248–61.

3. The note is printed in *FRUS*, 1952–1954, 7:199–202.

4. Dean Acheson, *Present at the Creation: My Years in the State Department,* (New York: Norton, 1969), p. 630.

5. April 3, 1952, cited in Werner Feld, *Reunification and West German-Soviet Relations* (The Hague: Martinus Nijhoff, 1963), p. 133.

6. James P. Warburg, *Germany: Key to Peace* (Cambridge: Harvard University Press, 1953), pp. 181, 197.

7. Ibid., p. 203.

8. That case is set out in detail in the official Soviet history of the period, A. A. Gromyko and B. N. Ponomarev, eds., *Soviet Foreign Policy,* vol. 2, *1945–80* (Moscow: Progress, 1981), pp. 161ff.

9. Quoted in Wolfgang Pfeiler, *Deutschlandpolitische Optionen der Sowjetunion,* Konrad Adenauer Foundation Research Report 63 (Melle: Ernst Knoth, 1988), pp. 41ff.

10. In Adenauer's letter to Ollenhauer, quoted in Feld, *Reunification,* p. 136.

11. *FRUS,* 1952–1954, 7:1181. The Eden plan is reprinted beginning on p. 1177, the Soviet security plan beginning on p. 1190. For Eden's own reflections on Berlin, see Anthony Eden, *Full Circle* (Boston: Houghton Mifflin, 1960), pp. 75ff.

12. Konrad Adenauer, *Erinnerungen, 1953–1955* (Stuttgart: Deutsche-Verlags-Anstalt, 1966), p. 528.

13. Strobe Talbott, ed., *Khrushchev Remembers* (Boston: Little, Brown, 1970), p. 394.

14. The proposal is reprinted in *FRUS,* 1955–1957, 5:516–19.

15. Quoted in Feld, *Reunification,* p. 108.

16. Ibid., pp. 149–50.

17. His speech is printed in Heinrich von Siegler, *Dokumentation zur Deutschlandfrage, von der Atlantik Charta bis zur Genfer Aussenministerkonferenze 1959,* with *Annexband: Verträge* (Bonn: Siegler, 1959), p. 618.

18. Quoted in George Kennan, *Russia, the Atom and the West* (New York: Harper and Brothers, 1957), p. 61.

19. His speech is reprinted in Department of State, *Documents on Disarmament 1945–59* (Washington: 1960), pp. 889–92.

20. This and the following quotes from Soviet notes and western responses are from Department of State, *Documents on Germany, 1944–1985* (Washington: n.d.), pp. 542ff.

21. At his press conference, November 26, 1958, quoted in Department of State, *Documents on Germany, 1944–1985,* p. 549.

22. These and other declassified documents cited in the remainder of this section are, unless otherwise indicated, from collections assembled by

the Nuclear History Program and edited by William Burr, David Rosenberg, and Georg Schild.

23. As reported in the *New York Times*, November 16 and 20, 1957, respectively, cited in Jack M. Schick, *The Berlin Crisis 1958–1962* (Philadelphia: University of Pennsylvania Press, 1971), p. 8.

24. See the *New York Times*, October 30, 1958.

25. In a speech on February 21, 1959, quoted in Schick, *Berlin Crisis*, p. 26.

26. Department of State, *Documents on Germany, 1944–1985*, p. 547.

27. Berlin to Secretary of State 412, November 27, 1958; for Dulles see Senate, *Documents on Germany, 1944–1961*, 87th Cong., 1st sess. (Washington: 1961), p. 406.

28. Memorandum of Conversation, Department of State, September 27, 1959.

29. Memorandum of Conversation, General Andrew Goodpaster, October 22, 1959. The following Adenauer quote is from David Klein, who as foreign service officer served as translator during the meeting; reported in Marc Trachtenberg, "The Berlin Crisis," in *History and Strategy* (Princeton, N.J.: Princeton University Press, 1991), p. 40.

30. Embassy Bonn to Secretary of State, January 14, 1959.

31. Department of State, *Bulletin*, June 1, 1959, p. 781.

32. Embassy Moscow to Secretary of State 2653, June 25, 1959.

33. See the *New York Times*, August 8, 1961, p. 8.

34. Embassy Moscow to Secretary of State, March 16, 1961.

35. *FRUS*, 1950, 4:674.

36. Memorandum of Telephone Conversation with the President, April 4, 1959.

37. Quoted in Renata Fritsch-Bournazel, *Confronting the German Question: Germans on the East-West Divide*, (Oxford: Berg, 1988), p. 124.

38. See Department of State, *Documents on Germany, 1944–1985*, pp. 1103–5, 1124–27, 1135–43.

39. As quoted in FBIS-SOV-71-63-18, April 1, 1971 (supplement), p. 21.

40. See, for instance, East German ambassador Horst Bittner quoted in *Red Star*, reported in FBIS, SOV, April 28, 1971, p. E3.

41. The remark was widely quoted. See, for instance, *The Economist*, May 12, 1990, p. 49.

42. The logic of the following discussion owes much to Ernest R. May, "Soviet Policy and 'the German Problem,'" *Naval War College Review* (September–October 1983).

43. See Hannes Adomeit, "The German Factor in Soviet *Westpolitik*," *Annals of the American Academy* 481 (September 1985): 15–28.

44. Bonn had been doing secret polling, not yet published and never shared with its allies, of West German visitors to East Germany. While hardly conclusive, the results suggested how much and how fast both economic contentment and political confidence had eroded after 1986–87.

45. See, for instance, Michael MccGwire, *Perestroika and Soviet National Security* (Washington: Brookings, 1991), pp. 360ff for a similar argument, though one more purposive in interpreting Gorbachev's actions, not to mention more optimistic about their outcome.

46. FBIS-SOV-90-129-S, July 5, 1990, p. 8.

47. The call was discussed by a Polish communist spokesman, Jan Bisztyga. See the *New York Times*, August 23, 1989; and *Izvestiya*, August 24, 1989, cited in FBIS-SOV-89-163, August 24, 1989, p. 19.

48. Printed in *Current Digest of the Soviet Press* 41, no. 40 (1989), 20.

49. Shevardnadze's remark is quoted in Stephen Sestanovich, "Gorbachev's Foreign Policy: A Diplomacy of Decline," *Problems of Communism* (January–February 1988): 11–12; Gorbachev's view appeared in the *Wall Street Journal*, October 28, 1988, p. A10.

50. See, for instance, the Soviet Foreign Ministry statement of March 14, 1990.

51. Valentin Falin, chief of the Central Committee's international department, suggested that Germany remain in both blocks. Shevardnadze did likewise, suggesting that "perhaps we should do some additional thinking on this." *New York Times*, April 11, 1990.

52. See the NATO communiqué, S-1(90)36, July 6, 1990.

53. In a nice summary of Soviet options, written in 1988, Wolfgang Pfeiler characterized a unified Germany in the western camp as "totally unacceptable" to Moscow. *Die Politische Meinung* 238 (May–June 1988): 26.

54. Christoph Bertram, "Ein Weltrekord der Diplomaten," *Die Zeit*, September 14, 1990, p. 4.

55. FBIS-SOV-90-129-S, July 5, 1990, pp. 8–9.

CHAPTER SIX
EUROPE'S PAST, EUROPE'S FUTURE

1. In his magisterial review of postwar West German foreign policy, Wolfram F. Hanrieder terms this clutch of American policies "double containment"—of both Germany and the Soviet Union, embracing the first

while deterring the second. See his *Germany, America, Europe: Forty Years of German Foreign Policy* (New Haven: Yale University Press, 1989).

2. See Philip C. Bobbitt, *Deterrence and Democracy: The History and Future of Nuclear Strategy* (New York: St. Martin's Press, 1987). Conversations with him have pushed my own thinking on this point.

3. Some other analysts of Europe were so flirting in the 1980s, however. See, for instance, the late Hedley Bull's "European Self-Reliance and the Reform of NATO," *Foreign Affairs* 61, no. 4 (Spring 1983): 874–92.

4. If this seems far-fetched, I had some company in this view for the Federal Republic before the Wall came down. See Harald Mueller and Thomas Risse-Kappen, "Origins of Estrangement: The Peace Movement and the Changed Image of America in West Germany," *International Security* 12, no. 1 (Summer 1987).

5. These statistics are from Hans-Joachim Braun, *The German Economy in the Twentieth Century*, (London: Routledge, 1990), pp. 237–51.

6. James W. Angell, *The Recovery of Germany* (New Haven: Yale University Press, 1932), pp. 287, 419.

7. John Maynard Keynes, *The Economic Consequences of the Peace* (New York: Harcourt, Brace and Howe, 1920), p. 99.

8. The classic recent statement of the interdependence case is Robert O. Keohane and Joseph S. Nye, Jr., *Power and Interdependence: World Politics in Transition* (Boston: Little, Brown, 1977).

9. For an extreme argument that the era now dawning will be dominated by relative gains as reckoned by nation-states or groups thereof, see Edward N. Luttwak, "From Geopolitics to Geo-Economics," *The National Interest* 20 (Summer 1990): 17–23.

10. Paul Bairoch, "Europe's Gross National Product, 1800–1975," *Journal of European Economic History* 5, no. 2 (Fall 1976): 296–97.

11. See Duncan Snidal, "Patterns of Cooperation in the Coming Multipolar World" (Unpublished paper, January 1990).

12. The classic source, truly classic, is Immanuel Kant: when "the consent of the citizenry is required . . . to determine whether there will be war," citizens will pause before embarking on "so risky a game." *Perpetual Peace and Other Essays* (Indianapolis: Hacket, 1983), pp. 107–43. The argument has been developed by Michael Doyle, "Kant, Liberal Legacies, and Foreign Affairs," parts 1 and 2, *Philosophy and Public Policy* 12, nos. 3, 4 (Summer, Fall 1983): 205–35, 325–53; and "Liberalism and World Politics," *American Political Science Review* 80, no. 4 (December 1986), 1151–69. For evi-

dence on this point, see Steve Chan, "Mirror, Mirror on the Wall . . . Are the Freer Countries More Pacific?" and Erich Weede, "Democracy and War Involvement," both in *Journal of Conflict Resolution* 28, no. 4 (December 1984); Bruce M. Russett and R. Joseph Monsen, "Bureaucracy and Polyarchy as Predictors of Performance," *Comparative Political Studies* 8, no. 1 (April 1975); and Melvin Small and J. David Singer, "The War-Proneness of Democratic Regimes, 1916–1965," *The Jerusalem Journal of International Relations* 1, no. 4 (Summer 1976).

13. Jack Snyder draws some of the possibilities and their connections. See his "Averting Anarchy in the New Europe," *International Security* 14, no. 4 (Spring 1990).

14. This is the pattern of politics described as "praetorian" by Samuel P. Huntington in his classic *Political Order in Changing Societies* (New Haven: Yale University Press, 1968).

15. Walter Russell Mead, "Coming to Terms with the New Germany," *World Policy* (Fall 1990): 601.

16. Quoted in Karl Schlögel, *Das Mitte liegt ostwärts* (West Berlin: Corso, 1986), p. 12.

CHAPTER SEVEN
A EUROPEAN GERMANY OR A GERMAN EUROPE?

1. This is a point that I came to appreciate from my friend and former colleague, Christoph Bertram. See his "European Security and the German Problem," *International Security* 4 (Winter 1979–80).

2. Ralf Dahrendorf, "The Europeanization of Europe," in Andrew J. Pierre, ed., *A Widening Atlantic? Domestic Change and Foreign Policy* (New York: Council on Foreign Relations, 1986), p. 32.

3. Gordon A. Craig, *The Germans*, (New York: G. P. Putnam's Sons, 1982), p. 190.

4. Richard Löwenthal, "Cultural Change and Generation Change in Postwar West Germany," in James A. Cooney et al., *The Federal Republic of Germany and the United States: Changing Political, Social and Economic Relations* (Boulder, Colo.: Westview Press, 1984), p. 34. The Weber quote is from ibid., p. 35.

5. Quoted in Gordon A. Craig, *From Bismarck to Adenauer: Aspects of German Statecraft* (Baltimore: Johns Hopkins University Press, 1958), p. 18.

6. Quoted in Gebhard Schweigler, "Domestic Setting of West German

Foreign Policy," in Uwe Nerlich and James A. Thomson, eds., *The Soviet Problem in American-German Relations* (New York: Crane Russak, 1985), p. 44.

7. *Spectator*, July 14, 1990, pp. 8–10.

8. In Bonn, March 20, 1990, text provided by German Press Information Service.

9. Quoted in the *Atlantic Monthly*, February 1937, p. 155.

10. These agreements echoed NATO's suggestions in its July 1990 communiqué. Hans Günter Brauch suggested an elaborate CSCE architecture—a political council supervising a verification center and a crisis control center, and a security council overseeing a military council and an arms production and export monitoring center. See his "German Unity, Defensive Defense and a New European Order of Peace and Security," in Hans Günter Brauch and Robert Kennedy, eds., *Alternative Conventional Defense Posture for the European Theater*, vol. 2, *NATO Strategy and Force Posture Alternatives* (New York: Taylor and Francis, 1990). Gregory Flynn and David J. Scheffer cataloged recent proposals and make one of their own, for a limited collective security treaty. See their "Limited Collective Security," *Foreign Policy* 80 (Fall 1990).

11. Richard H. Ullman's thoughtful book makes the opposite argument forcefully, that peace in Europe is "divisible": there will be conflict, especially in Europe's east, but not major war. His argument runs parallel in many respects to that of this chapter. See *Securing Europe* (Princeton: Princeton University Press, 1991).

12. He used the phrase often. See, for instance, *Vital Speeches* 60, no. 18 (July 1, 1989): 547.

13. Pierre Hassner, "The Priority of Constructing Western Europe," in Gregory F. Treverton, ed., *Europe and America beyond 2000* (New York: Council on Foreign Relations, 1989), p. 26.

14. See Uwe Nerlich, *The Atlantic Alliance at the Crossroad* (European Strategy Group, 1990), pp. 51ff. For another argument emphasizing NATO and CSCE as complements, see *The United States and NATO in an Undivided Europe*, Report of the Working Group on Changing Roles and Shifting Burdens in the Atlantic Alliance (Washington: Johns Hopkins Foreign Policy Institute, 1991).

15. Infratest for *Süddeutsche Zeitung Magazin*, January 4, 1991.

16. See my "West Germany and the Soviet Union," in Gregory F. Treverton et al., *Western Approaches to the Soviet Union* (New York: Council on Foreign Relations, 1987), pp. 11–12.

17. See Laszlo Lengyel, "Europe through Hungarian Eyes," *International Affairs* 66, no. 2 (1990): 291–97.

18. See William E. Griffith, *The Ostpolitik of the Federal Republic of Germany* (Cambridge: MIT Press, 1978), chapter 1.

19. For an intriguing and similar argument, see Josef Joffe, "The Revisionists: Germany and Russia in a Post-Bipolar World," in Michael T. Clark and Simon Serfaty, eds., *New Thinking and Old Realities: America, Europe and Russia* (Cabin John, Md.: Seven Locks Press, 1991), pp. 115ff.

A FINAL WORD

1. See, for instance, Joseph S. Nye, *Bound to Lead: The Changing Nature of American Power* (New York: Basic Books, 1990), especially chapter 6.

2. Memorandum by the Director of the Joint Staff, February 25, 1949, in Alfred D. Chandler et al., eds., *The Papers of Dwight D. Eisenhower*, 11 vols. in process, (Baltimore: Johns Hopkins University Press, 1970–), vol. 10, p. 516. Ernest May underscored this point for me, as well as pointed to this evidence.

3. *FRUS*, 1949, 1:347–49.

4. *FRUS*, 1947, 3:239.

Index

Acheson, Dean: European policies and, 31, 105–6, 121; Germany and, 67, 69, 70, 74, 75–76, 77, 110; North Atlantic Treaty and, 54–55, 73; Soviet Union and, 36, 54–55
Achilles, Theodore C., 44–45
Adams, Henry, 3
Adenauer, Konrad: European Recovery Program and, 99; Europe, postwar planning for, 61–62, 125; and Germany, reunification of, 138–39, 141–42, 178; Germany, West and, 67, 71, 110, 174; policies of, 138, 141–42; Ruhr Authority and, 104–5; Soviet Union and, 127, 128, 142
Agriculture, 114, 116, 117, 163
Alliance management, vii. *See also* North Atlantic Treaty
Allied Control Council (Berlin), 22
Andropov, Yuri, 147
Annäherung. See Detente
Arms control, 131–33, 189–90, 193
Atlantic alliance. *See* North Atlantic Treaty
Atlee, Clement, 58, 68, 107
Auriol, Vincent, 31
Austria, 66, 126, 146, 182
Austrian State Treaty, 146
Azerbaijan, 40

Bator, Francis, vii
Belgium, 109. *See also* Benelux countries
Benelux countries (Belgium; Netherlands; Luxembourg), 42, 48, 51, 102, 106, 108
Benes, Eduard, 40
Beria, Laurentii, 126
Berlin crises: of 1948, 49–50, 54; of 1953, 136; of 1958–61, 133–41, 142, 146, 174, 193

Berlin Wall: building of, 141; fall of the, 3, 15, 38, 92, 179. *See also* Germany
Bevin, Ernest: European Recovery Program and, 93; Germany and, 27, 74, 75; North Atlantic Treaty and, viii, 40–43, 47, 48–49, 65, 78, 204; Schuman plan and, 105–6; Soviet Union and, 58–59
Bidault, Georges, 33–34, 41, 48
Birthrates. *See* Demographic factors
Bismarck, 175, 176
Bizonia, 27, 28, 30, 31, 33, 34, 99
Bohlen, Charles E. ("Chip"), 45, 46, 50
Bonn treaties (1952), 125–26, 127, 130
Bowie, Robert, 71
Brandt, Willy, 138, 143, 177, 178
Brauch, Hans Günter, 229n.10
Bretton Woods (1944), 101
Brezhnev, Leonid, 144
Britain: continental strategy of, 57–59; economic factors in, 107, 164; emergency loan to, 56; European Coal and Steel Community and, 105–8; European Community and, 183; European Recovery Program and, 99; France and, 105, 106–8; and Germany, occupation of, 21, 26–27 (*see also* Bizonia); and Germany, rearming of, 65, 68, 74, 75, 76; and Germany, reunification of, 139, 142, 180–81; North Atlantic Treaty and, 40–44, 48–50, 51, 57–59, 75, 76; nuclear weapons of, 158; Organization of European Economic Cooperation and, 99, 107; post–World War II Europe and, 31, 43, 56–59, 89–90, 204; role of, 56–57, 107; United States and, 57–59. *See also* Western allies
Bruce, David, 73
Brussels treaty (1948), 48, 51, 52–53, 68, 91

231

Bulganin, Nikolai, 126, 128
Bund, 173
Bundy, McGeorge, 193
Burden-sharing, 54–56, 83, 84, 88
Bush, George, 181, 188, 191, 199, 214
Byrnes, James, 26, 27, 29–30
Byrnes Treaty (1946), 26, 27
Byroade, Henry, 66, 70, 110

CAD. *See* Civil Affairs Division
Canada, 49, 50, 51, 57, 76
CAP (Common Agricultural Policy). *See* European Community, Common Agricultural policy
Cartels, 110, 111, 112
CDU. *See* Christian Democratic Union
CFE. *See* Conventional Forces in Europe
Charter of Paris (1990), 187
China, 69, 128, 209
Christian Democratic Union (CDU), 61, 142, 150, 177, 180, 199
Christian Social Union (CSU), 177
Churchill, Winston: and Europe, defense of, 71; and Germany, post–World War I, 18; and Germany, post–World War II, 18, 21–22, 68; "iron curtain" and, 36
Civil Affairs Division (CAD), 21
Clay, Lucius, 22, 24, 25, 26, 31, 32, 33, 40, 66
Clayton, William L., 60, 214
Coal, 24, 31, 34, 103, 111, 112. *See also* European Coal and Steel Community
Coal and Steel Plan (1950), 75
Coalitions, 58, 65
Cold War: Europe and the, 38, 92, 97, 115, 128, 153–54; Germany and the, 24–25, 91, 129; nuclear weapons and, 155–60; Soviet Union and the, 113, 128, 154, 193–94; superpowers and the, 57; United States and the, 95, 115, 154, 210
Common Agricultural Policy (CAP). *See*

European Community, Common Agricultural Policy
Common Market, 153, 158–59, 160. *See also* European Community
Communism: European, Eastern, 167–8; French, 25, 34; German, 28, 34, 123, 134, 178; Polish, 149; spread of, 40, 46, 62, 65, 94, 97, 148, 209
Conference on Security and Cooperation in Europe (CSCE), 8, 10–11, 151, 157, 177–78, 182, 183–84, 185, 186–90, 194, 229n.10
Confidence building, 189–90
Conflict: democratic ideologies and, 166; ethnic, 167, 168, 190, 191; European Community and, 185; interdependence and, 10, 160–63, 165, 166–67, 168–69, 170; North Atlantic Treaty Organization and, 194; political, 167–70; Soviet Union and, 11–12
Congress, United States: European Recovery Program and, 44, 94, 98; German food subsidies and, 33; North Atlantic Treaty and, 50–51, 53–54, 55–56, 64, 79, 80–88; role of, 81
Connally, Tom, 82, 83, 85, 86
Constitutional issues, 81–82, 86, 87, 88
Containment, 33–36, 45–46, 66, 209, 213–14, 226–27n.1
Conventional Forces in Europe (CFE), 189
Council of Foreign Ministers, 41
Craig, Gordon, 174
CSCE. *See* Conference on Security and Cooperation in Europe
CSU. *See* Christian Social Union
Cuba, 140
Czechoslovakia, 40, 43, 65, 94, 97, 132, 143, 167, 184, 200

de Gaulle, Charles, 25, 114, 119, 141, 158

Democratic ideologies, 166
Demographic factors, 191–92, 196–97
Dependence/interdependence, 9, 10, 60, 91, 153, 156, 160–62, 163, 170, 172, 185, 186. *See also* Burden-sharing; Self-help
Detente, 119, 139, 143
Deterrence: conventional, 157; Europe and, 9, 42–43, 64, 157, 194–95, 199; mutual, 163–64; North Atlantic Treaty Organization and, 194–95; nuclear weapons and, 38, 155, 157, 158, 159, 160, 192, 199, 202–3
Dewey, Thomas, 86
Disengagement, 132
Douglas, Lewis W., 43, 50, 51–52, 105, 113
Douglas, Paul, 82, 83
Dulles, Eleanor, 137
Dulles, John Foster, 28–29, 31, 32, 36, 89, 113–14, 136, 137–39, 214
Dunkirk, Treaty of. *See* Treaty of Dunkirk

EAC. *See* European Advisory Commission
EC. *See* European Community
ECA. *See* Economic Cooperation Agency
Economic Cooperation Agency (ECA), 98, 100, 101. *See also* European Recovery Program; Organization for European Economic Cooperation
Economic factors: European Community and, 101, 117, 154, 160–61, 164–65, 181, 182, 212–13; European Recovery Program and, 6, 39–40, 42, 94–97, 99–101; in Europe, 46–47, 60, 113, 160–61, 162, 168–70, 191–92, 204; exchange rates, 101; free markets, 99, 100, 169; in Germany, 22, 161–62, 181, 182, 195–96; global, 212–13; of postwar reparations, 17; security and, 6, 7,

72, 116–18, 162, 163; in Soviet Union, 146, 147; tariffs, 102, 108, 113; in United States, 95–96, 112, 117–18, 196, 207–8. *See also* Communism; individual countries by name
ECSC. *See* European Coal and Steel Community
EDC. *See* European Defense Community
Eden, Anthony, 19, 68, 90
Eden plan (1954), 127, 129, 130, 139, 142
Eisenhower, Dwight D.: Berlin and, 138; Germany, collapse of, 19; North Atlantic Treaty Organization and, 76, 85, 87–88; nuclear weapons and, 136–37; postwar Europe and, 64, 209
Elections, German, 121, 123, 127, 129, 130–31, 134, 138, 139
Ellender, Allen J., 87
EMU. *See* European monetary union
EPU. *See* European Payments Union; European political union
Erhard, Ludwig, 100, 104
ERP. *See* European Recovery Program
Espionage, 49
Ethnic groups, 167, 168, 190, 191, 197, 200, 204
Europe: Cold War and, 153–54; defense/security of, 4, 10–11, 38–39, 41, 42, 43, 44–45, 48, 58–59, 61–63, 129, 131, 132, 139–40, 155, 183–95, 202–4, 206–7; dependence of, 3, 9, 60, 91, 153, 155, 160–61; divided, 7, 61–62, 143, 149–50, 153 (*see also* Germany, divided); *Europe des états*, 171; future of, 4, 8–12, 154–55, 156–60, 170–72, 187–95, 203–5, 211; Germany and, 15–16, 22, 32, 143, 203; human rights in, 178, 200; integration of, 6–7, 25; nuclear weapons and, 158–59; occu-

Europe (*cont.*)
pation of, 18–19; politics in, 46–47; recovery of, 22; shaping of, 15–16, 56–57; Soviet Union and, 37, 157–58, 203; strategic track of, 159, 160; United States and, 27, 38–39, 43, 47–48, 57–60, 61–62, 172, 206–14. *See also* Europe, Eastern; Europe, Western; individual countries by name

Europe, Eastern, 9, 13, 91, 92, 97, 153, 157, 159–60, 167–70, 183, 190–92, 194, 199–203, 211–12. *See also* Germany, East; individual countries by name

Europe, Western: army of, 71–74, 75, 77–78, 110 (*see also* Pleven plan); defense/security of, 65–68, 69, 79, 115–18, 129–31, 183–86, 204–5, 212; economic integration of, 100–101, 160–61; European Recovery Program and, 99, 100–101; federated, 89–90, 91, 104, 108, 172; future of, 207; immigration to, 200–201; independence/prosperity of, 78, 83, 91, 92, 100–101; Soviet Union and, 94, 129–30, 157; United States and (*see* United States: Europe and); United States military in, 64, 72–74, 75, 77, 78–88, 153–54; West Germany and, 65–68. *See also* European Recovery Program; North Atlantic Treaty; individual countries by name

European Advisory Commission (EAC), 20

European Coal and Steel Community (ECSC), 6, 25, 88, 91, 101, 102–14

European Community (EC): Common Agricultural Policy (CAP), 115, 117; economic factors and, 101, 117, 154, 160–61, 164–65, 181, 182, 212–13; Eastern Europe and, 10, 169–70, 185, 187–88, 207; Germany, reunification of, and, 181–83, 197; 1992

program, 114, 181–82; North Atlantic Treaty Organization and, 188; role of, 10, 56, 160–61, 187–88; security factors and, 183–84, 185, 188; shape of, 183; shared institutions of, 165–67; Soviet Union and, 202; United States and, 91, 114–15, 166. *See also* Common Market

European Defense Community (EDC), 88–90, 125–26, 127–28

European monetary union (EMU), 182, 213

European Payments Union (EPU), 101, 111

European political union (EPU), 182

European Recovery Program (ERP): background of, 39–41, 46, 47, 60, 92–93; economics of, 6, 95–97, 98, 101, 214; logic of, 93–95, 211–12; Mutual Security Program and, 97–98; North Atlantic Treaty and, 42, 44, 54, 57–58, 97. *See also* Economic Co-operation Agency; Mutual Security Program; Organization for European Economic Cooperation

European steel cartel (1926), 112–13

Fascism, 17

FDP. *See* Free Democratic Party

Federalism: European, 89–90, 91, 104, 108, 172; world, 38

Federal Republic of Germany (FRG). *See* Germany, West

Finland, 182

Finnish-Soviet pact (1948), 49

First charge principle, 23

Foreign Affairs, 27

Foreign policies, 53, 79–80, 94, 175–76, 178–79. See also *Ostpolitik*; *Realpolitik*; *Schaukelpolitik*; *Westpolitik*

Forrestal, James, 51

Fox, William, 57

France: communism in, 25, 34, 94; economic factors in, 72, 102, 164; European Coal and Steel Community and, 102–8, 109; European Community and, 204; German policies of, 25, 31, 33–34, 92–93, 94, 102, 104, 107, 156, 164–65, 204–5; and Germany, occupation of, 23–24, 39; and Germany, rearming of, 64, 65, 68, 74–78, 88–91, 110–11, 124, 127; and Germany, reunification of, 139, 142, 181, 195; military of, 66, 71–72; North Atlantic Treaty and, 49, 55, 59, 65, 188; North Atlantic Treaty Organization and, 67, 71–72; nuclear weapons of, 158; political instability in, 25; United Kingdom and, 105, 106–8; United States and, 59, 65, 71–72, 77, 112. *See also* Pleven plan; Schuman plan; Western allies

Free Democratic Party (FDP), 180

Freedom trains, 15

FRG (Federal Republic of Germany). *See* Germany, West

Fulbright, William, 87

Gaitskill, Hugh, 131–32

GATT. *See* General Agreement on Tariffs and Trade

GDR (German Democratic Republic). *See* Germany, East

General Agreement on Tariffs and Trade (GATT), 115, 117

Geneva meetings, 129–30, 139

Genscher, Hans-Dietrich, 28–29, 139–40, 150, 180, 181, 199

Gerhardt, H. A., 70

German Democratic Republic (GDR). *See* Germany, East

Germany, divided: Bizonia and (*see* Bizonia); Brussels treaty and, 48; centralized agencies in, 22, 25, 28, 35; currency reform in, 34, 35; economic policies in, 22–23, 24, 26, 32, 34, 96; effects of, 173–74; end of, 15, 119–22, 145–52; industry of, 28, 110;

neutrality/demilitarization of, 30, 39, 59, 67, 123–24, 125; occupation of, 21–27, 34, 111; planning for, 7, 16–21, 27–34, 35–36, 60–62, 65, 93; reparations and, 17, 19, 20, 22, 26, 30, 32–33, 35; Soviet Union and, 134–35, 136, 145–46; western allies and, 139. *See also* Berlin

Germany, East: Berlin and, 135–36, 137; economy of, 195–96; fall of, 15, 149–52, 179–80; Germany, unification of, and, 130, 180; integration of, 182; living conditions in, 142, 143, 144, 146–47, 178, 226n.44; recognition of, 144, 178; refugees from, 141; Socialist Unity Party (SED) in, 25; Soviet Union and, 8, 71, 124, 126–27, 133–37, 144–46, 147–49; *Volkspolizei* (peoples' police) in, 66, 71; western allies and, 136, 144

Germany, unified: demographic factors of, 196–97; dependence of, 155–57, 172, 202; domestic policies of, 176, 178, 197–98; Eastern Europe and, 200–201; economic factors of, 181, 182, 195–96, 200, 202; European Community and, 117, 181–83, 195, 197; European security and, 140, 155, 184, 203–4; foreign policies of, 198–99; future of, vii–viii, 11, 195–99; Germany, East and, 120; Germany, West and, 139; history of, 173–76; North Atlantic Treaty Organization and, 140, 150–51, 181, 184; nuclear weapons and, 9–10, 158–59, 160, 199, 202; politics of, 197–98, 202; post–World War II planning for, 26–29, 30, 32, 60, 62, 119–32; prewar, 17–18, 161, 164, 168; rearming of, 121–22, 150–51, 198; Soviet Union and, 120–31, 135, 140, 152, 155–56, 175–76, 199, 202; strength of, 172–73; United States and, 12, 117, 131, 176, 199;

Germany, unified (*cont.*)
Warsaw Pact and, 140; western allies and, 120–31, 139, 150. See also *Ostpolitik*; *Westpolitik*
Germany, West: Cold War and, 156–57; economic factors in, 96, 111, 117, 162, 195, 196; European Coal and Steel Community and, 102–5, 106, 109; European Community and, 165–66; European defense and, 24, 38–39, 64, 65, 74; European Defense Community and, 89; European Recovery Program and, 99; federal police in, 74; France and, 61, 104, 110–11, 117, 156; German reunification and, 15, 27, 125, 142–43, 180; Germany, East and, 177; North Atlantic Treaty and, 16, 39, 42, 53, 61, 64; North Atlantic Treaty Organization and, 65–68, 90, 104, 109–10, 120, 122–23, 124, 125–26, 127, 128–29, 132–33, 144; Organization for European Economic Cooperation and, 99; *Ostpolitik* and, 141–44; rearming of, 65–78, 104, 109–10, 121, 122, 123–24, 156 (*See also* individual countries by name); recovery of, 92–93, 102, 134; Soviet Union and, 141–45, 177, 199; stability of, 66–67; United States and, 27, 64, 111, 178–79, 199; *Wirtschaftswunder*, 100, 103. See also *Ostpolitik*; *Westpolitik*
Gillette, Guy, 88
Gorbachev, Mikhail: Europe and, 203; Germany, East and, 15, 126, 144, 145, 149, 152; and Germany, reunification of, 145–52; Germany, West and, 144; reform movement of, viii, 8, 15, 147–48, 152, 179
Greece, 31, 40, 57, 94, 114, 184
Group of Soviet Forces in Germany (GSFG), 145, 147
GSFG. *See* Group of Soviet Forces in Germany

Harriman, W. Averell, 98, 140
Hassner, Pierre, 193
Helsinki Final Act. *See* Conference on Security and Cooperation in Europe
Herter, Christian, 136, 142
Hickenlooper, Bourke, 55
Hickerson, John, 41–42, 44–45, 51–52, 53, 78
Hitler, Adolf, 54, 161
Hoffman, Paul G., 98, 100–101, 113
Honecker, Erich, 147–48, 149
Hoover, Herbert, 80, 84, 209
Humphrey, Hubert, 140
Hungary: communism in, 40, 149; disengagement of, 132; ethnic groups in, 167; nuclear weapons and, 160; security of, 184; United States and, 211; West Germany and, 15
Hussein, Saddam, 199

Indochina, 66, 71
Interdependence. *See* Dependence/interdependence
International Agreement on the Ruhr (1948–49), 24–25
Inverchapel, Lord, 44, 45
Iraq, 188, 205
"Iron curtain", 3, 36
Ismay, Lord, (Hastings, Lionel), 153
Isolationism, 13, 86
Israel, 209
Italy, 52, 76, 102, 106, 109, 182

Japan, 14, 35, 66, 154, 208, 211, 212
JCS 1067, 18–19
JCS 1067/8, 22
Jebb, Gladwyn, 44, 51, 52
Johnson, Louis, 73, 76
Johnson, Lyndon, 141

Kaiser, Jakob, 61, 62
Kant, Immanuel, 227n.12
Kazakhstan, 192–93

Kennan, George, 27–28, 35–36, 45–46, 50, 56, 66, 94, 97, 132
Kennedy, John F., 136, 137, 141
Keynes, John Maynard, 161–62
Khrushchev, Nikita, 126, 128, 135–36, 140–41, 144, 146
Kiesinger, Kurt-Georg, 142–43
Knowland, William, 84
Kohl, Helmut, 28–29, 150–51, 156, 170, 177, 179, 180, 182, 199
Korea, 65, 69, 88, 92, 103, 109, 110

Labour Party, 107
League of Nations, 8, 11, 17
Le May, Curtis, 85
Lend-Lease, 40
Lippmann, Walter, 36
Lodge, Henry Cabot, 83–84
Lovett, Robert, 43, 44, 51
Löwenthal, Richard, 61
Luxembourg. See Benelux countries

McCarthy, Joseph, 80
McClellan, John, 87
McCloy, John J., 66, 70–71, 73, 110–11
McElroy, Neil, 137
Maclean, Donald, 49, 50
Malenkov, Georgii, 126
Malta, 187
Marshall, George C.: European Recovery Program and, 39, 41, 93, 214; Germany and, 30, 31, 32, 33, 34, 36–37, 76; North Atlantic Treaty and, 48, 86
Marshall Plan. See European Recovery Program; Mutual Security Program
Masaryk, Jan, 40
Mauriac, François, 179
Mazowiecki, Tadeusz, 149
Medium Term Defense Plan (1950), 65
Mende, Erich, 131
Mexico, 210
Middle East, 96, 210. See also Persian Gulf War

Military: aid for, 98; armies, 166; of European Community, 188, 206–7; of Germany, 198; politics and, 85, 186; presence of, in Europe, 4, 12–13, 27, 55, 64, 66, 72–88, 153–54, 190, 191, 193, 207 (see also North Atlantic Treaty); of Soviet Union, 145, 147, 151, 156, 183, 192, 193–94
Military alliances. See North Atlantic Treaty
Mitteleuropa, 171, 175, 183
Mitterrand, François, 145, 182
Moch, Jules, 76–77
Mollet, Guy, 146
Molotov, V. M., 26, 27, 32, 33, 35, 41, 126, 127–28
Monnet, Jean, 75, 102, 103, 106, 112
Monroe Doctrine, 52, 54
Montgomery, Viscount Bernard Law, 58, 68
Morgenthau, Henry, 18–19
Morse, Wayne, 82
Moscow Conference (1947), 29–36
MSP. See Mutual Security Program
Murphy, Robert, 31
Mutual Security Program (MSP): European Security Program and, 97. See also Economic Security Program

NATO. See North Atlantic Treaty Organization
Netherlands, the, 76, 109. See also Benelux countries
Neutrality Act, 54
Nitze, Paul, 66
North Atlantic Council resolution, 77–78
North Atlantic Treaty (1949): background of, 41–53; military and, 55; negotiation of, 53–56; terms of, 90–91; United Kingdom and, 40–44; United States and, 44–56; West Germany and, 16, 38–39, 53, 81. See also individual countries by name

North Atlantic Treaty Organization (NATO): army of the, 70–71, 74–91; European Community and, 188; European security and, 129–30, 153, 184–86, 190, 194; and Germany, reunification of, 150–51, 181, 184; Germany, West and, 65–68, 70–71, 74, 124, 125–26; nuclear weapons and, 133, 192, 193; role of, 4, 10, 194, 212; Soviet Union and, 120, 122–23; United States and, 194, 206–7

Norway, 48–49, 51, 65, 76, 182

NSC-68, 66, 83

NSC-71, 67–68

Nuclear weapons, 9, 63, 65, 83, 90, 132, 136–37, 138, 151, 155–60, 163–64, 183, 192–93, 202, 205

OEEC. *See* Organization for European Economic Cooperation

Oil, 96

Ollenhauer, Erich, 127

Ollenhauer plan, 132

Organization for European Economic Cooperation (OEEC): establishment of, 99; role of, 101–2. *See also* Economic Cooperation Agency; European Recovery Program

Ostpolitik, 141–44, 176–79

Paris treaties (1954), 127

Parties, political: North Atlantic Treaty Organization and, 79–80, 86; post–World War II, 36–37, 81

Persian Gulf War (1990), 188, 205, 208–9

Petersberg Agreement (1949), 67

Pleven, René, 74

Pleven plan (1950), 88, 102, 103, 110, 205. *See also* European Defense Community

Point 4, 31. *See also* Truman doctrine

Poland: communism in, 40; disengagement of, 132; emigration from, 197; Germany, relations with, 17, 143, 180, 199, 200–201; nuclear weapons and, 159–60; security of, 184; Soviet Union and, 149, 194–95; United States and, 211

Portugal, 114

Potsdam Conference (1945), 22, 23, 24, 25

Power, balance of: in Europe, 43, 54, 55–56, 60–61, 157, 160–65, 172, 201, 203; Germany and, 143, 176, 203; North Atlantic Treaty Organization and, 186; Soviet Union and, 203; United States and, 59–60, 208

Quebec Conference (1944), 18

Rakowski, Mieczyslaw, 149

Rapacki, Adam, 132

Rapacki plan, 132–33

Rapallo agreement (1922), 9, 175

Realpolitik, 175–76

Relief efforts, 60. *See also* European Recovery Program

Reparations, German: economic effects of, in Germany, 17, 19, 35; Moscow Conference and, 32; Potsdam Conference and, 22, 23, 32; Soviet Union and, 20, 22, 26, 30, 32, 33

Ridley, Nicholas, 180–81

Rio de Janeiro formula, 45, 52

Risk-aversion, 124, 126

Romania, 40, 126, 146, 160, 167, 201

Roosevelt, Franklin D., 16, 18, 20, 21, 37

Rostow, Eugene V., 28, 29, 30, 33, 34, 35

Ruhr: France and, 24; Germany and, 104; post–World War II, 17, 18, 23–25; Soviet Union and, 33

Ruhr Authority, 104, 105

Russell, Bertrand, 186

Russell, Richard, 86

Russia. *See* Soviet Union

Saar, 23–24, 34, 104

Schaukelpolitik, 174, 175

Scheel, Walther, 143

Schmidt, Helmut, 177

Schumacher, Kurt, 62, 105

Schuman, Robert, 25, 49, 75–76, 77, 102–3, 110

Schuman plan, 102–8, 110, 112, 204. *See also* European Coal and Steel Community

SED. *See* Socialist Unity Party

Self-help, European, 54–56, 57–58. *See also* Dependence

Shevardnadze, Eduard, 130, 148, 149–50, 152, 203

Shinwell, Immanuel ("Manny"), 76–77

Short-range nuclear forces (SNF), 193

Single European Act (1986), 101

Skybolt affair, 114

Smith, Laurence, 87

SNF. *See* Short-range nuclear forces

Social Democratic Party (SPD), 105, 111, 125, 142, 177, 178, 180, 198

Socialist Unity Party (SED), 25

Soviet Union: Berlin and, 135–37, 140–41; Cold War and, 14, 154; Conference on Security and Cooperation in Europe and, 185; crisis in, 11–12, 151, 158, 183, 191, 193, 199–200, 201–2, 207, 210; economic factors in, 146, 147, 152; Europe and, 37, 43, 46, 48–49, 67, 68, 129–30, 132, 157–58, 172, 184, 202; Germany, East and, 8, 66, 71, 134–35, 136, 144–45, 148–49, 154, 175–76; and Germany, reunification of, 120–31, 145–52, 155–56, 181, 202; Germany, West and, 136, 140, 141–45; military of, 145, 147, 151, 155, 156, 183, 192; North Atlantic Treaty and, 40–41, 43, 51, 58–59, 61, 65; North Atlantic Treaty Organization and, 83; nuclear weapons of, 11, 157–58, 163–64, 192–93; postwar Germany and, 25–26, 28; post–World War II

reparations and, 20, 22, 26, 30, 32–33; reform movement in, viii, 8, 15, 147–48, 152, 179, 192; United Kingdom and, 58–59; United States and, 35–36, 83. *See also* Gorbachev, Mikhail; Stalin, Joseph

Spaak, Paul-Henri, 40, 138

Spain, 114, 170

SPD. *See* Social Democratic Party

Stalin, Joseph: death of, 146; Europe and, 5; European Recovery Program and, 97; Germany and, 7, 120–21, 122–23; North Atlantic Treaty and, viii, 49–50, 54, 63, 91; postwar Germany, planning for, 19, 20, 22, 36; western allies and, 119–20, 121, 122–23, 124

Steel, 103, 110, 111, 112. *See also* European Coal and Steel Community

Stimson, Henry, 18

Strategic Bombing Survey, 28

Strategic Concept (1949), 65

Strauss, Franz-Joseph, 137, 177

Superpowers, 57, 61, 146, 188

Sweden, 159, 182

Switzerland, 182

Taft, Robert, 55, 56, 80, 81, 83, 86, 88

Tariffs, 102, 108, 113, 115. *See also* Economic factors

Teheran Conference (1943), 20

Thatcher, Margaret, 107, 170, 180–81, 183

Third force, 60–61, 107, 125, 142

Third World, 69, 210

Thompson, Llewellyn, 141

Tory Party, 107

Trade. *See* Economic factors

Treaty of Dunkirk (1947), 38, 42, 45

Treaty of Rome (1957), 117

Truman, Harry S: Brussels treaty and, 48; James Byrnes and, 29–30; and Europe, military in, 64, 73, 81, 85, 86; North Atlantic Treaty Organiza-

Truman, Harry S (*cont.*)
tion and, 79; and postwar Germany,
planning for, 22, 23, 24, 67–68, 69
Truman doctrine, 31
Turkey, 31, 57, 94, 99, 184
"Two-plus-four" powers, 150, 187

Ukraine, 160, 192–93
Ulbricht, Walter, 134, 137, 144, 147
UN. *See* United Nations
Union of Soviet Socialist Republics
(USSR). *See* Soviet Union
United Kingdom. *See* Britain
United Nations (UN): Benelux countries
and, 48; European nations and, 188–
89; superpowers and, 57
United States: Cold War and, 154; economic factors in, 14, 95–96, 112,
117–18, 196, 207–8, 211; Europe
and, 4, 5–6, 13, 27, 38–39, 43, 47–
48, 57–59, 60, 61–63, 72–74, 78–
88, 114–18, 172, 206–14; European
Coal and Steel Community and, 112–
14; European Community and, 166;
European Recovery Program and,
95–97, 99–100, 117; foreign policy
of, 53, 79–80, 94, 176, 206, 213–14;
future of, 12–14, 210–14; and Germany, occupation of, 21, 23, 26, 27,
29–34, 39, 111; and Germany, rearming of, 65, 66–68, 69–71, 72–78;
and Germany, reunification of, 180;
military of, 27, 55, 64, 66, 72–74,
78–88, 193; North Atlantic Treaty
and, 41–42, 44–56, 57–58, 64, 78–
88, 90; North Atlantic Treaty Organization and, 194, 206–7; nuclear
weapons and, 136–37, 163–64; politics of, 78–88; post–World War II
France and, 25; power of, 59–60,
208; and reparations, post–World
War I, 23; and reparations, post–
World War II, 30–33; Soviet Union

and, 35–36, 83; strategies of, 82,
117, 209–10. *See also* Congress; European Recovery Program; Western
allies
USSR (Union of Soviet Socialist Republics). *See* Soviet Union

Vandenberg, Arthur, 44, 51, 54, 55–56,
113
Versailles Treaty of 1919, 17, 19, 161–
62
Violence. *See* Conflict
von Brentano, Heinrich, 138

Wall, Berlin. *See* Berlin Wall
War. *See* Conflict: interdependence and
Warsaw Pact (1955), 128, 130, 132,
140, 144, 185, 189
Weber, Max, 175
Wehner, Herbert, 121–22
Western allies: Berlin and, 137–38; Eu-
rope and, 132; Germany, East and,
136, 144; and Germany, unification
of, 120–31, 150; *Ostpolitik* and, 141;
Joseph Stalin and, 119–20, 121,
122–23, 124
Western European Union (WEU), 68,
90, 127, 130, 188, 205, 212
Westpolitik, 138, 176–77
WEU. *See* Western European Union
Wherry, Kenneth, 82, 85, 86
Wilson, Woodrow, 167, 191
World War I, 16–17
World War II, 16–17

Yalta Conference (1945), 20, 35–36
Yeltsin, Boris, 148
Yugoslavia, 167, 187–88, 189, 191,
207

Zwischenkultur, 174–75